TECHNOLOGICAL FORECASTING

A Practical Approach

MARVIN J. CETRON

With a foreword by
RALPH C. LENZ, JR.

and with a critical appraisal by
EDWARD B. ROBERTS

TEXT EDITION

tfi

TECHNOLOGY FORECASTING INSTITUTE
a subsidiary of
GORDON AND BREACH, SCIENCE PUBLISHERS
New York   London   Paris

"A company's way of handling new ideas has a critical effect on the quality, novelty and daring of ideas its staff members will offer. This effect, like a feedback in an electronic circuit, can work to stabilize the typical output of the organization or it can work to neutralize or disrupt its functioning depending on the way management's actions are perceived by the research workers."
— W. P. LOTHROP, S. KINGSBURY, AND L. W. BASS

FOREWORD

The methods available for technological forecasting range from the quite simple to the very sophisticated. These methods have been described rather extensively in the literature (see the Bibliography) and the diffusion of this knowledge is widespread. Until recently however, in spite of the wide choice of methods and general availability of information, there were very few sterling examples of technological forecasting prepared and *used* for research and development planning. Some of the documentation purportedly developed to describe technical trends may be judged best by weight or volume, rather than by too close a look at actual content. Practical application of technical trend forecasting must therefore deal with the reasons for the scarcity of useful results, with the shortcomings of some typical forecasts, and with suggested remedies—such as those expounded in this book—for overcoming these difficulties.

As Marvin Cetron explains, examples of useful technological forecasts are scarce because of widespread resistance or neutrality towards the subject. The greatest benefit of forecasting lies in its use as guidance for the activities of large organizations, yet it is axiomatic that large organizations will exhibit resistance to innovations which require individuals to change. Not enough of the key individuals in any organization have thought introspectively concerning the primary objectives of the business in which they are engaged, yet this is where technological forecasting must start if it is to be useful. A business whose objective is to produce better light bulbs will make a forecast different from that of a company whose objective is to provide devices for illumination of work, study, and play areas. Assignment of responsibility for technological forecasting to a staff element, without full involvement of the key line personnel throughout the organization, inevitably results in poorly developed forecasts which are seldom used.

Useful forecasts are also rare because of the overwhelming problems of data gathering. Most theorists in the field of forecasting have gathered performance data for a sufficient number of cases to explain or validate the methods of forecasting which they propound. In practice it may often be observed that data for parameters of performance which would be useful for measurement and prediction of progress are very difficult to obtain. Performance is sometimes not measured at all, is often not measured at regular intervals, is frequently measured under varying conditions, and is usually recorded in several different places. Thus, without a clear and specific knowledge of the exact limits of present and past performance, it is not unusual to find a reluctance toward projecting or publishing forecasts of future performance in the same areas.

The development of a useful quantitative forecast, using even the simplest methods of trend forecasting, is likely to become a lengthy research project. Data must be standardized and validated, and influential factors must be examined for their influence on the trend. The amount of work required for development of the data base for a good forecast is a primary factor in the scarcity of useful forecasts. Executive pressures and the desire to be on the technological or trend forecast "band-wagon" are probably responsible for the relative abundance of poor and inadequate forecasts.

To some extent the wide variety of forecasting methods available contributes to the lack of good examples of practical applications. Most of the methods, if rigorously applied, should produce good examples. However, many of the techniques lend themselves readily to careless application and inexact analysis, which then often degenerates into a narrative forecast to the effect that some unspecified degree of progress will occur by some indefinite future date. Good forecasts are often submerged in the mass of poor material, so that the scarcity of good examples is compounded by the difficulty of the search through large quantities of material labeled as forecasts of future trends, to find the few which are useful.

The shortcomings of forecasts prepared without the full involvement of key personnel may be observed in the opening section of the forecast documents. This section may be a brief preface by the staff responsible for collection of the material. If so, the forecasts will usually be no more than a catalog of all R&D work currently underway in the organization, with a brief statement of the intended results. If the preface is signed (but not written) by the principal executive, it will usually be an innocuous set of platitudes without specific attainable objectives. If written by the principal executive, the prefatory statement may range from a clear-cut personal statement of organizational objectives downward to hyperbolic description of future grandeur.

Whatever the nature of the prefatory statement, a set of forecasts which is not preceded by a quantitative expression, or forecast, of major performance objectives is likely to be a collection of unrelated individual technical trend forecasts, ranging in quality from poor to fair. Experience has shown that intra-organizational forecasts made in the absence of clearly defined major objectives to which the senior executives are committed, and made without a context of overall technical performance trend forecasts, are unlikely to be fulfilled and are of limited utility in research and development planning.

Failures in selection of proper parameters for forecasting are evidenced most often in the selection of improvement factors for which no quantitative measure of performance has been identified. Basic research may logically claim exemption from the requirement to quantify or predict gains, but applied research and development should be able to determine factors of improvement for which gains in performance are both useful and measurable. Problems in defining measurable standards of performance are often symptomatic of poor management, particularly if control rests in the hands of those who cannot define the degree of improvement which would be useful to achieve. That is, if improvement is not measurable by some standard, then it is impossible to determine the degree to which perform-ance can be improved, nor if any improvement at all can be effected, and the value of the effort to be expended is moot. Determination of one quantitative measure of improvement for a forecast in a given technical area is worth three pages of adjective-loaded narrative, yet all too many voluminous fore-cast documents exemplify this failure to quantify performance.

Even when adequate quantitative measures of performance have been identified, many attempts at forecasting are evident failures because of the sketchiness of the data presented. Straight, wavy, broad, or narrow lines drawn obliquely upward, without evidence of specific data points, often conceal inadequate re-search concerning actual performance achieved at given points in time. Many forecasts lose credibility because they convey all too clearly the impression that they represent freehand drawings by persons more-or-less expert in the technical field of the fore-cast. "Freehand" technical trend predictions of this nature are the graphical counterpart of narrative descriptions of progress and have only slightly more value.

The shortcomings of most organizational attempts at tech-nological forecasting do not lie in the methods selected, but rather in the failure to use any method whatsoever, or in the random, haphazard use of variety of poorly understood methods. The assembly of large groups of people concerned with imme-diate problems, motivated by special interests, and constrained by administrative schedules, is not conducive to preparation of good forecasts, even though it may achieve other worthwhile ends. Most such forecast attempts, and many other organiza-tional approaches to forecasting, are characterized by unneces-sary and misleading pictures of future concepts, by exhaustive descriptions of current projects and by irrelevant and non-performance oriented background. The forecast portion of such documents frequently consists of detailed discussion of a few major projects to be undertaken and lip-service to the need for progress in other areas. Where the documents are organized by technical disciplines, the forecast is often merely a statement to the effect that continued progress is likely if increased funding is provided for further work in the area. Such efforts indicate very little, if any, attempt to apply available methodology to the forecasting process.

Another typical failure in the use of methodology is the extrapolation of progress from the *point* of current achievement, even though most would normally recognize the absurdity of extrapolating from a single point. Thus, even if considerable effort is expended in identifying a quantifiable measure of improvement, and present capabilities are carefully determined, the forecast fails to establish a *rational* basis for its prediction of progress. This approach to forecasting is easily detectable by its graphical presentation of progress, with the current year as its origin.

With this background of scarcity of good examples in organizational forecasting, and in view of the common shortcomings of so many forecasting efforts, the following remedies, covered at length by the author, may be offered for improvement in future attempts.

An obvious starting point is the necessity of *commitment by the principal executives* to the ideas that the organization must plan for the future, that the plans must be based on a reasonable forecast of the future, and that forecasting can best be accomplished by a *rigorous use of specific methods*. Only that organization in which the principal executive is out front and leading the way, is properly attuned for the job of creating a technological forecast.

When the commitment and an appropriate viewpoint toward technical forecasting by the principals of the organization have been established, the next step is the formulation of specific objectives for the future. These objectives must be formulated concurrently with and in context with a forecast of the general future situation applicable to the organization. Hard decisions on priority of objectives and availability of resources must be made and clearly spelled out at this point, with platitudes, generalities, and equivocal support of all possible objectives carefully expunged. The objectives and the general forecast must deal successfully with the questions, "What is the fundamental business of the organization now?," "What changes will take place in this business?," and "What business do the members of the organization want to be in?" This formulation of objectives and the general forecast is then furnished to all participants in the forecasting process as direction and guidance for their efforts. If it is found to be in error, it may be challenged and amended, but, as amended, it must *remain* the basis for the final forecast product.

The determination of the specific parameters of performance which collectively contribute to achievement of the major objectives of the organization is the next major task in the technological forecasting effort. The participants in this effort must include the people who directly control the research or development which improves performance in the technical area under consideration. Incentive to work seriously at the task of identifying all of the significant performance factors will be enhanced if the participants understand the principal executive's commitment to the basic objectives and the role of the technological forecast with respect to those objectives. In particular, the knowledge that allocation of resources for research and development will be based upon quantifiable improvements to be expected will serve as sufficient incentive for most participants. The fact that the leaders in other technical areas have identified specific performance factors can serve as a useful competitive spur for those individuals who plead difficulty in establishing specific objectives and performance parameters for their field of interest.

Problems in data gathering could best be remedied by national or international programs to establish standards and conditions of performance for all of the major technologies and to gather and publish such data on a regular basis. Over a period of time this data would provide the same type of baseline for technological forecasting as that provided by business and financial statistics for economic forecasting. Until such programs are established, the next best remedy would be the collection and publishing of performance data on regular basis by major industrial and scientific organizations. To some extent such data is availale now as a basis for trend analysis, and certainly should be used whenever it can be found.

Short of the above panaceas, the only remedy for the problems of data gathering is the insistence upon research to obtain valid performance data representative of the trend of achievable performance, and adequate review of the data presented to insure that standards of accuracy are met in all areas of the technical forecast.

The quickest way of resolving the problem of appropriate methodology for any given set of forecasts is to select one specific method, provide a short introduction of the technique, establish a standard format, and follow through with review to insure that standards are met by each forecast. Until an organization or group has successfully completed and documented one complete forecast, the best choice of methods is probably to choose the simplest.

Many esoteric techniques of exploratory forecasting are available and others are receiving continuing research. However, the organizational application of more complicated methods is unnecessary and even unwise until a sound foundation of forecasting capability and interest has been built on the basis of consistent use of the simpler techniques. Effective forecasting can be accomplished if continuing efforts are made to improve substandard forecasts on a systematic basis. Very little can be expected from one-time or short-term efforts.

If the forecasting effort has received the necessary level of support, interest, and involvement throughout the organization so as to result in the development of sound objectives, a satisfactory structure of technical areas and tasks, and a complete set of valid technical trends adequately interpreted, then of next concern is the use of this information in research and development planning.

A vital step in the practical application of technical trend forecasting, and planning based on such forecasts, is determination of the people to whom the forecast and the plan should be presented. This should include everyone who is expected to have a "piece of the action," and therefore consideration should include superior levels in the organization, subordinates who will be expected to carry out the plan, co-level department heads, counterpart staff elements, industry or government agency participants, ultimate users, special interest groups, legal, regulatory of political representatives, and the general public. Since most of these people will be involved at some stage in the execution of the plan, the primary question is the order, timing, and nature or the presentation.

This book by Marvin Cetron is a "touchstone" which will serve to guide those who would desire meaningful forecasts and meaningful use of those forecasts. It is hoped that these chapters will encourage involvement and interest by planners at all levels in technological forecasting, forecasting, that is, which is based on comprehensive rationalization and dedicated effort. Only then can it be expected that the true utility and merits of this methodology will come into focus, and contrast. Our treasure is not limitless; the problems that need solving seem boundless. We must evolve and utilize systems that conserve the former to better address the latter. This book points way.

RALPH C. LENZ, JR.

Dayton, Ohio
January 20, 1969

Of all sad words of tongue or pen, the saddest are these: "It might have been!" —JOHN GREENLEAF WHITTIER

PREFACE

Technology forecasting is now white hot. As we all know, anything with such a high temperature will have its component elements in violent agitation. So it is today with technology forecasting, a young science, still much of an art, and giving off much more heat than light. The protagonists vary widely, a not unusual situation in an emerging interdisciplinary field, and run the gamut from (a few) knowledgeable quantitative practioners to incompetent Charlatans.

Besides, being in its formative years, technology forecasting has the handicap of having been spawned into the "Community." Its acceptance would have proceeded more smoothly had its origin been in the hallowed halls of Academia. Technology forecasting seems to me a modern Prometheus. Having stolen from the gods the fire which it bestows upon men, it now awaits the coming of Hercules so that it may be unchained for use.

Hopefully what I have done here is to synthesize the most important concepts in technology forecasting into a logical sequence that can be utilized by the practioner.

A Technological Forecast is the prediction with a level of confidence of a technical achievement in a given time frame with a specified level of support. Such a forecast is a tool for planning and decision making—though the forecast itself is not a plan. The art of technological forecasting is new and, consequently, there is no universally adopted approach to forecasting methodology. In this book, I review current philosophy and various forecasting techniques, as well as the practical utilization of forecasting in military and industrial planning.

Government and industry are developing many new ways to forecast future technical developments, but the payoff comes when these projections are incorporated as part of the R&D planning process. This is done on two levels: When deciding on future work in a specific development project and when assigning priorities to the over-all R&D effort. Systems being developed in the Navy and other branches of the Federal Government are able to integrate technological forecasts with data on future needs, probabilities of success, and potential funding levels. The computerized result could be a complete ranking of all ongoing and potential projects according to their over-all worth. But care must be taken to ensure that the computer printout retains its role as a servant and not a ruler of managers.

In this book, I try to give an integrated view of the most significant, practical aspects of not only technological forecasting but also of how the technological forecast can be used in decision making. The book is aimed at a wide cross-section of those with the need to know about technological forecasting and its application. These may include, with no order of priority intended: students in engineering and management schools who take courses in planning, management theory or operations research; managers or other R&D specialists who are intensively studying technological forecasting, planning and/or allocation of resources; managers in technological areas who are responsible for the planning job, who must consider ways of incorporating new techniques, opportunities or revamping and allocating of resource systems; and, finally, those managers—whatever their current assignment—who are interested in the new methods of analysis and problem solving that are utilized in the techniques and case studies presented.

At this point, a few words of thanks and appreciation are in order. The thoughts and work that went into the creation of the methods depicted in this book are the results of the efforts of hundreds of gifted and dedicated men who have worked for years in a wide range of organizations. All I can say is that, if this book helps provide the same kind of foundation for work to be done in the future that they have provided for many in the past, I will be more than compensated for my meager efforts here.

A special note of thanks is due to Edmund B. Mahinske, who served as editor, chief inquisitor and representative of the potential reader. He, with the able assistance of my secretary, Miss Penny White, combined several of my published works and other rough draft information and returned what was considered material for a technological forecaster's book, appropriate for a wide range of interested readers.

I am deeply indebted to six individuals who co-authored a number of the articles utilized, in part, in some of the chapters of this book. They are: George Bernstein, Donald Dick, Joseph Martino, Thomas Monahan, Louis Roepcke, and Allan Wieser. In additon, I would like to express my thanks to Ralph Lenz, Jr., for the excellent Forward; to Professor Edward B. Roberts for his critical appraisal of Technical Forecasting; and to Dr. Bodo Bartocha for his help on BRAILLE. Each of these men has added to my knowledge and has given me the benefit of his time and experience.

My gratitude is extended as well to my business associates, for their help and cooperation in developing the first Navy Technological Forecast.

Naturally, I accept full responsibility for any errors of fact or logic that might appear.

I would also like to single out for special mention my son, Edward, for his help in developing the index.

Finally, this book is dedicated to the three women in my life: Gloria, Gertrude, and Blanche, without whom this book would not have been possible. They are thanked for the understanding and inspiration that only an author's wife, his mother and her mother can give.

MARVIN J. CETRON

Washington, D.C.
December 20, 1968

CONTENTS

APPENDICES

BIBLIOGRAPHIES

INDICES

ACKNOWLEDGEMENT

The author and the publisher wish to express their thanks to the copyright holders for permission to quote at length from the following:

Cetron, M. J., "Forecasting Technology," *International Science & Technology,* September, 1967. 83–92.

Cetron, M. J. and Weiser, A. L., "Technological Change, Technological Forecasting and Planning R&D—A View from the R&D Manager's Desk," *The George Washington Law Review—Technology Assessment and the Law,* Vol. 36, No. 5, Washington, D.C., p. 1091.

Cetron, M. J. and Monahan, T. I., "An Evaluation and Appraisal of Various Approaches to Technological Forecasting." *Technological Forecasting for Industry and Government,* ed. J. F. Bright; Prentice Hall, Englewood Cliffs, N. J., 1968.

Cetron, M. J. and Dick, D., "Practical Technological Forecasting Problems and Pitfalls," *European Business,* Fontainebleau, France; Winter 1969.

Bernstein, G. B. and Cetron, M. J., "SEER: A Delphic Approach Applied to Information Processing," *Technological Forecasting;* American Elsevier, N.Y.C.; Spring 1969.

Cetron, M. J., "Using Technological Forecasts," *Science and Technology,* July 1968, No. 79, pp. 57–63.

Cetron, M. J., Martino, J. and Roepcke, L., "The Selection of R&D Program Content—Survey of Quantitative Methods," *IEEE Transactions on Engineering Management,* Vol. EM–14, No. 1 (March, 1967), 4–12.

The complexities of nature will always limit man's knowledge to a smattering of truth. Science advances by the slow attrition of ignorance and by the constant recognition of its uncertainties.
—HENRY DeWOLF SMYTH

INTRODUCTION
Ce que sera, sera

Whatever will be, will be. Strange that these words should hold a ring of wisdom and serve to still the thoughts of an inquiring mind. Stranger that men of learning, in some ventures of adulthood, will not wean themselves of this false notion. The future need not be viewed as fatalistic as all that. These chapters have as their purpose the instillment of the idea that the future is ammenable to analysis, that it is susceptible to shaping, that certain eventualities can be encouraged, and that *whatever will be* is to a large extent affected by what *you* want it to be—provided you plan and commit resources to that purpose.

Normally one does not induce much argument by making the foregoing statement or one akin to it. For one should always plan for the future, one should always put his plan into action, and one should apply his resources along the way to achieve the goals beyond. This is logical; it is only practical to do so. But let it be proposed that we analyze the future of technology, much less plan for it, and the arguments flare into incandescence—the battle lines are drawn.

The nay sayers—many among the academic, scientific, engineering and managerial elite—are the new group which have succeeded their distinguished forbears of the past: Those who proposed closing the Patent Office as a needless expense because everything that could be invented had already come into being; those who opposed the change from sail to steam—the list is interminable. They have receded into the dark recesses of history, cast by the wayside. So too will the new group. Technological

Forecasting will be elevated to the esteemed position and recognition it deserves to become a critical component of our cultural fabric. We will wonder, one day, what all the fuss was about. We will wonder how logical progress was ever possible without it.

What does Technological Forecasting ask of you? Simply this: that you methodically formulate a basis on which plans for progress into the future may be laid toward achievement of certain goals you desire in that future. In so doing, analyses of technology are required, its history, its current status, and knowledgeable prognostications of its probable future, if left to its current trends. Knowing what your schedule of future goals are in terms of technical or operational capabilities, you should then be able to discern where and when technology will fail to meet your requirements. As some say, you will have identified the "barrier problems." Having this in hand, you can formulate a plan, knowing when and to what problems to apply your attention, emphasis and resources. The difficulty envisaged in overcoming the barrier problems will in large measure determine how early the problem must be addressed and the magnitude of resources to be applied —commensurate with the importance of the goal that is to be attained. It is possible that the difficulty of a barrier problem may be insurmountable. But in this event you will have been advised aforehand. Your decision to change goals will have been based on factual analyses, and you will have been saved the eventual agony of uselessly chasing a will-o-the-wisp.

Chapter I sets forth the *raison d'etre* and the philosophical basis for technological forecasting. The pace of technological progress in both the military and commercial worlds, the astronomical costs associated with competing alternatives, as well as the penalty awaiting a misguided choice, makes mandatory the need for analyzing the course of technology into the future. The survival and continued existence of corporate entities hinges delicately on the matter of producing such analyses and then employing them properly to create a plan for execution. If plans are not laid for the future, the negligent will find that others who did so will have arrived there sooner and that, for them, there is no longer a future. The approach to the analyses must not solely be intuitive; it is more important that it be analytical, methodical and comprehensive, to a degree that all possible futures, their barrier problems, their promises and their price tags come into focus for your selection. A competitor, you may be sure, will be doing the same. Competence, capability and resources will then determine the day. However, without technological forecasting, the day will have already been determined—superiority in competence, capability and resources notwithstanding.

Chapter II concerns itself with technological forecasting activity in the Federal Government and, more particularly, in the Department of Defense. Since science and technology have a crucial effect on the military posture of a nation, the military departments are experiencing a high tempo of activity in technological forecasting activity—as evidenced by this chapter. But in spite of the imposing strides made, the matter is still in an extreme state of flux. The point has not yet been reached where it is said, "This is it." However, the "hang-up" lies not so much with technological forecasting (though it has its set of problems) as with planning and resource allocation functions based thereon. Useful, viable forecasts can be and have been made as attested to in the appendices. Problems arise in formulating the algorithms and the quantification of values relative to effort contribution, utility, cost, importance and the like which enter the parameters of the algorithms. "Best" solutions of the algorithms yield *suggested* optimum resource allocations and plans for acceptance or modification (or rejection) by military planners in research and development. There is an understandable reluctance or wariness toward such machined "suggestions." And yet, the suggestions are merely processed quantifications of the technical, operational and managerial community judgments. Perhaps the algorithms are too esoteric and frightening; perhaps they are not comprehensive enough. But one must ask the eventual question, "What operates in its place—is this better or worse?" One thing may be said for the methodological approach of forecasting/planning/allocation: It, at the very least, provides an organized starting point for the human discourse leading to accepted plans and allocations.

Chapter III presents in layman's language the basics of technological forecasting techniques and provides an introduction into the idea of normative forecasting. The idea is presented that it is possible to hypothesize a requirement in the far future and then map the barrier problems that must be surmounted to reach that goal. The mapping forward of technological progress then yields the degree of congruence between what must be achieved technologically and that which may otherwise result. At the points of discrepancy one must address himself to timely actions that force congruence or, alternatively, change his goals.

Chapter IV was written to acquaint the reader with the mechanics of technological change so that he might more fully appreciate technological forecasting itself. Further, this material gives insight on how these processes might be modulated to advantage; this is gained by knowing how technological change operates.

The four discernible categories of technological forecasting techniques identified in Chapter IV are presented in considerable detail in Chapter V. Here we consider the use of correlation and regression analyses. For the serious student, it is suggested that these powerful techniques receive further study to gain an appreciation of their use and applicability. In this connection several additional topics in the same vein are amply discussed in current literature, i.e., Bayesian theory, Decision Tree Analysis and the Monte Carlo technique as employed in decision analysis. Chapter V really constitutes a forecaster's "primer." Not only does it detail the various forecasting techniques, but it discusses the most powerful tool the forecaster has in presenting his results and findings. Rhetoric is fine and necessary, but graphics are better and handier. They facilitate presentation, particularly to audiences which might be uninitiated in the basic technical parameters underlying the forecast. In such instances, the forecast must be translated into terms meaningful to the audience. For example, the submariner is not particularly interested in, nor does he necessarily appreciate, forecasts in terms of yield strength of steels; however, if recast in terms of how deep he may be able to dive, then, you gain his immediate attention and understanding. It would be wise to keep in mind the final admonition in this chapter: "Words, numbers, and esoteric formulae may cause the decision-maker to gasp, but a graph immediately gives him a perspective and facile grasp of all the interrelationships involved."

Chapter VI, likewise, is an important part of the forcecaster's "primer." A forecast is not a melange of words, figures and graphs. This chapter prescribes the nature of content and format of a forecast by way of a practical example, the Navy Technological Forecast. Perhaps the most important point made, however, is that regarding *structuring*. This is different than format and represents the mapping-out of attack on the area to be forecasted. What is implied is that a forecast is not just a "blob" of data, it has, in fact, a hierarchical shaping. Given the technological area to be forecasted, one must start from this general starting point to identify the component and sub-component technologies which "tree" downward from that point. The technological forecast, however, commences from the bottom of this tree to arrive at by synthesis the area forecast. This concept of "treeing-down" to arrive at the hierarchical components of a forecast is illustrated in Figure VIII–1.

The remaining chapters including the appendices following (except Appendix B) represent the "practical work" of the book. It is in this material that we come to grips with live, practical situations. Chapter VII and Appendix C are companion pieces. The former describes at length SEER, a variation of the Delphic technique under the general category of intuitive forecasting. Appendix C comprises a shining example of exactly what a comprehensive forecast looks like. This portion of the Navy Technological Forecast, initially described in concept in Chapter II, illustrates in live form the concepts of forecast content, presentation and structuring as treated in Chapter V and VI. The formulation of the type of material contained in Appendix C is the main end toward which the many words of this book are thrust.

Additionally, in order to show the ultimate end of all this forecasting business and its ultimate utility, material has been included that illustrates the final payoff. Chapters VIII, IX and Appendix A contain practical illustrations of the employment of quantitative methods to perform the functions of efforts (alternatives) selection and resource allocation, i.e., "Putting Forecasts to Work."

Finally, and most certainly not least, Dr. Edward B. Roberts "turns the coin over" to examine the opposition side. In doing this, he performs a vital chore in acting as a conscience to prevent us from becoming so enmeshed and enamoured with our forecasting methodologies that our minds become clouded to their limitations and proper uses. Further, his sharp and pointed words stem not from disdain, but more from his desire to see our methods improve. With technological forecasting and associated quantitative methods of selection and allocation in a relative state of infancy, half-cocked schemes can be ill afforded. Similarly, complacency with the capability of current methods must be shunned. We may rest confident, that with the sympathetic urgings, such as those by Dr. Roberts in Appendix B, and with the continued and increasing amount of effort now being expended in this field, maturation is looming into view.

TECHNOLOGICAL FORECASTING

Some people see things and ask why, I dream of things and say, "Why not?"

—ROBERT F. KENNEDY

CHAPTER I

THE CONCEPTUAL FRAMEWORK OF
TECHNOLOGY FORECASTING

Purpose

The purpose of this book is to promote the utilization of a
practical system of logical analysis which, when applied to
pertinent technology data, can result in credible and explicit
conclusions regarding the status and path prediction of a particular technological area of interest. The material ensuing in
this chapter examines, by survey and literature search, possible
forecasting techniques and conceptual approaches to technological forecasting. Scientific or engineering specialists who may be
asked to contribute inputs to forecasts but may have only limited
understanding of technological forecasting and its possible approaches and problems are conceived as the audience toward
whom the material is directed. The attempt herein is to clarify
a complex, controversial subject and to recommend increased
use of a number of techniques and a synoptic viewpoint that can
improve the credibility and utility of forecasts formulated by
these specialists. What follows will also be of interest to users
of such forecasts and, hopefully, will promote greater acceptance of these techniques by providing an explanation of the
rationale and methods of technological forecasting.

It will soon become obvious to the reader that much of the
content of this book is based on technological forecasting experiences in the United States Department of Defense (DOD), and
more particularly, in the Military Services thereof. The reason
for this stems from the fact that these organizations represent
the locale where the predominance of technological forecasting
activity, progress, and sophistication is found. This is not to say
that the techniques and principles to be described are not equally
applicable to similar problems in other locales.

3

Utility of Technological Forecasting

Because the cost of research and development projects is continually increasing, decision makers are forced to become increasingly cautious about approving requests for limited funds. The time has come to examine new approaches to the problem of gaining support for research and development efforts by means of convincing rationales.

One potential solution to this problem lies in obtaining more credible forecasting of technological advances. A technological forecast is defined as a prediction, with a level of confidence, of a technological achievement in a given time frame with a specified level of support. The use of a more explicit forecast, based on historical fact and clearly presented, will help to justify proposed program goals and will enhance chances of approval. Evidence that a goal has been identified and *is feasible* assists decision makers in evaluating the utility of a proposed program, and it may convince them that resources should be allocated to achieve that goal.

In addition, forecasting can aid systems planners by helping them to shorten the time between the achievement of a technological goal and use of the new knowledge in the development of future materiel, systems and capabilities. A reliable forecast of the imminent achievement of a technological goal may be reflected in new development plans, in changes to development plans, and in the timely allocation of resources for development and developmental facilities. The forecast may also identify potential problems associated with the achievement of the goal and lead to their timely solution. It should also serve as a vehicle for communication between technical personnel and planners. There is a need for consistency in the manner in which estimates of probable technical performance are prepared and documented. This is particularly important in military applications and for systems engineering personnel, who are required to combine forecasts from a number of technical areas into concepts for future systems.

Forecasting is not a new idea. Most government and private

institutions employ some means of predicting future events and expressing the degree of their confidence in the occurrence of these events. In most cases, their methods of forecasting are intuitive, and the forecast is expressed as a hunch or feeling. Although it is not intended to discount the intuition of responsible experts in a technical field, many of the methods to be discussed will assist these forecasters in supporting their judgments and in expressing their ideas more clearly. It is hoped that, by the presentation of better methods of forecasting, the number of irresponsible, intuitive guesses in the field of technological forecasting will be reduced and will thereby lead to more acceptable forecasting. The rapid, largely haphazard achievement of technological goals in the twentieth century, and the rising complexity and cost of continued technological advancement, have outdistanced the ability of military forecasters to forecast by using only intuitive methods. Better techniques of forecasting will benefit all of the military services.

There are several general areas in which technological forecasting could be improved. First, it must be credible and specific, and should be based on historical facts and realistic trends. The forecast must be comprehensive enough to include all relevant factors and information.

Secondly, the forecast should be useful and meaningful to its intended readers. For example, it should encompass a time span sufficient to cover the long lead time required for the development of a modern weapon system, and the parameters forecast should be relevant to the functions performed by such systems.

The forecast should be explicit. All estimates and predictions concerning future events should be precisely and definitely stated in narrative or graphic form.

In order to be authoritative and convincing to military decision makers, the forecast must be compiled by experts in the technical field being forecast, although the opinions of outside experts may, of course, be included.

Lenz (I–1) states that the qualities sought for methods of prediction are explicitness, quantitative expression, reproducibility of results, and derivation on a logical basis. Lenz also provides convincing answers to arguments against explicit forecasting by critically examining the following postulated viewpoints leading to conditions of no forecast:

— No forecast possible: Implies each action taken is unrelated to any past experience, present situation, or future intended action. The resulting error is the assumption that all action is then random.

— Anything can happen: external influences are viewed as random processes and decisions thus represent a gamble, with some knowledge of the odds and the stakes.

— The glorious past: assumes continuation of prior circumstances which may no longer exist.

— Implicit assumption that current circumstances will continue: results in a continual attitude of crisis and abrupt reversals of decisions with each change in external circumstances.

— Implicit assumption that existing trends of change will continue: fundamental errors arising from uncritical acceptance of such forecasts are usually not recognized because the unrecorded forecast is difficult to reconstruct after changes in circumstances have intervened.

— Course of action based on an intuitive feeling of future conditions: although implicit intuitive forecasting has been effective in guiding the actions of many successful men, it has the significant weaknesses that it is impossible to teach, expensive to learn, and excludes any process of review.

Lenz concludes that, since some estimate of future conditions is inherent in each managerial decision, the actual question is whether such an estimate should be made unconsciously as an implicit part of the decision or whether it should be arrived at deliberately and stated explicitly.

Conceptual Framework for Technological Forecasting

The complex subject of technological advance can be better understood by viewing technology as knowledge—knowledge of physical relationships systematically applied to useful arts and transferred through the following eight technology transfer levels:*

	Transfer Level	*Example*

Impact Levels

VIII.	Society	Implications of communications technology on society.
VII.	Social systems	Implications of communications technology on defense and other aspects of society.
VI.	Environments	The communications sector of industry.
V.	Applications	The market for communications systems.

Development Levels

IV.	Functional technological systems	Solid-state communications systems and functional sub-systems
III.	Elementary technology	Solid-state technology, integrated circuit technology, etc.
II.	Technological resources	Diffusion techniques, planar techniques, etc.
I.	Scientific resources	Recognition of natural phenomenon of semiconduction.

Within this framework, forecasting can range from very broad predictions to the effects of technology on segments of the economy or society as a whole, to relatively narrow, detailed studies of technological progress in only one technical area, and finally to the initial understanding of how a basic phenomenon can be applied to the solution of a practical problem. Forecasting at levels I through IV predicts the future applications of scientific and technical knowledge to the development of functional systems and is conventionally referred to as state-of-the-art projection, or exploratory forecasting. The prediction of the impact of advancing technology and the consideration/evalua-

* This framework was suggested by Harvy Brooks at the Conference on Technology Transfer and Innovation, held 16–17 May 1966 in Washington, D.C. Cited by Jantsch (I–2).

tion of possible future worlds (i.e., forecasting at levels V through VIII) can be classified as normative forecasting, using the term developed by Gabor (I–3). Normative technological forecasting first assesses future goals, threats, or missions, then considers the impact of the projected technology, and finally works backward to the present. In this conceptual scheme, exploratory forecasting becomes an input to normative forecasting, which in turn becomes the input to a technological plan that can commit resources to the implementation of the desired technology transfer and thereby "invent the future." The area to be treated in this chapter is exploratory forecasting, i.e., the vertical transfer of technology from levels I to IV.

There is evidence that the rate of technological development has been increasing in recent years. In *Technology and the American Economy* (I–4) Lynn concluded from a study of 20 major technological innovations that the incubation period—the typical time between a technical discovery and recognition of its commercial potential—has fallen from 30 years before the first world war to 16 years between the wars and to 9 years in the period 1945–1964. The time between this recognition of commercial potential and the initial commercial application, in turn, decreased from about 7 years to about 5 years.

Quinn (I–5) has stated that the transfer of technology can be better understood when viewed, not as pieces of hardware, but as knowledge of physical relationships systematically applied to the useful arts. This knowledge can vary over time from the initial concept of how a basic phenomenon can be applied to the solution of practical problems to knowledge applied to system components or complex systems. Quinn notes further that what may appear to be a stepwise function advance in a technology is usually nothing more than the accumulation of small advances not worth noting individually until they additively make a significant change in the total technology. Moreover, a given technology generally includes a variety of competing devices, each with a distinctive balance of performance and economic characteristics. Finally, of course, a specific process or product in a technology may fulfill quite divergent needs and perform very dissimilar functions for its various owners. It is this relative continuity in a technology's technical and economic characteristics and potential applications that makes technological forecasting possible.

This predominantly evolutionary advance by small steps has been pointed out by the studies of Gilfillan (I–6) and more recently by DOD Project Hindsight (I–7).

Nelson et al (I–8), in their analysis of the way in which technical advances occur, developed the following operational concept of technological knowledge.

The operational part of the body of technological knowledge is a set of techniques, each defined as a set of actions and decision rules guiding their sequential application, that man has learned will generally lead to a predictable outcome under certain specified circumstances. The stock of known techniques for achieving practical results is only part of the richer and deeper body of human knowledge, which includes, as well, a comprehension of the properties of things under various conditions, relationships among and between objects and properties, and broad frameworks of interpretation.

In many cases, techniques can be derived from the general body of understanding. In other cases, the technique is almost completely empirical, i.e., it works in a predictable way but it is not known why.

At any given time the stock of known techniques defines the set of products that can be made, and the known broad processes (and the range of variation within these processes) for making them. There are four principal constraints on the kinds and quantities of goods that an economy can produce per worker:

— The stock of technological knowledge, which limits the kinds of products man knows how to produce, and the various processes he knows for producing them.

— The education, training, and experience of the work force, which determines the extent to which this knowledge is embodied in people.

— The organization of firms and of the economy as a whole, which determines the effectiveness with which this knowledge can be used.

— The stock of physical capital and the availability of natural resources.

Within these limits, and given time to permit human material resources to be reallocated, there is a considerable range of choice concerning what and how much can be produced. Technological advances take the form of new product designs or new process routines. Examples of the first are the jet engine and penicillin; of the second, the oxygen process for steel making and the arc welding technique. Technological advances in the broader sense also include improved management techniques, such as statistical quality control or production control programming, and new concepts of organizing economic activity. At any given time technological knowledge exists to produce a considerably wider range of products or use a larger set of processes than, in fact, are being supplied or employed. Some of these have been well tested but are sufficiently close that a satisfactory program for their use could easily be specified, given the incentive to do so; the job would be considered routine engineering. Like the obsolete technologies, these are not in use because they are not economic under existing conditions of demand and supply.

In addition to the stock of presently operational techniques, at any time there is a considerable store of ideas reasonably well worked out but still short of operational, and an almost infinite stock of partial or embryonic ideas that are not even close to operational. Technology advances as these ideas are developed into operational form.

The quantity of resources required to make a design idea operational depends upon three key variables:

— The magnitude of the advance sought over existing comparable products.

— The nature of the product field, in particular the size and complexity of the system.

— The stock of relevant knowledge that permits new techniques to be derived or deduced, as well as the stock of available materials and components with which designers can work. At any particular moment, in almost all fields, a number of efforts are in progress aimed at creating new or improved products and processes. Some are aimed at various dimensions of product performance, others at reducing cost. Some reach for major advances, some for minor improvements. As a result, technology seldom is stagnant in any field. The pace of technological advance, however, varies strikingly from one product field to another, and from time to time.

Two broad factors lie behind the differing and changing rates of technological progress. First, there are differences and changes in the rewards for particular kinds of technological advance— demand factors that stimulate or repress efforts aimed at achieving them. Second, there are differences and changes in the stock of relevant components and materials and of knowledge, and in the number of people who possess the relevant knowledge— supply factors which permit or restrict certain kinds of advances. When only marginal modifications in a product or process are sought, the knowledge required need not extend much beyond existing technology. When the advances sought are greater, the inventor must see existing techniques within a significantly larger and perhaps a quite different context. Scientific knowledge has often been the key to that larger context.

The science based technologies and industries have a great advantage in achieving major advances in products and processes. Research aimed at opening up new possibilities has substituted both for chance development in the relevant sciences and for the classical major inventive effort aimed at cracking open a problem through direct attack. The post-World War II explosion of major advances in electronics, aircraft, missiles, chemicals, and medicines reflects the maturing of the science base in these industries as well as the large volume of resources they employ to advance technology.

James Bright, of the Harvard Business School (I–9), has noted seven important tides of technological change. These are:
— Increased transportation capability.
— Increased mastery of energy.

— Extension and control of life.
— Increased ability to alter the characteristics of materials.
— Extension of sensory capabilities.
— Mechanization of physical activities.
— Mechanization of intellectual activities.

To summarize, the evolution of knowledge in the various technology areas yields perceivable patterns of steady but piecemeal improvements in design, based on experience and exploitation of new materials and components and spiced by an occasional major advance. It is the analysis of these patterns that makes technological forecasting possible.

Technological Forecast Structure

Technological forecasting can mean different things to different people. The following classification system is proposed in order to provide a structure for further definition of the type of forecast envisioned:

1. Technology transfer levels involved.
2. Nature of forecast.
   a. Exploratory.
   b. Normative.
   c. Combined forecast and plan.
3. Field of forecast.
   a. Military.
   b. Industrial.
   c. Society as a whole.
4. Orientation of forecast.
   a. Describes future scientific and technological opportunities which can become available if selected by planners.
   b. Forecasts scientific and technological capabilities or events (choice by planners not included as a contingency).
   c. Forecasts impact of application of such capabilities.
5. Breadth of forecast—may range from either projections of the major forces of science and technology to projections

of narrowly defined specific design parameters such as horse-power per pound of power plant.

    6. Method of gathering inputs.

        a. Permanent in-house function assigned to pertinent field departments or laboratories but assembled by central group.

        b. Central "think" group (e.g., GE Tempo, RAND Corporation).

        c. Technical panel (in-house or supplemented by outside sources).

        d. Forecasting institute or consulting firm.

        e. Staff analysis group.

        f. Ad hoc study group.

        g. Scientific adviser.

        h. Research committee.

    7. Predominant forecasting technique utilized.

        a. Intuitive.

        b. Statistical.

        c. Cause and effect analysis.

        d. Analogy.

        e. Models and conceptual schemes.

        f. Others.

    8. Extent of "self-fulfilling" nature of forecast (i.e., degree to which forecast can stimulate action and thereby create the forecast effect).

If military research and development (R&D) planning is viewed in the conceptual framework previously given in the above classification scheme, exploratory forecasting can be looked upon as the presentation of future technological opportunities and threats, while normative forecasting might be considered as the goal-setting portion of long-range planning. The long-range plan then becomes a statement of goals and objectives and the proposed approaches to achieving these goals. The program is the final commitment of the organization to put its resources into the approaches outlined in the technical plan. More of these matters with regard to military R&D planning will be covered in the next chapter.

The Meaning of a Forecast

Modern management emphasizes consideration of future events at times of decision. In small organizations, the facts, projections, and probabilities may be the responsibility assumed by a single individual. In larger organizations and in a time of changing technology, the structure, facts, and probabilities are processed by more sophisticated information systems.

To accomplish long-range research and development planning, two fundamentals are prerequisite. First, one must have clearly in mind the future objectives to be achieved. Second, one must have a relatively clear knowledge of the anticipated state-of-the-art in the several supporting sciences and technologies at the time when they will be exploited to achieve these objectives.

A technological forecast is a realistic estimate, by technically knowledgeable persons, of the rate, direction, and extent to which a particular technology or group of technologies will develop in a specific period of time. Its purpose is to separate clearly the more likely technical states from the less likely.

A forecast is not a plan, it is not to be construed as a commitment that material or a technical achievement will be available at the time or in the form indicated, or that it will be developed at all. It will not predict breakthroughs nor will it describe the innovation.

Technical forecasting does, however, indicate that a significant advance is in the offing and suggests probable timing of the advance. Thus, by providing a continuing state-of-the-art assessment, a primary value of technical forecasting is the early recognition of a scientific development which in turn allows for timely response.

Technological forecasting alone cannot determine what will have been accomplished in science or technology by some future date. The technological future will be determined by a number of factors, including financial support, the number of scientists or engineers working in a particular field, the number of new ideas or innovations introduced into the field, and a communication or interplay factor among the men and ideas.

A technological forecast itself must communicate. It must stimulate operational minds, but within the bounds of technological feasibility. It must satisfy technical minds that it is reliable and relevant within professional standards. To reach both these minds, it must be presented concisely, quantitatively, and accurately.

The development and analysis of technological forecasts can be an effective influence in the creative thought processes which are essential to dynamic management. Each projection requires careful consideration of the factors which influence the indicated progress. As apparent inconsistencies and barriers become evident, attention and effort must be focused on their removal. The necessity for innovation is projected well in advance so that the usual procrastination in introducing change may be overcome.

In the long run, it is not enough that a technological forecast serve only general communication. It must find its way into the formulation of plans, programs, advanced designs, allocation policies, and other management functions. Continuous revision and feedback from users will be required to create a recognized valuable management tool. Since decisions usually tend to be made in the general direction of existing progress trends, one of the most important functions of the accurate technological forecast is to insure that such decisions do not result in "too little— too late" or in "too much—too soon."

Variation Among Technical Fields

Naval technology embraces a wide spectrum: ordnance, logistics, protection, communications, medicine, toxics, detection, environment, human factors, surveillance, to mention a few major areas. The basic and applied sciences feeding into these military technologies are even broader, perhaps as broad as almost all science and engineering. Furthermore, the science and research sponsored under one technology usually produces inputs to other technologies. Research in power sources, for example, could change the configuration of ordnance systems as well as transportation systems. Research in immunology could change medical practice or biological warfare vulnerability. Research in lasers could change communication systems and/or antipersonnel weapons. Micrometeorology research for chemical warfare also applies to surveillance, and so on.

There is a natural tendency for research and engineering sponsored under any one technology to be forecast in terms of applications to that technology. There is also a tendency for forecasts to include only the currently justified and sponsored research and engineering. While these tendencies are natural and always expected, they are prejudicial to the breadth of vision a forecast should possess ideally.

The initial attitude toward forecasting is quite different among the various scientific and engineering fields. It would be a dangerous oversimplification to characterize these attitudes by field in sharply-defined terms. But for the sake of illustration, and for sympathy with the forecasting specialist's problem, the following examples are given. The physicist is said to favor the random-breakthrough concept of future technology, which implies that one does not forecast, one waits until it happens and then sees how it affects applications. The engineer or applied scientist is sometimes accused of being reluctant to forecast because he tips his hand and gives development or patent possibilities to his competitors. The biomedical scientist is reluctant to forecast, it is alleged, because critical experiments, not parameter extrapolation, is the procedure for progress. The systems designer is leery of forecasts because component and subsystem progress depends on resource-allocation decisions made by people over whom he has no control.

One objective of formal forecasting is to develop a realistic and acceptable, common philosophy toward forecasting among technical fields.

Early Models

Technological forecasting has no established epistemology, no recognized theory or science of methods. At one extreme we find an apparent willingness to assign this function to the very imaginative science fiction writers; at the other, a suggested requirement for a very scholarly approach. Alexander (I–10) presents a very reasonable case for the "Jules Verne" school and gives evidence of the success of this approach. Gilfillan, in considering the prediction of invention (I–11) merely specifies some 38 principles of invention. These principles might, through the inductive method described by Bacon and illustrated in Darwin, yield a skeleton about which a forecast methodology could be built. In any event, the methodologies suggested by Alexander or induced from Gilfillan could be classed simply as "forecast by informed judgment."

Lovewell and Bruce of the Stanford Research Institute (I–12) suggest that the forecast can be accomplished by "thorough logical surveys of current and conjectured applications of science—and of their consequences," and describe such an approach in reasonable detail. Their primary departure from Alexander, more so than from Gilfillan, is to augment the simpler "informed judgment" approach by introducing a requirement for an explicit statement of the rationale leading to each prediction.

Lenz (I–13) departs from the essentially single point predictions of the previously mentioned and addresses a procedure for forecasting by "trend extrapolation." Here we find an indication that a model for technological forecasting might be built; that analytical techniques might be applied to assessing the technological future; that a tool can be derived to provide a means for assuring dispassionate application of the informed judgment of scientific and technical expertise.

The case is made for the relative roles for analysis and for judgment by Secretary McNamara when in speaking about system analysis, or, as he called it, "quantitative common sense," he said, "I would not, if I could, attempt to substitute analytical techniques for judgment based on experience. The very development and use of those techniques have placed an even greater premium on that experience and judgment, as issues have been clarified and basic problems exposed to dispassionate examination. The better the factual basis for reflective judgment, the better the judgment is likely to be. The need to provide the factual basis is the reason for emphasizing the analytical approach" (I–14). In precisely this sense can the general character of the desired technological forecast model be described: a tool to insure that factual bases are used for reflective "informal judgment."

Serious Science Forecasting and Science Fiction

The art and science of technological forecasting is young. It almost seems contradictory to the rigorous standards of evidence taught in professional education. It may seem closer to science fiction than to fact. For this reason, reputable professionals are often hostile to or skeptical of technological forecasts. Yet for the preparation of the Navy Technological Forecast, the best qualified persons were utilized. The very mind which has been steeped in the facts and figures of a field for years and which creates hypotheses, experiments, or designs "at the bench," is the one which can make professional conjectures with realism and restraint.

The technical expert is not asked to create science fiction. The laws of nature as known in his field are both the vehicles and the boundaries of serious projections. He is not asked to recite these laws or to write a text on what is known in his field. He is asked to sit back and think a little differently, synthetically instead of analytically. In order to plan his next experiment or design in everyday work, he sorts out critical issues which stand in the way of mental acceptance of a smooth-flowing set of propositions. This or that proposition or issue needs test or demonstration. In forecasting, he is encouraged to examine the same universe with the same rigor, but to visualize the implications of the confluence of laws, possible results of new experiments, and trends within limiting factors. This is not science fiction. It is just another mode of responsible professional thinking which heretofore was unverbalized and uncommunicated but which now, in the age of technological strategy and tactics, must be articulated and integrated with other information to maximize organizational survival and growth.

The "Breakthrough" Argument

There arises an argument: You cannot predict breakthroughs; therefore, why predict at all?

Breakthroughs rarely occur. Examples like incandescent filaments, penicillin, transistors, and lasers are often used. But if history is examined a little more closely, one will discover long intervals between a hypothesis based on fairly solid previous knowledge and a demonstration of fact or feasibility.

Breakthroughs are partial. They seldom are sufficient to change systems and applications overnight. They may affect components and methods, but these are tied in with larger systems which are rooted in the past and present by an environment of many other components and methods. Systems evolve into being; they do not suddenly jump into being.

Breakthroughs can be the expected products of only a very small fraction of the R&D effort. The majority of research and development progress is accomplished by small steps, tedious competent work, many frustrations, and incremental gains.

Breakthroughs may not be predictable in time of occurrence, but their effects can be estimated if they occur at predicted times.

This last point supports arguments for a fertile and well-integrated technological forecast as a document and source of information. Unless the future image is knit closely together, with the interactions between purposes, systems, and technology spelled out, the estimation of the impact of hypothetical or anticipated (in the sense of betting) breakthroughs is a wild and uncertain exercise. With all the information tied together, and the technological forecast a vital segment of the information, the impact of breakthroughs can be examined logically.

The "Status Quo Preservation" Argument

The argument is made that the future tends to fulfill an image, not because of any magic, but because the image is a focus for shaping events. Consciously or subconsciously, the image is used by persons to organize otherwise chaotic bits and pieces of experience and information. Raw data are converted into information when the sensory input is screened for its relevance to the image. Reconfiguration of the image is partly conditioned by the historical flow of sensory information. The course of history may well be interpreted as casually related to the succession of images of the future held by persons along the way.

Forecasters and users of forecasts must be aware of the possible implications of this argument because the technological forecast is a collection of images of the future, no matter how it is separated or consolidated. One of these implications is "preservation of the status quo." If a forecast is just a rehash of a long-range R&D plan (the latter having been prepared first and justified with a supporting program), then the forecast is being used to validate the plan. More properly, a plan is a consequence of the forecast and other factors, and the plan should change annually with the new round of forecast information, requirements information, and budget levels.

The forecast could be misused by management in such a punitive manner that the forecast is forced into the straitjacket of a commitment. If forecasters are held responsible for the truth of their forecasts, they will tend to be conservative in predicting progress and change and will underestimate the rate of change to keep it under control.

Sophisticated Prediction Models

With the state-of-the-art in technological forecasting as underdeveloped as it is, the Navy Technological Forecast (NTF) is not an attempt at sophistication nor is it a requirement that the forecasters develop sophisticated tools and techniques for forecasting. Years of "research on research" and "planning on planning" must precede a technology of technological forecasting. What is desired now is substantive information with as much breadth and reliability as possible, without knowing how to measure either.

Balance: Conservatism vs. Optimism

In the long run, the utility of a technological forecast will depend upon the good professional judgment of the forecasters. The judgment referred to is the technical judgment, not value judgment. A scientist or engineer may believe that a technology is feasible or likely, but disagree with the social/economic implications. When addressing the technical question, only the technical answer is desired.

The easiest way to undermine or unbalance a technological forecast is to address it only to technical questions which have obvious immediate payoffs. Safeguards must be erected against this possible shortcoming of a forecast.

Another serious problem of balance exists in the possibilities of overstatement and understatement. A very conservative forecast may imply low risk for the forecaster and high risk for the planner. A very optimistic forecast may have high risk to the forecaster and low risk for the planner. However, these risk statements may be reversed when the natures of the risks are examined.

Conditions and Contingencies

Trends convey the semantics of growth, development, evolution, progress, and direction. The planner needs, in addition, a sense of the boundaries and restrictions, a sense of proportion and likelihood. All too often, a technological forecaster may show vistas and scenery without the road map and the hazards along the way. Whereas good salesmanship is supposed to favor the vista approach, sincere judgment is desired in the technological forecast. The sincerity of a forecast can be conveyed by an honest and communicative appraisal of the conditions, contingencies, rates, phase changes, limitations, and complexities which impinge upon the trend. Graphics are useful adjuncts to the written word in showing these limitations.

Sometimes applied research, and often basic research, is

characterized as "inner motivated," meaning that the path of progress depends on the results at each step. A forecaster may be reluctant to nominate the final path in prospect because he does not know the specific results at each step. On the other hand, he may know the general objective and the possible alternatives at various junctures in the branching process.

The trend of technology in terms of naval applications may, in some fields, be conditioned by forces outside the control of the in-house R&D community. The trend may depend on the reaction of relatively disinterested parties. One example may be the synthesis of pharmaceuticals or the engineering of complex biomedical instrumentation. Industry R&D governed largely by consumer markets will be the main source of technological advances for many naval applications. The forecaster's problem is to describe the likely progress of industry in response to the consumer market and to anticipate the incidental advances for naval application.

REFERENCES

I −1. Lenz, R. C., Jr., *Technological Forecasting,* 2d Edition, Aeronautical Systems Division, AFSC, ASD–TDR–62–414, Wright-Patterson AFB, Ohio: June 1962 (AD408–085).

I– 2. Jantsch, Erich, *Technological Forecasting in Perspective,* Working Paper DAS/SPR/66.2, Organization for Economic Cooperation and Development, Paris, France: October 1966.

I– 3. Gabor, Dennis, *Inventing the Future,* Secker and Warburg, New York, 1963, Pelican Book A663, Penguin Books, Harmondsworth, Middlesex: 1964.

I– 4. U.S. National Commission on Technology, Automation, and Economic Progress, Report, Volume I, *Technology and American Economy,* Washington, D.C.: February 1966.

I– 5. Quinn, James Brian, "Technological Forecasting," *Harvard Business Review,* March/April 1967.

I– 6. Gilfillan, S. Colum, "The Prediction of Inventions," in: U.S. National Resources Committee, Technological Trends and National Policy, Part I, Section II, pp. 15–23. U.S. Government Printing Office, June 1937.
——, *The Sociology of Invention,* Follett Publishing Co., Chicago, Illinois: 1935.
——, "The Prediction of Technical Change," *The Review of Economics and Statistics,* Volume XXXIV, November 1952, pp. 368–385.

I– 7. Chalmers W. Sherwin and Raymond S. Isenson, "Project Hindsight, "
       Science, Vol. 156, 23 June 1967, pp. 1571–77.
I– 8. Richard R. Nelson, Merton J. Peck, and Edward D. Kalachek,
       Technology, Economic Growth and Public Policy, Washington,
       Brookings Institution, 1967.
I– 9. Bright, James R. (Ed.), *Research, Development, and Technological
       Innovation,* Richard D. Irwin, Homewood, Illinois: 1964.
I–10. *The Wild Birds Find a Corporate Roost,* T. Alexander, Fortune Mag-
       azine, Vol. 1.XX, pp. 130ff (Aug. 1964).
I–11. *The Sociology of Invention,* S. C. Gilfillan, Follet Publishing Co.,
       pp. 5–13 (1935).
I–12. *How We Predict Technological Change,* P. J. Lovewell and R. D.
       Bruce, "New Scientist," Vol. 13, pp. 370–373 (1962).
I–13. Ibid 1 supra.
I–14. "McNamara Defines His Job," *New York Times Magazine,* April 26,
       1964, pp. 107ff.

Weapons determine tactics; tactics do not determine weapons.

　　　　　　　　　—HANNIBAL (et sequitar)

CHAPTER II

TECHNOLOGICAL FORECASTING IN THE DEPARTMENT
OF DEFENSE AND OTHER GOVERNMENT AGENCIES

SCIENCE AND TECHNOLOGY are having an increasing influence
on the military posture of nations (II–1). The pace of technological change greatly affects the short and long term environment and with it strategic planning in the Department of Defense (DOD). It is obvious that a need exists for a comprehensive look into the future to forecast what the force structure of
the service might look like in ten to twenty years.

The Services, to be effective, must be able to anticipate and
lead the course of events, not merely react to events as they
occur. Every individual and organization must think ahead in
order to prosper, but the concerns of the military tend to be
larger than those of others, and the results of its actions may
determine U. S. survivability as well as committing itself to some
future course of action for greater periods of time. Thus, for
DOD, the ability to be future oriented is singularly important.

In order to establish long-range objectives for the United
States in matters of domestic and foreign affairs it is necessary
to project the political-social-economic environment over the
next twenty years. The military's part in this postulated world
situation should also be identified as a responsibility to meet any
eventuality at any time. To provide optimum military worth
from limited resources is the goal of all DOD Research, Development, Testing and Evaluation (RDT&E) which must be
directed to the achievement of long-range as well as short-term
goals.

The expansive growth of technology in the mid-20th century
has posed a dilemma to the military planner which is well stated
in the Rockefeller Fund report (II–2):

"All is not well with present United States (military policy); strategic concepts lag behind developments in technology and in the world political situation . . . Systems of budgets, appropriations, and fiscal managements are out of gear with the radically accelerating flow of military developments. . . .

"Four factors—the importance of a growing industrial base, the crucial role of lead-times, the increasing significance of forces in being, and the necessity of a versatile military establishment—impose on policy makers an unparalleled problem of choice. It is further complicated by the explosive rapidity with which technology is developing . . . Moreover, each new weapon system costs more than double its predecessor which it replaces at shorter and shorter intervals.

"This technological race places an extraordinary premium on the ability to assess developing trends correctly . . ."

Purpose of a Military Technological Forecast

The purpose of a military technological forecast is to help in resolving the above dilemma by making technological trends more explicit to planning personnel in the operational and technical communities.

The science of technological forecasting is very new. Consequently, as of now, no formal approach to forecasting methodology has been developed. This chapter will review current philosophy and state-of-the-art techniques employed in projecting technological advancements, especially in the military environment. A technological forecast is a tool for planning and decision-making, but it is not a plan. A forecast could be a plan if a commitment were made to apply resources to eventuate the forecast. Technological forecasting alone does not determine what will be accomplished in the future in the Research and Technology areas. The environment will be generated by many other criteria such as budgeting policies, technological breakthroughs in other areas, and probably most important, the sociopolitical environment. This does not mean, however, that we shouldn't forecast because a technological forecast does give the opportunity to the operator to select the portions of the forecast which he would want to implement. After this selection is made and the resources applied, he is in a better position to insure that these decisions do not bring the technological building blocks to the systems arena either too early to be utilized or too late to be incorporated in that particular system.

Advantages of Technological Forecasting to the Military RDT&E Program

RDT&E within the military services is characteristically conducted as a dialogue between the Users Interest represented by the tactical side of the house and the Producers Interest represented by the technical side of the house. Plans are the result of "negotiations" between the two interests. The planning process is a continuing iterative interchange. Through this process the trade-offs are made which will result in the maximum military capability for the Operating Forces that are possible within the limits of available resources.

If the military is to meet its operational needs in the future, early decisions are vital; it takes an average of eight to eleven years to get today's technical developments into the Fleet, Air or Field. A technological forecast which identifies, in terms of military relevance, future opportunities arising from advances in science and technology, will provide one element on which the necessary dialogue can be structured.

A meaningful forecast would assist in the projection of military policy and force structures to meet anticipated enemy threats. It would find extensive use in:

— Projecting U. S. technological capabilities during the forecast period. It would identify technologies which would enhance the operational capability and effectiveness of the military.

— Providing the necessary input into a technology/capability matrix to define Exploratory Development Goals (EDG's) and systems configurations to meet and/or exceed the projected enemy threat. Scientific and technological areas which have intuitively high pay-off not directly responsive to the projected threat would be identified.

— Making better postulations of the enemy threat during the forecast period by identifying U. S. technological capabilities which may be assumed to be within an enemy's potential. Complete interpretation, understanding and establishment of the threat are considered to be outside the responsibility of the Technological Forecast.

— Serving senior management by presenting strengths and capabilities of military scientific and technical efforts.

By formalizing the inputs from the technical community to the definition of long-range military capabilities, the forecast could be used in preparing the following planning documents:

- Joint Long Range Strategic Study (JLRSS)
- Navy Strategic Study (NSS)
- Air Force Systems Command's Planning Activity Report (PAR)
- Army Basic Strategic Estimate (BASE)
- Army Combat Development Objectives Guide (CDOG)
- Navy Mid-Range Study (NMS)
- Navy Mid-Range Objectives (NMRO)
- Air Force, Army and Navy General Operational Requirements (GOR)
- Air Force Technical Objective Documents (TOD's)
- Army Qualitative Material Development Objectives (QMDO's)
- Navy Exploratory Development Goals (EDG's)
- Air Force, Army and Navy Tentative Specific Operational Requirements (TSOR)
- Air Force, Army and Navy Advanced Development Objectives (ADO)
- Air Force, Army and Navy Specific Operational Requirements (SOR)

A formal forecast would provide inputs to feasibility studies at all levels in the military's operational and technical communities. The forecast would make available to the laboratories and technical offices projections of the state-of-the-art in supporting areas outside their immediate scientific or technical expertise. It would identify technological areas which have high potential in sensitive development areas. A moderate improvement in some technical areas, for example, can have a high impact on operational effectiveness, whereas a large technical gain in other areas may not improve an operational capability. It would also identify the extent of interdependence of the various technical disciplines and areas in which component developments are compatible or augment one another. When more than one function contributes to an end-item development, a reasonable forecast can be employed to determine the relative burden on the projected state-of-the-art in each contributing area. Hence, the projected forecast would be valuable in preparing Proposed Technical Approaches (PTA) and Technical Development Plans (TDP).

The generation of the military technological forecast would be the responsibility, primarily, of the various in-house laboratories. It is anticipated that in its preparation attention would be directed not to linear extrapolation of current programs, but to all military areas of scientific and technical expertise.

The forecast, being generated by laboratory personnel, would strengthen the laboratories' planning functions by encouraging longer-range projections of scientific and technical capabilities and would provide greater communication with higher echelon planners. Fluctuations in program planning and funding can be reduced by having better predictions which would improve operational capabilities based on anticipated advances in technology.

Technological Forecasting in the Military Services

ARMY

The Army Long Range Technological Forecast (LRTF) is prepared under staff supervision of the Chief of Research and Development. It is intended to describe knowledge, capabilities and examples of material which science and technology can be expected to produce if supported by orderly programs of research and development. The document is used by operational and organizational planners, the combat developments system, and long range research and development planners in the Department of the Army in formulating new concepts, requirements and plans.

The Long Range Technological Forecast is currently published in three volumes, as follows:

Volume One, "Scientific Opportunities," discusses the opportunities and limitations in both nonmaterial- and material-oriented research which will affect future technical capabilities of the Army. Where research effort to increase knowledge in a specific area is needed but not now in prospect, the area and the requirements are described.

Volume Two, "Technological Capabilities," describes the technical capabilities which are foreseen as achievable in areas vital to the provision of future high-performance material.

Volume Three, "Advanced System Concepts," includes examples of material systems which might be provided if the capabilities described in Volume Two are achieved.

The Commanding General, U. S. Army Materiel Command, formally compiles and consolidates Army-wide critiques and contributions to this Forecast with the close cooperation of the Army Research Office on behalf of the Chief, Research and Development. The relationship of the Army Long Range Technological Forecast to Army planning documents is shown in Figure II–1. The Forecast is one input to the "Basic Army Strategic Estimate." It is used by the Combat Development Command in the preparation of doctrinal studies, Qualitative Materiel Development Objectives, and qualitative Materiel Requirements cited in the Combat Development Objectives Guide (CDOG).

In addition to the ALRTF, the Army conducts a series of Forecasts-in-Depth intended to provide an insight into specific technological fields, for use by persons within and outside the Department of the Army who have need for such background information. A Forecast-in-Depth (FID) is primarily an ency-

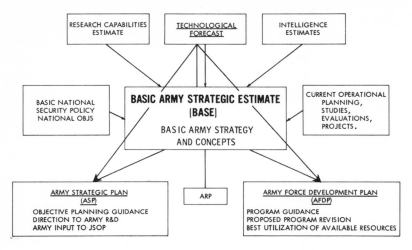

Figure II-1. Role of Forecast in Army Planning.
(Source: AMC Phamphlet 705-1, Volume I, January 1966)

clopedic summary of the current knowledge, a projection of the expected technological environment during the next 20 years, and an analysis of the research effort required to attain the most promising materiel aspects. Its purpose is to enable scientists and technically and operationally oriented individuals to communicate relevant ideas and learn of potentialities in a given field.

A Forecast-in-Depth, while generally comprehensive, is not exhaustive. Hence, the treatment may properly be considered an over-all introduction to the current state-of-the-art and a 20-year extrapolation of the technological environment. An extensive bibliography is included.

AIR FORCE

In the Air Force it has become a tradition to prepare technological forecasts by periodically convening large groups of scientists and engineers from government laboratories and from the scientific and industrial community. Such groups have been assembled in an approximately five-year cycle for periods of concentrated study extending over several months. The two most

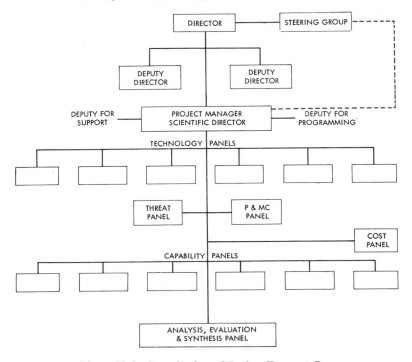

Figure II–2. Organization of Project Forecast Group.
(Source: Air Force Project Instruction Manual, 1963)

recent technological forecasting studies conducted by the Air Force were the Woods Hole Studies of 1957/58 and Project Forecast in 1963. Both of these were broad-scope studies involving many fields of technology of interest to the Air Force. Both produced a series of reports which contained technological forecasts for periods ten to fifteen years into the future.

Figure II–2 shows the organization of the latest major Air Force effort, Project Forecast. The forecasting of technology was done by the Technology Panels identified on the chart. The project organization was used as a mechanism for relating the forecast to military capabilities, the threat, and national policy considerations, through specific panels established for this purpose.

In the interim period between formal technological forecasting studies, the panel reports are distributed throughout the Air Force, where they are used as reference material in Air Force planning documents such as the following:

— *Office of Aerospace Research Five-Year Plan.* The Office of Aerospace Research (OAR) is responsible for the Air Force research program. Since OAR tasks are generally of a long-term nature, its goals must be forecast against relatively uncertain visions of the future. Nevertheless, in the interest of maximum economy and effectiveness in the use of our national resources, the OAR intends to proceed along carefully plotted courses of action. This year's (1968) Five Year Plan sets forth organizational and research objectives for FY 1969 through FY 1973, describes courses of action for their accomplishment, and presents studied estimates of the requisite resources.

— *AFSC Planning Activity Report.* The Air Force Systems Command's Planning Activity Report is the principal document for reporting on development planning activities under the control of Headquarters, Air Force Systems Command. It provides descriptions, funding, schedules, and pertinent progress milestones for development planning activities that (1) lead to the development of a new system or new equipment for the operational inventory, (2) lead to the submission of a Proposal for an Advanced Development Program to demonstrate the technical feasibility of a subsystem or building block and/or to establish the confidence level in an experimental system or equipment which may be incorporated into the operational inventory, (3) examine an operational mission or function in depth to identify system concepts that may improve the operational capability to perform the mission, and (4) examine specific technological advancements to determine their potential applications to the various Air Force missions or functions.

— *RTD Long Range Plan.* This plan, prepared by the Air Force Directorate of Laboratories (DOL), formerly the Research and Technology Division (RTD), considers the management of Air Force Exploratory and Advanced Development programs. It is prepared by scientists and engineers in the Air Force laboratories. It is an attainable plan in that it describes how DOL will allocate the resources that it may realistically expect to have available over the next decade. The plan is oriented toward achieving the level of technology required to attain future Air Force capabilities, many of which were identified by Project Forecast. It also recognizes that a major objective of the Directorate is to build and maintain a strong in-house technical capability in the Air Force laboratories. DOL's plan is not unalterable; breakthroughs will occur, and efforts that prove unfruitful will be terminated. On the whole, however, the plan represents a coordinated picture of where DOL is going in the next decade.

     — *Technical Objectives Documents.* These are prepared by the Research and Technology Division, AFSC, to provide means of communicating with science and industry and to describe means of communicating with science and industry and to describe the Air Force's objectives in each of 36 different technical areas. As is the case in any selective grouping of science and technology, it is difficult to draw sharp boundaries between areas and thus overlaps occur within the documents.

     — *Technology for Tomorrow.* The fifth and latest edition of this document was published by the Aeronautical Systems Division, AFSC, in 1962. (At present only a reference document, it may be reinstated by the Research and Technology Division, AFSC.) It was a presentation of motivational concepts outlining the approach to an optimum plan. It was a guide to the organization and selective application of resources and capabilities for aggressive support of the Air Force's long-range technical mission. The contents and organization of the document reflected the fact that a cohesive detailed plan existed collectively in the minds of the engineers, scientists, and management personnel who have contributed to its formulation.

NAVY

     Intuitive prediction of technological capability was common in routine planning activity in the Navy technical community (see Figure II–3), but in February 1968 a formalized coordinated forecast was instituted.

     Figure II–3 also illustrates the functional status of the tech-

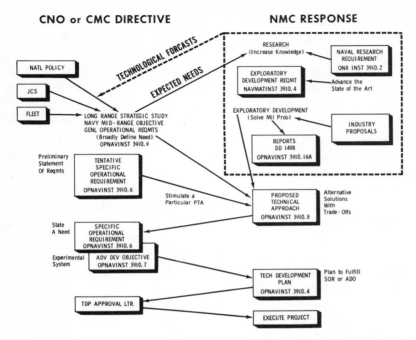

Figure II–3. Technological Forecasting's Position in Navy
Planning. (Source: OPNAV Instruction 3900.8C).

nological forecast within the flow sequence of planning documents. It is shown that requirements are assessed against feas-
ibilities as referenced to time, with two important planning
criteria outputs

— Technological constraints or limits imposed which
serve to define feasible performance in relation to desired performance.

— Implications for the orientation or emphasis shifts in
defined areas of research and development.

During the past two years several informal meetings were
held by representatives of the Chiefs of Naval Operations, Material, Development, and Research to discuss the desirability of
producing a formal Navy Technological Forecast. Two groups
composed of various Navy representatives were then established
by the Chief of Naval Research and the Chief of Naval Develop-

ment to conduct investigation studies relative to utility, techniques, and implementation of technological forecasting. The groups concluded that the Navy would realize definite benefits at all management levels by the application of meaningful forecasts in planning, research, technology, and operational systems development programs.

The Chief of Naval Development has assumed the responsibility for the entire Navy's technology forecasting with the aid of a small group designated the Technological Forecasting Group reporting to him.

The resultant Navy Technological Forecast (NTF) consists of a loose-leaf document in three parts containing individual prognostications of pertinent advances, capabilities, limitations or developments which the naval scientific and technological community can be predictably assured of having available during a forthcoming 20-year period. This document describes scientific knowledge, capabilities in technology, and examples of subsystems, components, or systems which science and technology should expect to produce during this period. The NTF is divided into three parts for convenience of the user.

   • *Part I—Scientific Opportunities:* Describes significant projections of research in the physical, engineering, environmental and life sciences normally associated with the RDT&E 6.1 planning categories. The advances and limitations in scientific research defined in Naval Research Requirements which are relevant to future technological capabilities of the Navy are discussed.

   • *Part II—Technological Capabilities:* Contains the significant projections of applied research and development which normally are included in RDT&E 6.2 planning categories. This section of the forecast covers a broad spectrum of research and development ranging from basic technologies (e.g. Power Conversion) to functional capabilities (e.g. Deep Ocean Technology).

   • *Part III—Probable Systems Options:* Relies heavily on the first two parts to suggest examples of subsystems or systems which could be developed if the capabilities described in Parts I and II above are achieved. The examples included are supported by realistic projected capabilities.

Additional information on the Navy Technological Forecast can be found in Chapter VI.

MARINE CORPS

The Marine Corps presently employs the Navy Technological Forecast and the Army Long Range Technological Forecast, interpreting them in terms of specific Marine Corps applications. In addition, under Marine Corps sponsorship, the Syracuse University Research Corporation engaged in a study (Project 1985) in 1963–1964, entitled, "The United States and the World in the 1985 Era," which examined "projected national objectives and policies, the international and domestic military, economic, and technological factors affecting the United States in the 1985 area." It is planned that the Army Long Range Technological Forecast will continue to be used in areas in which Marine Corps interests parallel those of the Army, and that the Navy Technological Forecast will meet the needs of the Marine Corps in most other technical areas.

A Communications Media

There is a need for improvement in communications between the operating and technical communities within the military. The Technological Forecast is designed to provide a vehicle that can partially fulfill this need. Figure II–4 illustrates the framework whereby the tactical-technical dialogue takes place through an upward flow of technical capabilities, forecasts, and systems concepts which meet with the objective of mating with the constraining downward flow of missions, technological goals, and operational requirements. The scientific community "proposes" technological capabilities while the operational community "disposes" to fulfill strategic and tactical needs.

A technological forecast of scientific and technical capabilities can constitute a vital part of the over-all tactical-technical dialogue. The forecast can assist in establishing guides for mili-

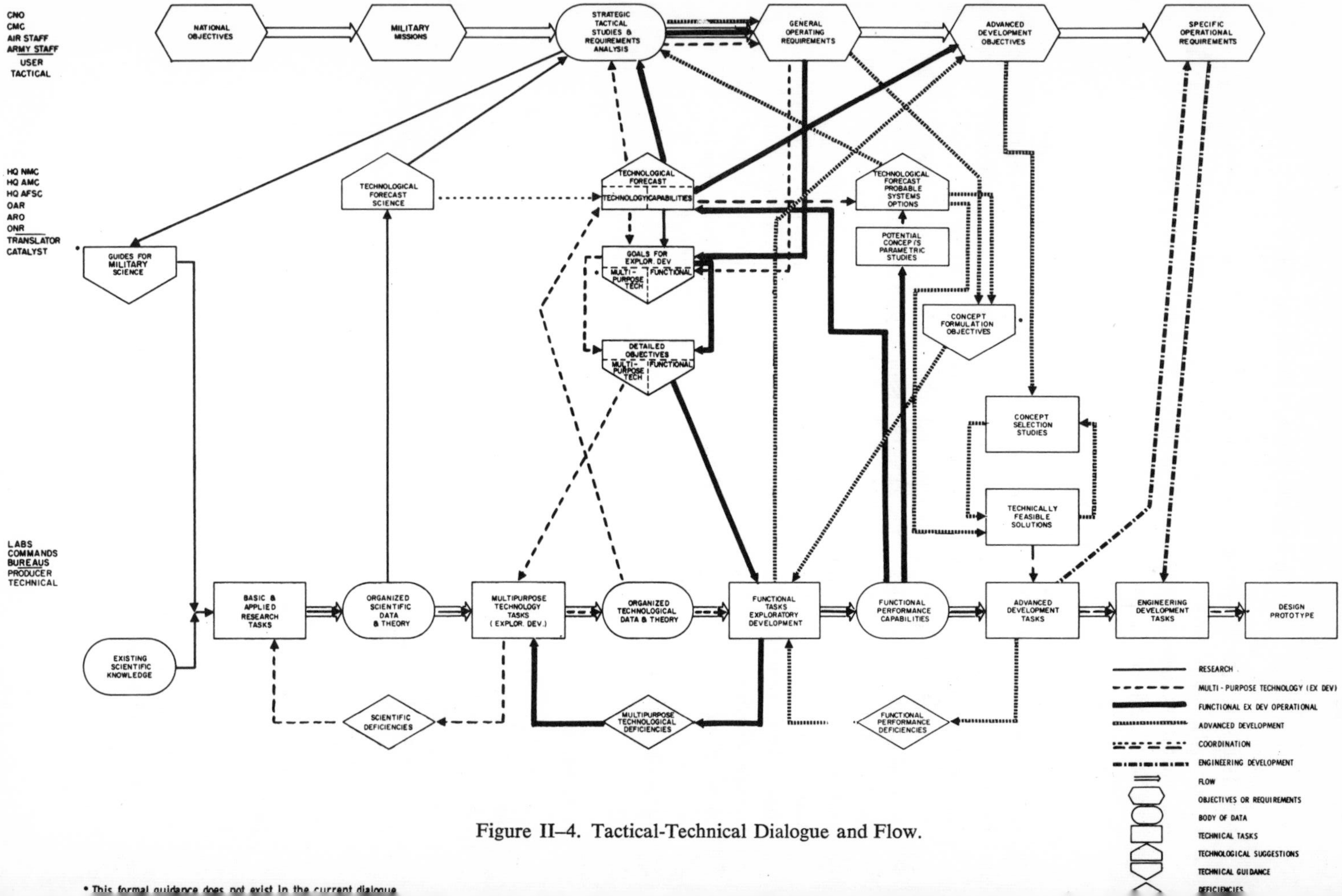

Figure II-4. Tactical-Technical Dialogue and Flow.

* This formal guidance does not exist in the current dialogue.

tary science and goals for exploratory development by making available capabilities leading to concept suggestions for use in developing requirements. What may be seen from this chart is that the goals translate tactical requirements into technical objectives and the forecast translates technical capabilities into strategic possibilities.

The forecast and the goals form a two-way street. Ideas and desired capabilities which are gained in developing the goals might show up as missing in the forecast. Conversely potentials which would otherwise not be considered in the plan will turn up in the forecast. If the forecast is good, it can be a repository of avenues of technical approaches from which choices can be made in developing the goals.

It can be seen from a proposed R&D planning sequence in Figure II–5 that Technology, including Technological Forecasting, as well as Threat and Policy determinations, play a major

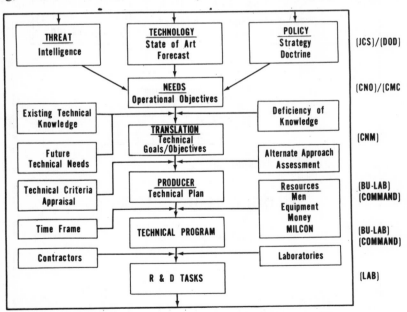

Figure II–5. Proposed R&D Planning Sequence in the Navy
(Source: A Proposal for a Navy Technological
Forecast, May 1966).

role in developing Operational Objectives. An analysis of these operational objectives and current and projected technology result in Goals for Exploratory Development and/or technical objectives. The goals/objectives are then appraised technically and alternate approaches are considered prior to being incorporated into the technical plan. This technical plan when approved would serve as a basis for the procurement of resources, as well as the generation of the technical program. This procurement and program generation should go on concurrently so that the time frame could be sharply reduced. The technical program

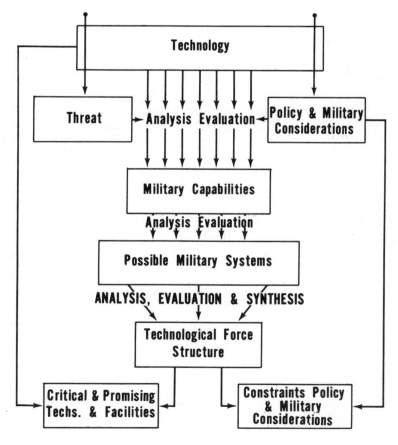

Figure II–6. Project Forecast Flow. (Source: Air Force Project Instruction Manual, 1963).

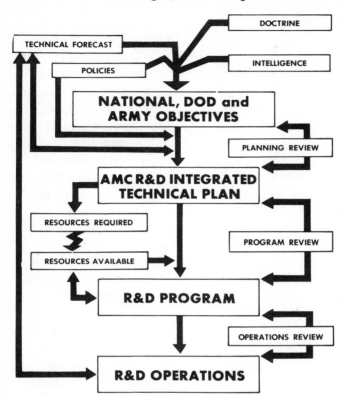

Figure II–7. R&D Planning Interrelationships in the Army
(Source: AMC Pamphlet 705–1, Volume 1, January 1966).

is then broken down into R&D tasks and performed either by government or contractor groups. The crucial point in this whole R&D planning system is the feedback concept in which the technical information generated in the R&D tasks is fed back into Threat and Policy where it may affect the Operational Objectives. In other words, the whole planning sequence is an iterative one and dynamic technological forecasting is not only an ingredient but indeed a catalyst.

Figure II–6 and Figure II–7, respectively, illustrate the functional status of the technological forecasts in the Air Force and Army Long Range Planning framework. The forecast functions and utilization are seen to be analogous for all three services.

Technological Forecasting in Other Government Agencies

ATOMIC ENERGY COMMISSION

The Atomic Energy Commission did their first Technological Forecast during 1964, having been told by the Joint Congressional Committee on Atomic Energy that they would no longer be funded on a piece-meal basis unless they had "a Policy for National Action in the Field of High Energy Physics." In responding to this directive, the Atomic Energy Commission made use of a report generated in 1963 by the Physics Committee of United States.

In essence, the report said the following: We have won six Nobel prizes since 1957. Unless we increase our $50 million yearly budget to at least $150 million for the next five years and increase $300 million and possibly a half billion in the 1970 time frames, we will fall behind the Russians.

Subsequently, they made a Technological Forecast on equipment and facilities which includes a $6 billion national effort over the next 15 years to discover the nature of all matter. The report, which was generated in-house, vigorously supports the view of the high energy physicists of the United States and makes the following specific points:

— A high energy proton accelerator of approximately 200 billion electron volts (Bev) be developed and operated as a national facility. (The largest accelerator now in operation is a 33 Bev machine at Brookhaven National Laboratory on Long Island. The Russians are building a 70 Bev machine.)

— Accelerators now in operation at the Argonne National Laboratory in Illinois be upgraded in intensity.

— Studies be made of a future national accelerator in the range of 600 to 1000 Bev. Construction of such a machine, which would cost roughly $1 billion and be 2 miles in diameter, should be started in Fiscal 1971 for use in Fiscal 1980.

  President Johnson commended the AEC for "a well-considered program," but did not commit the Administration to specific AEC plans.

"The field of high energy physics," Mr. Johnson said, "like

all research in basic science, is ever changing . . . We must not be so bound to our guidelines that there is no flexibility to respond to the changing needs of the program and to changing fiscal needs and resources.

"We will continue to compare the needs in this field with those of other scientific needs. In turn, the needs of science as a whole will be assessed in the light of other demands on Federal resources."

FEDERAL AVIATION AGENCY

Last year FAA undertook the establishment of a long range planning system and attempted to determine the policies and identify the goals which would be their operating guidance. As part of these goals and in order to develop guidance to direct the future course of the FAA, it was concluded that an environmen-

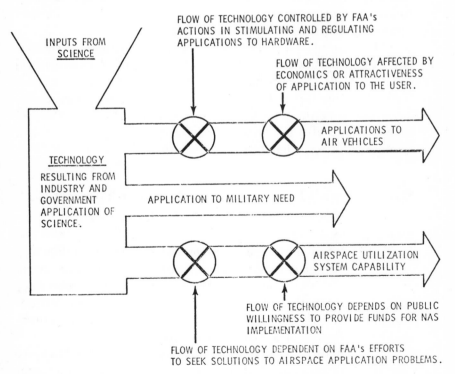

Figure II–8. FAA Technology Relationships.

tal forecast was necessary, that a technological forecast was also necessary and that, with an amalgamation of these, a long range plan could be developed.

It might be helpful here to show diagrammatically the Agency's relationships to, and control over, application of technology. (See Figure II–8.)

NATIONAL AERONAUTICS AND
SPACE ADMINISTRATION

NASA has a highly organized planning program to provide sales and research guidance support. The Prospectus 1964 and Annex A and B which they have compiled is more of a plan— a summary documentation of experiments which need to be and could be done in a specific time frame and at a predicted cost. Technological forecasting (called Division Prospectus) is done to arrive at these proposals but is a NASA privileged document (probably very preliminary at this stage).

There are plans to set up a 50-man team of discipline specialists at Ames Research Center, Moffett Field, to monitor and summarize the state-of-the-art and expected advances in chosen fields. They are not to do any directing of research in these areas, however. In addition, NASA holds an annual "state-of-the-art" review where all their experts are brought together to present summaries of what has been learned during the year.

Composition, Character and Content of a Forecast

The format of a forecast should be flexible—largely determined jointly by the personnel preparing the Forecast and the User. The information presented should include the following:

— *Background Including Present Status*—The background should briefly highlight the evolution of the technology being forecast with emphasis on relevance to military technological needs. The present status should present the state-of-the-art of the category as a basis for Forecast projections.

— *New Capability or Technical Approach*—The proposed functions, characteristics, or concepts of any new item should be presented including limitations which might exist. Where appropriate, tabular or graphical presentations should be used to show merits of competing items. Functional diagrams should be included in describing the technical approach.

— *Forecast*—The forecast should graphically display a projection of anticipated advances of the items as a function of time up to 20 years. This projection should be a quantitative

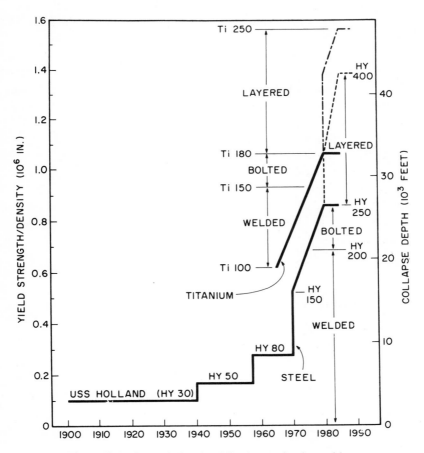

Figure II–9. Strength Levels of Steel and Titanium with
Corresponding Pressure Hull Collapse Depth.
(Based on Weight/Displacement Ratio of 0.6).

expression of achievable parametric limits, where possible showing the level of confidence in the validity of the projection. Supporting and qualifying narration should be minimized.

— *Potential Significance to the Military*—Where appropriate, the value of the items forecast should be appraised in light of military relevance. As an example (Figure II–9) we may express yield strength/density with time, which is meaningful to the scientific community. However, a more meaningful expression for the military community would be collapse depth versus time. The values in Figure II–9 are hypothetical for illustrative purposes only.

— *References*—For the convenience of the user who may want to obtain further information, the reference section should list associated R&D organizations making important contributions, names of outstanding experts, and references to reports or literature supporting the forecast material.

— *Categorization*—The following items should be included in the military forecast:

> *Science and Engineering*
> Physical Sciences
> Engineering Sciences
> Environmental Sciences
> Life Sciences
>
> *Subsystems/Components/Technology*
> Vehicles/Installations
> Weaponry/Armament
> Surveillance/Target Acquisition/Navigation
> Communications/Command & Control
> Countermeasures
> Logistics
> Target Environment
> Power Conversion
>
> *Systems*
> Strategic
> Tactical
> Amphibious

Antisubmarine
Fleet Defense
Space

In order for the technological forecast to be utilized, the forecast must be credible. Indeed the more credible the forecast is, the more it will be utilized and vice versa. The more it is utilized the more time and effort will be applied in making it credible. It is important that the individual or organization that generates the forecast be identified with the forecast because the credibility depends on the good professional judgment of the forecaster(s) in that organizational segment. The researcher or technologist must not become ego-involved with the socioeconomic implications and whether he agrees or disagrees with them but must forecast what is feasible in a given time frame. This means addressing oneself to a technological area and the technological area only, leaving the social implications to the sociologist.

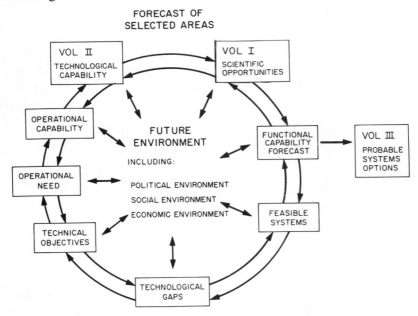

Figure II–10. A Dynamic Approach to Technological Forecasting.

Future Environment

It can be seen from Figure II–10, "A Dynamic Approach to Technological Forecasting," that even though this chapter has dealt primarily with the periphery of this "ferris wheel," there is a hub. Whether we jump on this ferris wheel at the "operational need" box (the tactics determine the weapons or Forecast in Depth concept), or start with the "scientific capability" box (the weapons determine the tactics or "building blocks") the objective or output of this exercise is to develop future, feasible systems. The more iterations we go through the clearer the future environment becomes. This is important because these feasible systems options are being generated to be used in the future environment. In turn the future environment itself is being addressed with emphasis by numerous organizations throughout this country. This fact is attested to by the listing contained in Appendix D.

Summary

A military technological forecast would benefit long-range military planners at all echelons. The scope of work should include significant projected capabilities in all areas of science and technology relevant to military activities. Updating of the forecast should be a dynamic process as the needs exist. A complete updating should be accomplished after approximately two to three years.

"Finally, there is the responsibility . . . to set out deliberately to invent the future. Whether there is to be a future probably hinges on whether there can be developed an inventiveness with respect to human affairs that will keep pace with the ingenuity of the technicians" (II–2).

REFERENCES

II–1. Statement by Chief of Staff, General Curtis E. LeMay, March, 1963.
II–2. The Rockefeller Fund, National Security—The Military Aspect, January, 1958.

How to give individual men the evidence they need to make sensible judgments about the kind of world they want to live in and how to give them the power to make their judgments stick, that is the unfinished business of the next third of a century. —ELTING MORISON

Chapter III

FORECASTING TECHNOLOGY

It is necessary to emphasize one important point, if no other: It no longer suffices to look *toward* the future. Rather, we must look *at* the future. There is a difference—a difference not too dissimilar from that between life and death. While looking *toward* the future implies the usual human emotions of hope or resignation, looking *at* it implies "going" there, examining the possible future(s), and then preparing oneself accordingly—today.

This chapter will discuss the techniques by which one may "go" to the future and examine it and thereby give confidence to the decisions one makes today—and prevent the catastrophes of tomorrow. But, first a few more words of admonition for our brothers who might be complacent about the future.

The unknown is the great deceiver of men and the abettor of false diviners. Nations and civilizations have sacrificed their existence as a consequence of reliance on tenuous mumbo jumbo, gods, ideologies and platitudes, passed off convincingly as gospel.

Today we have this new nemesis of the unknown, more lethal and speedier in its work of dispatch than those faced in the past. It is the future. It is an unsympathetic Reaper who wields a scythe of technological progress, cutting down those who take unremitting root in the present.

Often heard are the words that those who do not heed the past are doomed to repeat it. If one's company or one's nation does not face this new nemesis with clear methodical, dedication of effort and attention, it, too, may be relegated to a dusty, forgotten niche in history. The experience with the unknown is clear.

For example, our nation, at this moment, faces one particularly vital challenge (perhaps the last in a series of these challenges) to probe the future. There is a great, but somewhat muted debate raging as to whether we should or should not build an antiballistics missile (ABM) system. Unfortunately, the argument revolves about the question, *"Will* they build an ABM system?" More properly, the question should be posed with the auxiliary verb "can" rather than "will." In matters of great import, we must act on that which *can* be; we should not wait for certainties, for then it is far too late. The technique of technological forecasting is a means by which one may determine what *can* be. It is hoped that this technique will be employed and its results heeded.

A note of warning here: Technological forecasting by itself will not generate a complete picture of the future. Similar forecasting in the areas of sociology, politics, economics, resources, morals, ethics, etc., must be acquired, for these will have an effect on the action taken in connection with the technological forecast, just as the reverse is true.

Methods of Deriving the Forecast

As stated previously, a technological forecast is a *prediction, with a level of confidence, of a technical achievement in a given time frame with a specified level of support.* A technological forecast is *not a plan.* It is a tool for planning and decision-making. It is emphasized that technological forecasting should

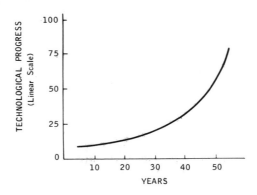

Figure III–1.

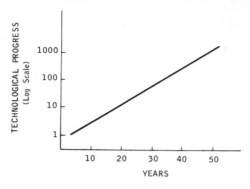

Figure III–2.

consist of a systematic analysis which, when applied to specific technical data, will yield a consistent, quantitative technological conclusion, no matter which competent person performs the analysis.

The most obvious method of technological forecasting is to assume that the rate of technological progress experienced in the immediate past will continue. This is not a very accurate method and it is probably the one we use unconsciously when we are called upon to make intuitive forecasts of the future. While this method may be used to predict over short time spans —say a year or two—it is extremely dangerous to use beyond that. Technological progress does not have a linear characteristic. It is best likened to the growth of a snowball rolling down

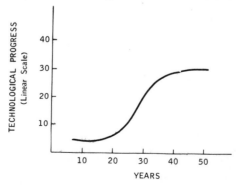

Figure III–3.

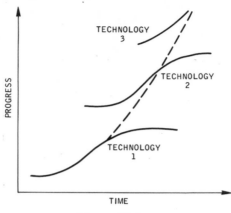

Figure III–4.

a mountainside, picking up mass and velocity. If we were to plot technological progress, its representation by the curve shown in Figure III–1 would be close to the truth. (The second curve in Figure III–2 is simply a plot of Figure III–1 using logarithmic ordinates.)

A skeptic will point out that these curves are wrong. After all, we all know that if you follow the history of some particular technology, the progress looks like that represented in Figure III–3. This is true—as far as it goes. But what really happens is that technological progress in a field (here you must broaden your sights) is a series of steps, a concatenation of the progress of the technologies comprising it. The situation, then, is as depicted in Figure III–4.

Just about the time a dominant technology begins reversing its progress slope, a new approach begins its inception and take-over. Be warned, then: "When things have gone about as far as they can go," one should have already been looking at other—possibly latent—technologies as new avenues of approach.

Forecasting by Growth/Analogies

The growth-analogy method of forecasting is permissible so long as its time span of application and its limitations are recognized. The method recognizes that progress in a specific technology, or particular avenue of approach toward a given capability, has an exponential characteristic initially, changes its slope, and then tapers off toward a horizontal asymptote. The point one should recognize is that this is a short term prediction characteristic for a specific avenue of approach. It is good for a few years—ten years at most—but no more. The velocity curve of a falling body and of its subsequent terminal velocity, shows this characteristic. Population growth is the same: It has the S-shaped characteristic; it, too, flattens out until new forces come into play, e.g., medical advances, new food production methods, etc. And so it is in any specific technology. Each technology experiences an initial period of slow growth. Finally its potential is recognized, money and effort are poured in, problems are resolved, and what follows is a period of accelerated growth. Eventually, things "go about as far as they can go" and the growth rate decelerates.

Forecast of a Technological Field

Only a shortsighted person will want to limit his forecast to a specific technology. Rather, his interest should lie in what is going to happen in a particular field. An example of this process is seen depicted in Figures III–5 and III–6, which show the acquisition and improvement of successively more efficient sources of light.

One may reasonably question the validity of the continued exponential extrapolation depicted in the first of these curves. This question can be best answered in two ways. First, historical experience demostrates such an extrapolation to be appropriate. Second, reflection upon the growth factors at play indicates that until some physical limit is reached, an increase in capabilities in a technological field is to be expected. For instance, one expects an exponential increase in the number of working scientists, and an exponential increase in the number of technical periodicals and published papers, a similar increase in the funded support of research, and the discovery of new technologies or

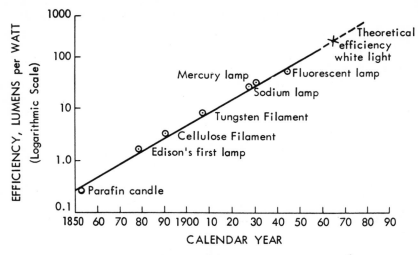

Figure III–5. Functional Capability Trend of Illumination.
(Semilog Plot).

the exploitation of some latent technology. A microscopic examination of historical growth would not reveal the smooth, day-
by-day enhancement suggested in the first light-efficiency curve
(Figure III–5). In fact, a continuing series of perturbations is
what really happens, as in the second curve—a series of steplike
advances and plateaus. The curves show the growth curve of the
conventional incandescent bulb and the fluorescent lamp, both
current techniques for converting electrical power into illumination. Growth points are identified to indicate the manner in
which the plot has been prepared. The shape of the curve shows
a rather limited growth during the early experimental years of
the technology, then literally an explosion in increased efficiency,
and, finally, a tapering off as the growth curve appears to approach an asymptote. The relationship between this plot of technological advance and that of a technological field is apparent.
Each specific technology contributes just a small portion to the
overall growth.

Both types of plots have their value and use. The microscopic
view, as in the second plot (Figure III–6) provides information
on specific technologies and indicates when those particular ave-

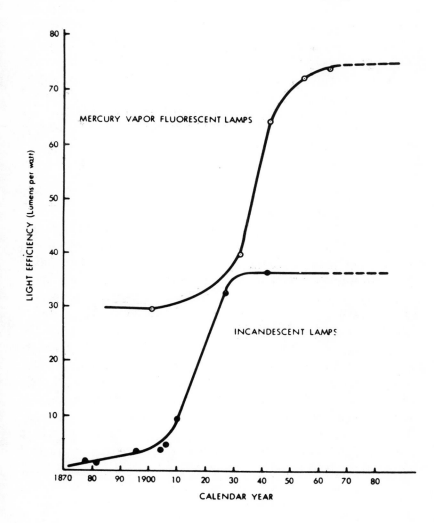

Figure III–6. Technical Capability Trends. (Source: General
Electric Lamp Bulletin, January 1956).

nues have been exploited, so that serious attention should now be turned to greener pastures. The macroscopic overview, on the other hand, is a picture of the general trend; its extrapolation (short of physical limits) opens the curtain on the far future.

If one desires to take a long-range look into the future, he must first tackle the problem by forecasting the technological fields, as described in the previous section. Then he must apply the technique of dynamic forecasting which will be discussed presently. On the one hand, a forecast of a technical field yields a picture of its probable future if no actions are taken to affect its natural course. Dynamic forecasting, on the other hand, allows a view of its future (or rather, futures) if the value of influencing factors is permitted to vary.

We now make an important shift in the context of our discussion. Supposing we were to postulate an antiballistics missile system of given capabilities. The question raised by military planners is, "When can we have it?" The question, "When can *they* have it?," is not much different, for as recent history shows there are no proprietary rights to technological capability. Well, when can we or *they* have it? Advances in acquisition and improvement of systems are directly related to the technologies employed in constructing them. Since we know which of the technologies and technological fields contribute to the building of a system, and if we are armed with forecasts thereon, we can make reasonable predictions to answer these questions. Further, we can identify the critical paths or critical technologies that interpose the greatest obstacles to achieving the system. By dynamic forecasting we can reach conclusions concerning where and how much effort must be applied to arrive at the postulated system in a given time.

Dynamic Forecasting

Up to this point we have been discussing technological forecasting on the basis of basic, qualitative concepts. We will continue in this vein, leaving it to subsequent chapters to provide in depth examples.

Up to now, the discussion of forecasting methodology has been based strictly on historical extrapolations. As stated earlier, this can be dangerous. Remember, in important matters, one particularly wants to know what *could* be made to occur in the future. In other words, by means of the technique we are about to address we will recognize that we have some influence on the future, i.e., we can go beyond simple, historical extrapolation. We want to know to what extent we can influence progress into the future as a function of the resources at our disposal, where those resources are to be applied, and the gains that will result. This is dynamic forecasting. As one would expect, it requires the use of expertise in *identifying* all the factors that will be involved, in quantifying those factors, and then in mixing them together—"playing them against each other" in order to determine what solutions answer our questions.

In this method, technological progress is based upon mathematical expression of the influence of those factors over which control may be exercised. For instance, these factors might include the number of people trained for a given research and development task, the number of people employed to perform that task, and the facilities provided. The effect of each of these factors and the feedback relationships are combined in equations which provide a prediction of the technological progress to be obtained from a given input. The greatest difficulty in this method of technological forecasting is the determination of the input factors. These weightings—or "transfer coefficients," as they are called—convert quantities of the input variables into quantities which are meaningful in measuring technological progress. For instance, let us say we have an input factor such as gallons of fuel. This factor has no *real* meaning until we convert it to hours of operating under varying conditions. In most cases, the transfer coefficients will necessarily be based on the empirical relationship which has existed in the past between the input and output factors.

Let us take a familiar example to show how dynamic forecasting is done implicitly every day. The individual may not even realize that he is using the same trade-off procedure that the forecaster uses in dynamic forecasting. Consider the meticulous restaurateur who has the interests of his clientele at heart, but who also must keep one eye on his profits. If he itemizes his various dishes and then assigns a value to each, he is able to judge how well he is going to serve his customers, as well as his pocketbook. But he must not stop here. He also has a reputation in fine cuisine to uphold and he must attach a value to this. Weather has a great deal to do with what people eat. So has the visual appeal of food. So has atmosphere. The restaurateur might want to enter the effect of the stock market, and even the international situation, into his equation. To be sure, these factors are intangibles. Nonetheless, they can be assigned value, i.e., they can be quantified. The value that is assigned to any of these variables is its transfer coefficient. When we put all these factors (together with their transfer coefficients) into a single expression, we have what is called an algorithm. It is not an exact mathematical expression because it is nothing more than quantified, subjective judgment. However, once so expressed, an algorithm can be manipulated mathematically in order to optimize any variable. For example, the restaurateur can optimize profit or minimize cost by holding reputation constant while he varies some other factor.

Some of the questions a forecaster must ask himself are: What are all of the factors by which I can influence the outcome? Is the outcome worth the price I must pay to influence the factor or variable? The beauty of dynamic forecasting is that the problem is now expressed mathematically, and this expression can be subjected to an infinite number of solutions and consequences from which one may make a choice. Sounds easy? How about the quantification of the transfer coefficients? There's the real difficulty.

Forecasting for the Military

The procedure for a military forecast is relatively simple in concept. The processes involved may start with the present being given and then work toward deriving the various futures. Or they may start with a number of postulated futures and work backword to derive the achievements which must be met in order to insure that those futures will be attained.

As an example, let's work forward: First we take stock of the current status of the various technological fields, their histories and recent advances. By use of the methods already mentioned, applied by experts in those fields, the expected capabilities in each field can be projected for a given period in the future. These component capabilities can then be combined as building blocks from which possible future military-system capabilities can be derived. We are now in a position to ascertain which of the technologies are most in need of attention; at this point we also have a feeling for how much effort will be required in order to develop needed capabilities.

We could just as well have started at some point in the future and worked backward: System capability or operational parameters would be set down by our military commanders for the given time period. Or the commanders might have made their needs known by postulating a future threat. In either event, the future capability of the systems desired by our military forces would have been defined. We would then break down these future needs into the requisite status of the technologies for the given period; then we would forecast for what must transpire in these technologies in order to get from here to there, and whether it looks as if we can get there at all.

Technological forecasting does not offer a guaranteed answer to the future, but a forecast—if diligently arrived at—will assist in the projection of military capabilities to meet any enemy threat. In addition, forecasting will alert one to the need to explore new approaches with which to continue the improvement in operational capability—such as advanced laser weapons, or surveillance techniques, or a total system such as the Polaris submarine and its missiles.

Forecasting also provides the necessary input into a technology/capability matrix to define goals for R&D and systems to meet (or exceed) a projected enemy threat. In this way, it is possible to identify those scientific and technological areas which have high payoff not directly responsive to the projected threat. For example, you might forecast when it will be possible to detect and classify a periscope at x nautical miles under conditions known as "sea state 4," i.e., when wave heights reach 8 feet. Or the forecast might involve the technology of air-cushion vehicles. For example, let us look at the performance curves shown in Figure III–7. The lower curve shows the performance improvement that can be expected in air-cushion vehicles if no radical technological developments are introduced between today and 1985. The top curves, on the other hand, show what could happen to performance if a single known technique were to be perfected and applied—in other words, if the captured air-bubble idea were to be exploited.

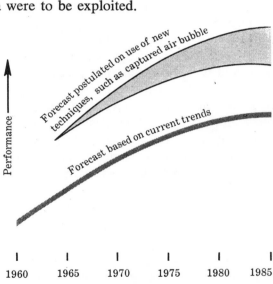

These curves show a 1963 forecast of performance of air-cushion vehicles. In lower curve, we see how performance was expected to improve if no major innovations were incorporated in air-cushion vehicles. In the top curves, however, it was shown how performance could be increased significantly if ways could be found to apply skirts and trunks to these air-supported vehicles. For example, if such vehicles could ride on captured air bubbles, the forecast indicated that performance might be improved two-fold.

Figure III–7. Projection of Air-Cushion Vehicle Performance.

We should take note of a couple of other things that fore-casting provides for the military. For one, it enables the refine-ment of postulations of an enemy threat during the forecast period, by identifying U.S. technological capabilities which may be assumed to be within an enemy's potential. For example, even if the U.S. elects not to develop an antiballistics missile system, information regarding the U.S. technological capabilities in this area would nonetheless continue to be useful, both in the mili-tary arena and in the political arena. Second, forecasting serves senior management in the military by calling attention to the strengths and weaknesses in capabilities of military efforts in science and technology.

Forecasting for Industry

By now, you have probably recognized some of the ways by which technological forecasting can be useful in industry:

• To steer development programs into areas which could utilize new technology to reduce costs or increase profits, such as using a new plastic instead of a metal.

• To focus on areas where a new demand might exist or a product improvement might be required to protect one's share of a market. For instance, what is the potential market for elec-tric engines for automobiles?

• To aid in the planning of research and development programs to meet both short- and long-range corporate goals. Should we spend money on fuel cells or nickel-cadmium bat-teries for deep-diving submersibles? Should we invest in laser research or in new chemicals for use in a retina operation?

• To assist in developing performance standards for new products, techniques, and materials. By knowing what is fore-cast, one can set standards and either select current materials and process them with existing equipment, or decide instead to select a new material or a new processing technique.

• To help identify new opportunities and possible com-petition in the technological arena which might modify corporate goals. If your competitor holds a patent in an area where you presently have a large market share, you may want to get a new product or diversify.

   • To aid with the scheduling of resources and new technology so that they converge in the manufacturing area in a timely manner so that opportunities are not wasted.

Summary

Assume that we have been willing to expend the effort needed to acquire forecasts of the type described and that the forecasts which were generated exhibited the technical prescience ascribed to them. We would then be in possession of an oracle which, instead of predicting the future, would predict all *possible* futures and the directions by which one might elect to proceed into the future of his choice. Here, the word "choice" is used loosely, for in many instances, the future to which one must proceed is not a matter of choice, but a matter of survival. This technological oracle knows no masters but those who would take the pains to seek it. In truth it is a lethal weapon that handicaps those who do not approach it—or, having approached, do not heed it. A technological forecast for a given field of interest postulates conceivable future systems of stated capabilities; it then details the component technological advances that must be achieved in order to gain the postulation.

Secretary of HEW, John Gardner, said, "No society is likely to renew itself unless its dominant orientation is to the future . . . In a society capable of renewal, men not only welcome the future and the changes it may bring, but believe that they will have a hand in shaping that future."

Innovation is the basic function of management, whether of industry, politics, science or the arts, and management must coax or coddle it into being. —WILLIAM T. BRADY

CHAPTER IV

A VIEW FROM THE R&D MANAGER'S DESK

TRADITIONALLY the managers of research and development, as contrasted with other managers in industry and government, possess a unique position in relation to technology. Where most managers must plan to meet technology change, the R&D manager additionally must plan technological change. Thus he not only plans for the inevitable, but he can alter the future of technology through planning and control. It should be emphasized that he can do this only when adequately supported with the necessary resources.

The R&D manager sees technology as a three-legged stool with planning and control, technological change, and technological forecasting comprising the three legs. Like the stool, a proper technological environmental balance is acquired when each is present in proper proportion and are mutually aiding. Today's technological complexity and competitive urgency gives compelling reason for the R&D manager to be informed about each of these three factors in order that he may enhance achievement of his organization's goals. More important, because his position in the technological environment favors him with knowledge gleaned from views of the future, his contribution to and involvement in formulating and changing those goals will be of critical necessity.

Accordingly, this chapter will delve into the mechanics of technological change in some detail; it will also provide further insight concerning technological forecasting techniques.

Technological Change

Technological change is the link between the past state-of-the-art and its present and future states. An understanding of the phenomena of technical change, how and which factors influence it and how to measure it are requisites to preparing credible technological forecasts. An understanding of technological change is required also to develop plans and to institute controls that will direct the course of technological change in a manner which will be beneficial to the organization and, in the case of government R&D, to the general advantage of the country.

Occurrence of Technological Change

Since technology is the application of a body of knowledge to useful purposes, technological change, then, is the transfer of new knowledge from those who originate it to those who can apply it (IV–1). Dr. Fabricant describes technological change in one sense as, "the net change in the social stock of useful knowledge" (IV–2).

Philip Reily reports that information transfer during technological change occurs in three steps: *Invention* (the act of conception, the association of a technological possibility with a potential need); *Innovation* (the introduction of a new idea to the economy); and *Diffusion* (the spreading of the new technology through the whole industry) (IV–3). The transfer of information may occur horizontally within each step as well as vertically between each step. For example, the transfer of information of an invention using A and an invention using B can result in an invention using both. When horizontal transfer occurs in the first two steps, the volume of information transferred and the rate at which it is communicated is in lesser proportion. When diffusion occurs in the last step, it generally occasions, or gives impetus to, a rapid spawning of other useful, possibly competitive, end products.

Dr. Fabricant suggests that there is another way of viewing technological change. In one approach it may be viewed as a change in the stock of useful information, but viewed alternatively, it may be taken as the effects stemming from the transfer of information (IV–4). Although the second sense of technological change facilitates measurement, it does not provide the immediate insight required by management to plan for and control change. It can provide change trends against varying social, economical and political backgrounds. From these, the manager can develop algorithms concerning what, how and why change takes place and use these as references in preparing technological forecasts.

Thus, there are two concepts from which a meaning of technological change may be derived: 1) net formation and transfer of information, and 2) the effects of this net transfer of information.

What Are the Factors That Influence Technological Change

Since change occurs in three phases, it is convenient to examine the influential factors in each of these steps. The total of these factors provides a description of what influences technological change as a whole.

The formation of new information and its rate of transfer in its commercial aspects are concerned with the discovery of a marketable product or process and the time it takes to market that product or process. While early inventions such as X-rays for examining the body were serendipitous, products and processes are now so complex that it is erroneous to assume that inventions such as the transistor and nuclear energy as a power source could be discovered without deliberate application of scientific principles to the solution of specific problems. Thus it appears that to stimulate the inventive process, the first step in technological change, it is necessary to pinpoint need and/or potential markets.

Factors affecting the communication of available technical knowledge and market needs to the inventor, in turn, affect technological change. The inefficiency of technical information storage, communication and retrieval needs to be emphasized. A recent article reported that Leonardo Da Vinci had developed a system of ball bearings to reduce friction in machinery. It was not until 1920 that Sperry Gyroscope, independently, came up with the same idea (IV–5). According to a study conducted by Bell Telephone Laboratories, the time between discovery and the application of a new product is becoming shorter (IV–6). On the other hand Philip Reily reports "The core of the problem is that even in our enlightened world of today, it takes on the average 25 years or more for new science to be put to broad use" (IV–7). See Table IV–1.

One explanation for the decreasing interval between invention and application is the enormous increase in human and financial resources devoted to stimulating technological change. This factor leads directly to two others: how the resources are applied and the quality of the resources (human experience and training). Quality also refers to the mental attitude that society has for accepting or rejecting change. The position of special groups, e.g., social, economic (unions) and political, is an important consideration in trying to determine influencing factors on technical change.

TABLE IV–1
TIME LAG BETWEEN PRODUCT DISCOVERY
AND APPLICATION (IV–8)

Innovation	Year of Discovery	Year of Application
Electric Motor	1821	1886
Vacuum Tube	1882	1915
Radio Broadcasting	1887	1922
X-ray Tubes	1895	1913
Nuclear Reactor	1932	1942
Radar	1935	1940
Atomic Bomb	1938	1945
Transistor	1948	1951
Solar Battery	1953	1955
Stereospecific Rubbers & Plastics	1955	1958

Clearly government through its tremendous investment in R&D has acted to stimulate the inventive process. The largest proportion of government R&D expenditures in the past have been allocated to defense and space projects, consequently, the transfer of new knowledge has been progressing slowly into the civilian economy. Civilian applications of defense and space technology, however, are being accelerated to the extent that government efforts are being aligned to promote vertical technology transfer for social needs.

This vertical technology transfer, or "coupling" as it is now called, is being scrutinized by NASA as well as the DOD agencies, and the following list, suggested by Harold Davidson of the Army Research Office, indicates significant methods for further "speeding-up" this coupling process (IV–9).

— Periodically develop a list of problems and needs pertinent to the laboratory or research agency and make these available to the scientist so there can be more relevant research.

— Periodically evaluate the outputs of each laboratory against military needs.

— Add liaison and coupling activities explicitly to the goals and missions of organizations.

— Add liaison and coupling activities explicitly to the job descriptions of pertinent individuals such as project monitors.

— Appoint two small groups of liaison individuals, one group to establish links between labs and basic research agencies and another group to strengthen the coupling between labs and operations.

— Provide better opportunities for coupling activities by scientists, such as special symposia, by bringing scientists and technologists together.

— Insert translators, especially between science and technology.

— Encourage the creative scientist where possible to follow his work beyond the research stage into development, possibly as a consultant.

— Try to select scientists for both in-house and contract or grant work who are at home with both science and technology.

— Recognize and otherwise reward individuals for their successful coupling efforts in challenge areas.

— Consider (with some caution) the possibility of programming a coupling effort.

— Study good and bad examples and find out why the

crucial differences exist and what they would mean in terms of overhauling the present system.

— Encourage face-to-face conversation between technical people rather than or in addition to going through the chain of command.

— Minimize the physical space barrier between scientists and technologists—house them together or close by whenever possible.

Mr. Davidson also suggests some other means to overcome the barriers to vertical technology transfer (IV–10).

— We need more study on fundamental principles, such as the methodology of coupling and the preparation of a reference text on the subject. Also we need a methodology for evaluating coupling techniques.

— We need to sell the doctrine of coupling to the scientist, the engineer and the production man.

— We need information on how to motivate scientists, engineers and production people to effectively communicate with each other.

— We need to gather the limited knowledge and experience in successful coupling.

— We need to evaluate the successes and failures of the recognized coupling efforts underway in industry and government and learn from them.

— We need to study the role of the academic world in the coupling process since they are prime producers of basic knowledge.

Table IV–2 indicates the increasing trend of government sponsorship of R&D and Table IV–3 shows the breakdown of 1967 R&D expenditures by industry and by company versus government contributions. Technological change may be restrained by special interest groups as well as by the absence of financial support. For example, button manufacturers shrewdly and strongly opposed the zipper, invented in 1879. It did not reach the market for 30 years (IV–11).

Even within private industry there are impediments. Carl Barnes has noted that 60% of the presidents of the 200 largest

TABLE IV–2
FEDERAL R&D EXPENDITURES (IV–12)
(*Based on figures from federal budgets*)

Fiscal Year	Total Federal Budget Expenditures (millions of dollars)	R&D & R&D Plant (millions of dollars)	% of Total
1940	$ 9,055	$ 74	.8
1941	13,255	198	1.5
1942	34,037	280	.8
1943	79,368	602	.8
1944	94,986	1,377	1.4
1945	98,303	1,591	1.6
1946	60,326	918	1.5
1947	38,923	900	2.3
1948	32,955	855	2.6
1949	39,474	1,082	2.7
1950	39,544	1,083	2.7
1951	43,970	1,301	3.0
1952	65,303	1,816	2.8
1953	74,120	3,101	4.2
1954	67,537	3,148	4.7
1955	64,389	3,308	5.1
1956	66,224	3,446	5.2
1957	68,966	4,462	6.5
1958	71,369	4,990	7.0
1959	80,342	5,803	7.2
1960	76,539	7,738	10.1
1961	81,515	9,278	11.4
1962	87,787	10,373	11.8
1963	92,642	11,988	12.9
1964	97,684	14,694	15.0
1965	96,507	14,875	15.4
1966 (estimate)	106,428	15,963	15.0
1967 (estimate)	112,847	16,152	14.3

United States corporations have expressed dissatisfaction with the "lack of creativity at the bench" (IV–14). His more significant conclusions on the problems retarding the inventive process and their solutions are:

— Actual products of research are only potential new products or processes, and before becoming commercially successful, they must be sold to management.

— Selling to management requires skill, persistence and

TABLE IV–3

1967 INDUSTRIAL R&D EXPENDITURES (IV–13)

(*Based on I–R and National Science Foundation figures*)

Industry	Company Funds (millions of dollars)	Total R&D (millions of dollars)
Aircraft and missiles	$ 700	$ 5,700
Electrical equipment and communications	1,350	3,800
Chemicals and allied products	1,600	1,900
Motor vehicles and other transportation equipment	1,250	1,400
Machinery	1,100	1,400
Professional and scientific instruments	365	650
Petroleum refining and extraction	400	440
Primary metals	250	280
Fabricated metal products	190	215
Rubber products	150	215
Food and kindred products	160	175
Stone, clay and glass products	150	170
Paper and allied products	85	90
Textiles and apparel	45	50
Lumber, woodproducts and furniture	5	15
Other industries	400	600
TOTALS	$8,200	$17,100

courage, and for every successful product that reaches the market there was a "champion" behind it—someone who risked his reputation.

— Management must provide sound screening procedures to weed out poor products, but they should not erect insurmountable barriers that will discourage the champion from pushing his idea.

— Some companies have insisted that all R&D products be need-oriented. These products are easy to sell, although they may not represent the more productive output which the scientist can provide. Barnes pointed out that products like neoprene, nylon, polyethylene, silicones, penicillin, Teflon, transistors and the Polaroid Land Camera did not come into being because there was a recognized need. The need came after the product was developed.

— To ensure that maximum productivity from industrial research is achieved, three types of research should be going on: 1) There must be research whose aim is to fill envisioned needs; that is, to develop a product or process for which a market can be developed. 2) There should be research aimed at making new discoveries—the formation of new knowledge. 3) Along with the other two types, there will be research that is oriented toward filling existing needs.

— Corporate management can promote creativity within the research laboratory by simplifying the process by which the inventor can make known his idea, but more so by providing incentive for the inventor. One positive move management can make is to remove from the corporate atmosphere the notion that an individual who earnestly tries and fails is worse than the individual who remains static. This feeling must be conveyed not only to the inventor but to line management, who must pass upon the ideas submitted to them.

— Management wants to accomplish two things as the result of an incentive program: 1) Maximize stimulation of invention to ensure technological progress. 2) Maximize utilization of worthwhile products or processes resulting from this technological effort.

— To insure that the patent system retains a measure of incentive for the inventor and that the employer's investment is protected, it has been suggested that in situations where the employer does not wish to pursue commercialization of the invention all rights to it revert back to the inventor.

Barnes' findings are true for the small laboratory as well as for the large corporation or the government laboratory. Therefore, his suggestion for three types of ongoing research warrants additional attention in respect to the part technological forecasting can play. It would generally be difficult to obtain authorization to do research in a profit-oriented laboratory without substantial evidence that the technology can be developed. The risk is doubly high in this situation, since technical success does not necessarily result in commercial success, and technical failure is always possible. In the case of a university or non-profit laboratory justification for such research may be easier to obtain since technology generally may better the life of the community, commercialization not being the ultimate criterion. In either case, however, the ability to forecast the degree of success within a specified amount of time with a specified allotment of resources can help to sell potentially successful ideas. This is one of the prime roles of technological forecasting.

Since innovation is primarily a risk-taking process, the key to its stimulation is encouragement of the entrepreneurial spirit. An economic environment must exist which offers sufficient financial rewards to the innovator if he succeeds, and one that diminishes the amount of loss if he fails. Creating such an environment is primarily the responsibility of the government. This responsibility has been recognized in part by special tax concessions given various industries. The industrial organization that is deeply involved in military or space R&D projects and subsequently enters into commercial production of a civilian version of the military product is at an advantage over the non-military competitor. This advantage stems from the fact that his risk of overcoming technical obstacles was minimized; his development and production engineering has been acquired under low-risk conditions. It is *not* being proposed that government R&D programs be further expanded to include all organizations in a particular industry, but some liberalization in regard to passing on information on proprietary techniques and processes developed under government projects could be considered in order to equalize the incentive to those companies not working on government projects. This incentive could promote greater diffusion of technical information during the innovation step of technological change.

A country's political situation affects many aspects of the innovation step. Import/export duties and policies, for example, can discourage the introduction of new products, because the acquisition of raw materials or other inputs required to produce the end-product may be adversely affected. A country whose raw materials or other resources are tied up in a war effort generally does not experience a sustained growth in leisure time or luxury products, and in fact some products that may be termed as necessities may be lacking. Even religious and social mores affect the innovation process. Innovations such as birth control pills and the development of techniques to transplant human organs have had to overcome strong social obstacles. For instance when the heart from a non-white was transferred to a white patient in South Africa in 1968 it raised racial questions.

Thus the total environment must be amenable to the new product or process for it to be successfully introduced, and subsequently gain widespread use. Widespread use, in turn, fosters new applications which eventually lead to the seeking out of improved products or processes, thus enhancing the growth in a particular technology. The difficulty in dynamic technological forecasting (introduced in Chapter II) is the quantification of parameters just discussed and the specification of the interrelationships of these parameters in a mathematical model as applicable to the rate and extent of technological change. The problem is a difficult one, but the results of a valid model will bear rich rewards.

Three steps in introducing a new technology, process, or procedure should be considered. Most new ideas go through the following stages prior to implementation:

— The idea is not feasible.

— It is feasible but it is not cost effective.

— It is feasible and cost effective and moreover I (the boss) thought of it first.

How Can One Measure Technological Change?

There are competing and widely differing means to measure technological change (IV–15). Although each measuring scheme provides a different indicator or a different view of what is taking place, together these indicators may provide a reliable means of determining the extent and rate of change.

There are two basic classes of measurement schemes. Each is associated with one of the basic concepts of technological change, i.e., the formation and transfer of information, or the effects of this formation and transfer. Neither class appears to be perfect. Table IV–4 summarizes some of the measurement schemes in use. The most popular measure is one associated with the "effects" definition and is the output per unit of labor and capital input, with allowance made for education (IV–16).

It is beyond the scope of this book to examine in depth the various measurement schemes and to recommend one for use. What is significant here is the fact that a valid and reliable scheme will provide the information required to test the theories regarding the interplay of the factors influencing technological change as proposed by the forecaster and as used in the preparation of the forecast.

TABLE IV–4

TECHNOLOGICAL CHANGE MEASUREMENT SCHEMES
(IV–17)

Class I: Information Formation and Transfer

Scheme   1. Uses the net charge from one period to another of expenditures on R&D.

2. Uses net change of number of technical workers in the labor force.

3. Uses the number of patents granted or applied for in a given period.

4. Uses a count of new developments appearing in a given time period.

Class II: The Effects of Information Formation and Transfer

Scheme   1. Denison's method:
Technological change = Change in real GNP minus (all accountable factors; such as, changing labor hours and increase in tangible capital stock, which contribute to the rise in GNP).

2. Kendrick's method:
Technological change = output per man-hour, in private economy; or output per unit of labor and tangible capital input, private domestic economy.

3. BLS (Bureau of Labor Statistics) method:
Technological change = Real product per man-hour, total economy.

Technological Change and Forecasting Techniques

Technological forecasts can be made for any of the three steps of technological change. A forecast made for the invention step is generally an estimate of technical potential, and one made for either the innovation or diffusion steps is a projection or prediction of technical application. Raymond Isenson offers the following as examples of each: 1) Technical Potential: In the year 2000 physicists will have the knowledge and techniques to harness fusion of hydrogen. 2) Technical Application: In 1972 the United States will fly a prototype of the supersonic transport (IV–18).

Thomas Monahan distinguishes the types of forecasts by levels and defines each level as:

Level 1: Forecast of functional capabilities, i.e., the end results, as opposed to the means of achieving the objective.

Level 2: Forecast of specific techniques, which enable a functional capability to be accomplished.

Level 3: Forecast of conceptual systems, which may be realized when technological capabilities are achieved.

Level 4: Forecast of technical areas, encompassing more than one functional capability in a broad discipline, each area comprehensive and sufficiently independent to preclude overlapping (IV–19).

It should be noted that these four levels correspond to subdivisions of the technical potential-type forecast described by Isenson.

James Hacke conceives technological forecasting as sharing the empirical, inductive character of natural science. Thus, since forecasting entails some of the important limitations and ambiguities of natural science, it realizes the same shortcomings, but on the other hand it also shares those characteristics which give empirical science its power. Forecasting is related to the scientific method through three characteristics:

— The forecaster can formulate testable hypotheses and then test them by applying them to historical events, and check prediction against actual results.

TABLE IV–5
CONCEPTS AND MISCONCEPTIONS OF FORECASTING
(IV–22)

Concept	Description
1. Prediction	Anticipation of future events without qualification. All if's and but's have been taken into account. Scientific prediction requires sufficiently complete and correct knowledge of the relevant variables, their interrelations and the process of change from the earlier to the later state.
2. Projection	This is basically the same as prediction except for one important difference. The projection includes qualification statements; such as, if this . . . then that. . . .
3. Program Plan	A course of action is charted towards a goal and modifications are made as necessary in the strategy and tactics of achieving the goal.
4. Propaganda	A climate of opinion is created favorable to achieving an objective.
5. Poetry/Primitive Projection	Includes visions, conjectures and speculation—not to be taken seriously.
6. Parroty	A simple repetition of what is fashionable to say.

— Technological forecasts need a precision apparatus to give the user some indication of how accurate the forecaster thinks he is and an objective indication of how accurate the forecast is. Error limits should be given with the forecast.

— A general theory to explain forecasting methods and trends is needed. Some general principles should be formulated by induction and tested at each step (IV–20).

Since technological change is affected by a more complex array of factors during the innovation and diffusion steps, a forecast of a technical application involves a higher degree of uncertainty and consequently a lower confidence level than a forecast of technical potential.

What appears to be the best definition of a technological forecast, as contrasted with the conceptions and misconceptions summarized in Table IV–5 embodies the kind of information management seeks from a forecast: "The prediction with a level of confidence, of a technical achievement in a given time frame with a specific level of support (IV–21).

The period over which a forecast should extend generally varies with the technical field and industry involved. The period should be long enough to allow management to form and initiate a plan to meet or alter the conditions which are forecast. Periods

TABLE IV–6
CLARKE'S FORECASTS (IV–24)

Year	Transportation	Communication Information	Materials & Manufacturing
1970	space lab lunar landing nuclear rocket	translating machines	efficient electric storage
1980	planetary landings	personal radio	
1990			fusion power
2000	colonizing planets	artificial intelligence	wireless energy sea mining
2010	earth probes	telesensory devices	weather control
2020	interstellar probes	robots logical languages	
2030		contact with extra-terrestrials	space mining
2040			transmutation
2050	gravity control space drive	memory playback	planetary engineering
2060		mechanical educator	
2070	near-light speeds		climate control
2080	interstellar flights	machine intelligence exceeds man's	
2090	matter trans-mitter	world brain	replicator
2100	meeting with extra-terrestrials		astronomical engineering

TABLE IV–7
WOLFBEIN'S FORECAST OF TRENDS (IV–25)

Agriculture: new and improved farm machinery and greater use of fertilizers and insecticides, new strains of livestock.

Instrumentation: greater use of numerical control machines.

Machinery: increased automation, mechanized materials handling.

Metals processing: the basic oxygen process of steelmaking, automation of the entire steel making process.

Transportation: higher speeds, larger size vehicles in all forms of transportation, mechanized traffic control and handling.

Power production: automatic control systems, low cost nuclear generation.

---

vary between 5 and 20 years (IV–23). The author advises a time span of 20 years, since it takes from 5 to 8 years for exploratory development to be incorporated into the market place and 15 to 20 years for research to become applied to the economy.

Quasi-scientific forecasting as done by Da Vinci, Verne and Clarke (see Table IV–6 for some of Clarke's forecasts) was possible since these individuals possessed unencumbered, imaginative minds with a scientific bent. As long as one remains within the general bounds of the laws of nature, he is safe in forecasting any technical achievement of the wildest scheme. It is quite another problem, however, to provide the kind of forecast defined. Since these visionary forecasts do not have a fundamental scientific basis, they cannot be taken seriously. Tables IV–7 and IV–8 illustrate some forecasts resulting from individual pools of technical experts. These forecasts were not devised by the Delphi method, which will be discussed in Chapter VII, but are the results of educated opinion drawn from selected experts.

There are four discernible categories of technological forecasts (IV–27):

1. *Intuitive Forecasting*
   a. Individual
   b. Consensus
      (1) Polls
      (2) Panels (USAF-Project Forecast & USN SEABED)
      (3) Delphi

TABLE IV–8

HAYDEN'S FORECAST BY POLLING FOR THE YEAR 2000
(IV–26)

Computer Domesticized: Two-way communication with a computer from the home, hearthside facsimile newspapers and magazines, automatic language translators.

Improved Mental Ability: Genetic engineering, electromechanical connection between brain and computer.

Longer Life Span: Increase through drugs life span by 50 years.

Nuclear Energy: Electrical power furnished by a dozen generating stations each with a capacity of 60,000 megawatts.

Transportation: Regularly scheduled commercial traffic to lunar colonies.

Solar Heated Houses: by 1985.

Politics: Automatic voting, on the spot casting of votes.

Sea Farming: by 2000.

---

2. *Trend Extrapolation*
   a. Simple
   b. Curve Fitting
   c. Trend Curves
   d. Systematic Curve Fitting
3. *Trend Correlation*
   a. Pre-cursor Events
   b. Correlation Analysis
   c. Regression Analysis
   d. Correlation Coefficient
4. *Analogy*
   a. Growth
   b. Historical

Integration of Technical Forecasts and Planning

Planning is the management function that generally precedes all organizational activity. How can R&D management optimize its planning function, i.e., obtain the best results from the resources it has to allocate? One method is to look into the future through the benefits of technological forecasts. Planning in R&D organizations involves a variety of decisions: which projects to start, which to continue at a slower or faster pace and which to stop; what kind of talent is required and what quantity should be hired or phased out; what new instruments and facilities are required or are no longer necessary. Three courses of action exist for the manager in the face of changing technology: 1) he can plan to accommodate the change, 2) he can plan to alter the estimated future technical environment, or 3) he can do nothing.

In developing both short and long-term plans, the planner must structure his forecast on a sound data base. Operations research, in its narrowest sense, is an essential ingredient of the planning process. In its broadest sense it may well pervade the entire forecasting process. By analyzing the data in terms of its short-term as well as its long-range potentialities, and its relevant environment, a pattern for the future may be established. If the approach to technical forecasting is purely sequential it is called "exploratory."

When the forecast is "needs oriented" it is termed "normative." In the normative forecast, goals, needs, objectives or desires are specified and the forecast works backward to the present to see what capabilities now exist or could be extrapolated to meet future goals. In some cases the goal may even force technology. Indeed, the remoteness of the goals and the priority they have may well determine how many concurrent approaches are pursued to meet the goal. Two good illustrations of normative forecasting are the Navy's "Polaris" Program and NASA's "Man on the Moon" Program. It should be noted that in both of these cases in which a needs oriented forecast was involved, resource availability was not the major problem.

Normative forecasting may be formalized and usually is. In fact, normative forecasting probably should be called "goal oriented planning." Most appraisal techniques that are utilized fall into two categories: those which use the decision theory approach of rating (subjectively or objectively) various criteria for success in order to arrive at an over-all figure of merit, and those which are based on economic analysis.

The advantage of both of these techniques is that totally dissimilar projects or programs can be compared; therefore, such methods have relevance to policy planning at both the national or corporate level. It must be remembered that in both of these techniques the data plus the analysis, either manual or computerized, furnishes only information. The manager must use the information and it is information plus judgment that renders a decision.

REFERENCES

IV– 1. Address by Philip K. Reily, "Technical Information Transfer and Economic Growth," Institute on Transfer of Technical Information, American University, Washington, D.C., Oct. 23, 1967, p. 13 (hereinafter cited as Reily).

IV– 2. Fabricant, Solomon, "Measurement of Technological Change," seminar on Manpower Policy and Program, Manpower Administration, U.S. Department of Labor, July, 1965, p. 7 (hereinafter cited as Fabricant).

IV– 3. Reily, *supra* note 1, pp. 10–11.

IV– 4. Fabricant, *supra* note 2, p. 6.

IV– 5. *Washington Post*, January 4, 1968, p. A–26.

IV– 6. Table 1 lists some examples of time lags between discovery and applications.

IV– 7. Reily, *supra* note 1, p. 10. A notable exception has been the proliferation of laser technology.

IV– 8. Wolfbein, Seymour L., "The Pace of Technological Change and the Factors Affecting it," O.E.C.D. North American Regional Conference on Manpower Implications of Automation, Washington, D.C., Dec. 8–10, 1964, at 19 (hereinafter cited as Wolfbein).

IV– 9. Davidson, Harold, "The Transfer Process from Science to Technology," Institute on the Worth of Planning and Control Processes in R&D Management, American University, Washington, D.C., Apr. 22, 1968.

IV–10. *Id.*

IV–11. Reily, *supra* note 1, p. 9.

IV–12. Danilov, Victor J., "$24 Billion for Research," *Industrial Research*, Jan., 1967, p. 53.

IV–13. *Id.*

IV–14. Barnes, Carl, "To Promote Invention," *International Science and Technology*, Dec., 1966, p. 67.

IV–15. Fabricant, *supra* note 2, p. 3.

IV–16. *Id.* p. 14.

IV–17. *Id.* pp. 7–15.

IV–18. Isenson, Raymond S. "Technological Forecasting—A Management Tool," *Bus. Horizons*, Summer, 1967, p. 37 (hereinafter cited as Isenson).

IV–19. Monahan, Thomas, "Current Approaches to Forecasting Methodology," *Symposium on Long Range Forecasting and Planning,*

U.S. Air Force Academy, Colorado Springs, Colo., Aug. 16–17, 1966, p. 26 (hereinafter cited as Monahan).

IV–20. Hacke, James, "A Methodological Preface to Technological Forecasting," *Symposium on Long Range Forecasting and Planning*, U.S. Air Force Academy, Colorado Springs, Colo., Aug. 16–17, 1966, pp. 46–48.

IV–21. Cetron, M. J., "Forecasting Technology," *Science and Technology*, Sept., 1967, p. 83 (hereinafter cited as Cetron). Many other authors have provided variations of the definitions and concepts expressed in the previous paragraphs. Appendix A summarizes some of the concepts and misconceptions of technological forecasting Siegel feels were in evidence around 1953. A current article in *Management Review* best sums up the concept of technological forecasting:

> Even the most sophisticated technological forecasting being carried out today is still an art, not yet a science, but it involves an understanding of the complex process of technology transfer, of the interactions between technological development and social and political change and, finally, of the impact of technological innovation on the total system within which it functions.

"Technological Forecasting," *Management Rev.*, Aug., 1967, p. 64.

IV–22. Siegel, Irving H., "Technological Change and Long Run Forecasting," *J. of Bus.*, July, 1953, p. 144.

IV–23. Cetron, M. J., *A Proposal for a Navy Technological Forecast*, Part I Summary Report, p. 4 (1966).

IV–24. Clarke, Arthur, *Profiles of the Future*, p. 232 (1962).

IV–25. Wolfbein, Seymour L., *supra* note 8, pp. 16–18.

IV–26. Hayden, Spencer J., "En Route to the Year 2000," *Management Rev.*, Nov., 1967, pp. 17–24.

IV–27. Cetron, M. J. and Monahan, T. I., "An Evaluation and Appraisal of Various Approaches to Technological Forecasting," First Annual Technology and Management Conference, Industrial Management Conference, Lake Placid, N.Y., May 22–25, 1967, p. 2.

There is also today a tendency to let the spectacular aspects of some kinds of technology lead us to give undue attention to those things which are glamorous, at the expense of those things which are important and badly needed.

—J. R. KILLIAN

CHAPTER V

FORECASTING METHODOLOGIES, SELECTION, AND PRESENTATION OF FORECASTING INFORMATION

Summary of Forecasting Methodologies

At this juncture it would be well to summarize and round out the descriptions of forecasting methodologies at our disposal. As stated in Chapter IV, these fall into four discernible categories as follows:

Intuitive Methods

One of the most direct and, at the present time, widely used methods of generating a forecast is to sample the opinions of one or more persons knowledgeable in the specific technology or technical area under consideration. When more than one forecaster is involved, the forecast is built on a consensus or on a composite of estimates.

— *Individual or "Genius" Forecasting.* There is considerable merit in a forecast made by a single individual who is expert in his special area, not only in depth in the underlying scientific disciplines or technologies, but who is openminded in taking a synoptical view of the functional area to which his expertise has direct application.

— *Consensus.*

*POLLS. To overcome the difficulty inherent in a single estimate which may be poor, it may be well to combine the judgments of several individuals who are active in the field. It is presumed that a realistic forecast can be obtained by cancelling out the errors of individual predictions, but this is not necessarily the case, especially if the sample is poorly drawn.

*PANELS. The panel approach to technological forecasting,

91

in which individual experts are brought together, provides for a desirable interaction among their several opinions. Project Forecast of the Air Force and Project SeaBed of the Navy are two interesting examples of successful panel operations.

*DELPHI TECHNIQUE. The Delphi technique is directed to the systematic solicitation of expert opinion. Instead of using the traditional approach toward achieving a consensus through open discussion, this technique "eliminates committee activity altogether, thus —— reducing the influence of certain psychological factors, such as specious persuasion, unwillingness to abandon publicly expressed opinions, and the bandwagon effect of majority opinion." It replaces direct debate by a carefully designed program of sequential individual interrogations (best conducted by questionnaires) interspersed with information and opinion feedback derived by computed consensus from the earlier parts of the program. Both the inquiry into the reasons and subsequent feedback of the reasons adduced by others may serve to stimulate the experts into taking into due account considerations they might through inadvertence have neglected, and to give due weight to factors they were inclined to dismiss as unimportant on first thought (V–1).

Delphi is *used* in forecasting; contrary to a current misconception, it is not a forecasting technique. More properly it should be described as an elegant method for developing a consensus; it is a polling method employed for systematic solicitation of expert opinion. Delphi not only uses technological forecasting, but it also incorporates a "need" orientation which tends to mask the forecast. Figure V–1 shows the result of an opinion poll on "Scientific Breakthroughs." The illustration shows when, in the opinion of a group of experts, these breakthroughs are likely to occur. See Chapter VIII for a specific example of Delphi which was modified to suit the particular user group.

Trend Extrapolation

— *Simple Extrapolation*. The most obvious method of technological forecasting is to assume that whatever has hap-

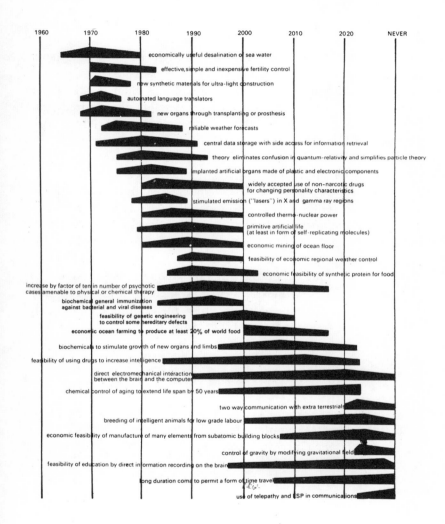

Figure V–1. A Delphi Consensus of Scientific Breakthroughs.
(Source: Gordon, R. J. and Helmer, O., *Report on a Long Range
Study*, Report P–2982 Rand September 1964)

pened in the past will continue to happen in the future, provided there are no disturbances. While it is not a very accurate method, it has the advantage of objectivity.

The method is applicable to forecasting functional capabilities. If the field of interest of the forecast centers on man's ability to communicate, appropriate data sets might be "frequency spectrum exploitable" or "number of intelligence bits per hour per mile of separation between communicators." Such a set of data does not explicitly concern itself with whether the desired function is to be accomplished by cable, microwave, teletype, or a Telstar satellite. One or more of these techniques must be implicitly involved. The growth is considered in terms of cumulative time or calendar year.

— *Curve Fitting with Judgment.* Technological progress, as we are currently witnessing, more than likely proceeds in an exponential manner similar to the law of acceleration under the influence of gravitational forces or to the phenomenon of biological growth. Initial advance is exponential, followed by a continued diminution of the rate of advance as "maturity" is approached. The synthesis of several fields of progress, each occurring at different intervals, may result in an exponential advance for a functional capability. Initially the technique tends to experience a period of slow growth. Finally, its potential is recognized, money and work are poured in, problems are resolved, and an accelerated growth occurs. Eventually, limiting factors are encountered, the growth rate decelerates, and the curve asymptotically approaches some upper value, which should be defined when the limiting factor is known.

— *Trend Curves.* Several types of trend curves may be described:

*Linear increase with flattening as a limit is approached.

*Exponential increase with no limit in the time frame under consideration.

*S-shaped curve, the normal characteristic of specific maturing technologies.

*Double-exponential or even steeper increase, with subsequent flattening, characteristic of some functional capabilities in areas of concentrated research and development.

*Slow exponential increase followed by sudden much more rapid increase, with eventual flattening.

— *Systematic Curve Fitting.* To calculate and project trends quantitatively, one may use one or more empirical equations:

*Straight line or first degree polynomial, in instances in which growth is characterized by a linear increase or decrease:

$$y = a + bx$$

*Parabola or second degree polynomial, in instances in which growth is characterized by one bend, either upward or downward:

$$y = a + bx + cx^2$$

*Exponential, in which growth is a geometric function with respect to time (or other controlling parameter):

$$y = ae^{bx}$$

If the empirical data to be used in making the projection are reliable, the above equations may be used, together with the technique of least squares, to project future values of significant parameters.

To determine the parameters (constants) of the desired polynomial a set of "normal" equations is derived by a squaring and minimizing procedure.

Trend Correlation Analysis

The trend of a technical parameter which is complex and difficult to predict by itself may be more easily expressed as a result of a relationship between two or more other trends. Whereas time-dependent trend extrapolation attempts explicit forecasting, interrelationships between parameters can be explored on a much more general level if they do not have to fit into an explicit time frame. Nevertheless, they may represent extrapolations of reality beyond present capability or estimates, in the instance of future technologies.

In order to use two or more trends to determine a third, the predictor must have available a number of primary trends which are related to the technical field of interest. To these he must add a knowledge of probable relationships that might arise from combinations of such variables. The predictor may then select the relationship and the primary variables which influence the desired technical improvement. The trends of the primary variables may be projected on the basis of any techniques which appear appropriate. The prediction is then completed by projection of the unknown variable on the basis of the relationship between the primary variables.

— *Precursor Events.* Forecasting by analysis of precursor events uses the correlation of progress trends between two developments, one of which is leading the other. But it must be obvious that the two developments are logically related to each other, such as the research and development effort applied to combat aircraft eventually also bears fruit in the transport sector. Figure V–2 illustrates this relationship.

— *Correlation Analysis.* "Correlation" covers problems dealing with the relationships between two or more variables, specifically, the degree of a certain special type of relationship among them. In practical problems, it is often more important to find out what the relation actually is, in order to estimate or predict one variable (the dependent variable) from knowledge of another variable (the independent variable); the statistical technique appropriate to such a case is called regression analysis, or often least squares. When consistent correlations can be found, the method offers an objective approach to forecasting.

When more than two variables are involved, we have "multiple correlation." Any number of "causal" factors can be handled by multiple correlation, as long as there are more observations than factors. While the procedure cannot be described graphically for more than two causal factors, or independent variables, the formulas and ideas are essentially the same. It is most desirable that all factors be employed which have a bearing

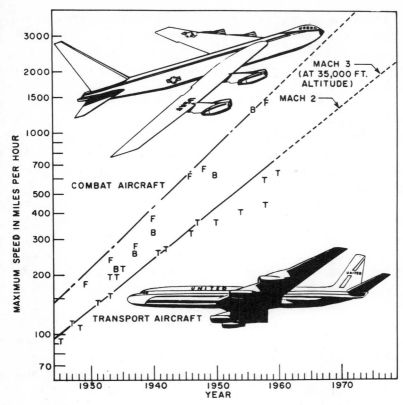

Figure V–2. The Precursor Relationship: Comparative Speed Trends of Combat and Transport Aircraft (Source: Adapted from Lenz: Technological Forecasting).

on the outcome and that any relationships among two or more which are known "a priori" be defined.

Analogy

According to Lenz attempts to develop a theory explaining why technical progress should proceed in an exponential manner date back at least as far as 1907 to the theory advanced by Henry Adams, who compared the acceleration of progress with the effect of a new mass, introduced into a system of forces previously in equilibrium, which is induced to accelerate its motion until a new equilibrium is established. The accumulated information would then be seen as analogous to the speed, and the second derivative of information over time is analogous to an acceleration (assumed constant).

Growth Analogy. Pearl's work on the analogy of population increases to the growth of biological organisms has been cited above. To support his thesis Pearl includes the rate of increase of fruit flies within a bottle, the rate of increase of yeast cells in a given environment, and the rate of cell increase within white rats.

De Solla Price includes technological forecasting within the larger framework of all growth phenomena in science, including the number of scientists or papers, etc. This analogy has some merit in that it gives a symmetrical curve normally, without further assumptions. He also examines the growth of length of a beanstalk over time. Ayres proposes autocatalytic chemical processes as a model.

Hartman derives his model from a single analogy with reaction processes in a gas, from Hartman's "gas," the molecules are scientists and pieces of information, both occurring at a given volume density. The scientists "molecules" do not move significantly, whereas the information "molecules" move with assumed constant velocity in random directions. A useful reaction (i.e., the generation of new information) is supposed to occur when the scientist "molecules" have a "reaction cross-section" on being hit by the information "molecules." In criticizing Hartman's model it is to be noted that his basic assumption that information gain is proportional to the amount of existing information ($dI/dt = kI$) holds only where (a) ideal communication between all investigators and all sources of information can be assumed and (b) every opportunity presented by this communication can in fact be exploited. The model may be a useful approach to research and development in a specific field or within a small or medium-sized research group.

Historical Analogy. To study the impact of a new

technology on functional capability it may be desirable to consider what lessons history may have for us. For example, General Electric Company (TEMPO) (V–2) could make a forecast of the relative contributions to the energy input to the United States to be made by various sources in the decade out to 2060, in which they estimate the contributions to electricity to be made by nuclear fuels, using the same type of growth curves which they observed for fossil fuels and hydroelectric power in the period 1800–1960.

What Should Be Considered in Selecting a Methodology?

The forecasting approaches previously presented ranged from intuitive through complex correlation analysis as a means of structuring the data. Which technique is best depends upon the circumstances under which the forecaster is working and his needs, the reliability, completeness, and quantitative precision of the data base, the purpose of the forecast, the length of the forecast period, and the time available for generating the forecast. Likewise the technique selected should be compatible with and adaptable to the information available, i.e., "a micrometer should not be used to measure a sewer pipe."

Conversely there is a very real need for improvement in the level or degree of sophistication with which many technologies are treated by forecasters. For example, the most unsophisticated forecasting technique is obviously the genius or intuitive type. It has been variously estimated that 80%, 90%, or even 95% of all forecasting done by the military services until recently was of the genius type. Frequently, insufficient historical data precludes the use of more sophisticated techniques, however, in many other instances substantial quantities of reliable data are available for analysis but are not used. As a result, the level of confidence which can be ascribed to the forecast is frequently less than desirable.

When valid data is not fully utilized, because of an unsophisticated forecasting technique, we say that a Type I forecasting error has been made. If on the other hand, a sophisticated technique is used utilizing imprecise and incomplete data, we say that a Type II forecasting error has been made. In either case a wrong decision or error in judgment has occurred and the resulting forecast is of questionable value. Of the two types of forecasting errors, Type I is far more common especially when subject matter specialists are called upon to prepare inputs to forecasts.

The major requisites of good forecasting can be reduced to: 1) a reliable data base (which normally consists of the scientific and technical specialists knowledge in the subject matter area as well as any supporting data); 2) astute judgment and common sense on the part of the forecaster; and 3) understanding of available forecasting techniques and how and when to apply them. The primary gain from the use of such techniques is the greatly improved insight one obtains into the nature and inter-relationships of influencing factors and into the sensitivity of solutions to their consistent frame of reference, distinct alter-native technical solutions to a given operational problem. In effect, the techniques provide the tools whereby the technical knowledge and judgment of the forecaster can be applied to logical, systematic thinking about the pattern of development of the particular technology.

Techniques for Presenting Trends

On pages 46, 47 and 48 of Chapter II, the composition, char-acter and content of an adequate forecast were detailed. Little was mentioned concerning the graphic content—a very impor-tant element. Words without pictures are as weak as pictures without words. In the first instance, the reader is asked to visu-alize what is spread out in rhetoric and probably exists in the mind of the writer. In the second instance, pictures imply a logic which may not be identical with that of the accompanying syntax. The technological forecast should be a proper combination of the two modes of expression.

Time-Dependent Trends

Figure V–3 depicts a *time-dependent trend*. The payload ratio of flying belts is shown as it is expected to increase in the future. Conventional fuel is a barrier at one level of performance and exotic fuels at another level of performance. The improvements between barriers are those expected in the usual history of applied science and engineering going from the demonstration of feasibility to the futility of incremental improvements. The Figure implies that current new fuel research would break out in 1963. It also implies that between 1965 and 1970, competition will exist between the underdeveloped new configuration and the overdeveloped old configuration. The broad areas indicate the confidence interval. Real time in this case as the

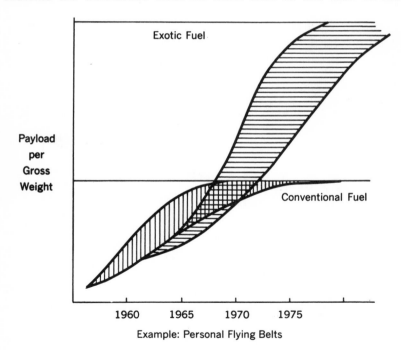

Example: Personal Flying Belts

Figure V–3. Time-Dependent Trend (Source: Army Long Range Technological Forecast).

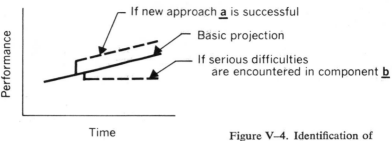

Performance

If new approach **a** is successful

Basic projection

If serious difficulties
are encountered in component **b**

Time

Figure V–4. Identification of
Anticipated Results if Se-
lected Special Circumstances
Occur (Source: Pardee-
Research Program
Effectiveness).

independent variable of progress makes a certain amount of sense.

Figure V–4 is a similar set of curves which identifies antici-pated results if selected special circumstances occur. The trend of a critical parameter (in this case the thrust-to-weight ratio of

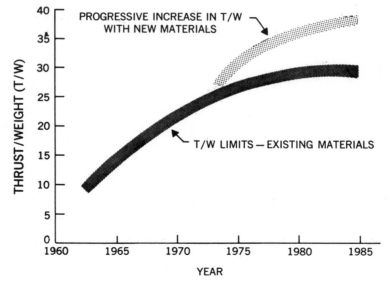

Figure V–5. Trends in Thrust—To Weight Ratio of
Dependent Lift Engines (Source: Army Long
Range Technological Forecast).

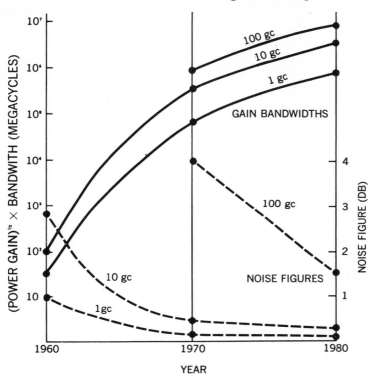

Figure V–6. Projected Development of Solid-State Amplifiers
(Source: Army Long Range Technological Forecast).

lift engines) is shown in Figure V–5. Uncertainty (because of technology or funding limitations) is shown by the broad line. The impact of new techniques (in this case, materials) is also shown.

The case of a development involving the projection of two critical parameters (in this instance, power gain bandwidth and system noise of solid-state amplifiers) is shown in Figure V–6.

The projection of a critical parameter in technology, in which specific milestones in research and development are identified, is shown in Figure V–7. The actual and anticipated gains in certain characteristics of air cushion vehicles are reported. Air cushion vehicles performance, in terms of a factor of merit, is projected for a vehicle with a bare bottom and with a skirt

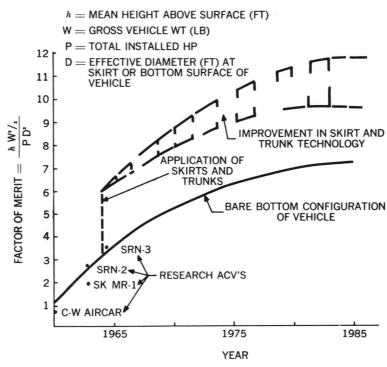

Figure V–7. Air Cushion Vehicle (ACV) Performance (Source: Naval Ship Research and Development Center).

and trunk system. Significant improvements in ACV performance have resulted from the development of skirts and flexible jet extensions. Aerodynamic problems associated with these developments have been largely resolved, but finding suitable materials for the air cushion devices is a continuing problem.

The projection of the critical parameters in each of several alternative techniques, showing specific developments in perspective, is shown in Figure V–8. As shown, considerable improvements in specific impulse have been made in solid and liquid propellants, especially in recent years. However, no one parameter in itself can be used as a basis for comparison of the various propulsion systems. Solid propellants have lagged liquid propellants in specific impulse values for years. This trend will con-

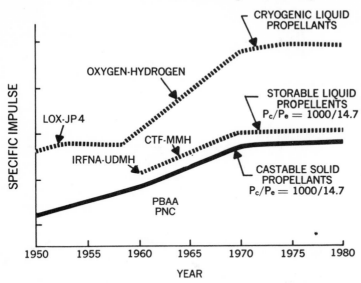

Figure V–8. Predicted Improvements in Specific Impulse
(Source: Army Long Range Technological Forecast).

tinue, due to the need for compromising performance in order
to attain certain physical and ballistic properties in the solid-
propellant grain. Solid-propelled motor designs, however, are
sufficiently less complex and lighter in weight than liquid-pro-
pelled systems that over-all advantage can result from the selection of somewhat less energetic solid-propellant combinations.

Parameter-Dependent Trends

In other cases, the identification of real time is less precise.
Often the real times of occurrence of steps of progress are dependent on one or more factors (parameters or variables). Figure V–9 depicts a *parameter-dependent trend*. The gal/day of
desalinized ocean water is hard to put on a time-scale of expected
progress. Many factors affect this progress, two of which are the
cost of power and the diffusion rates of membranes. These effects
are not independent. Their joint occurrence would determine the
performance characteristics of constructable diffusion desaliniza-

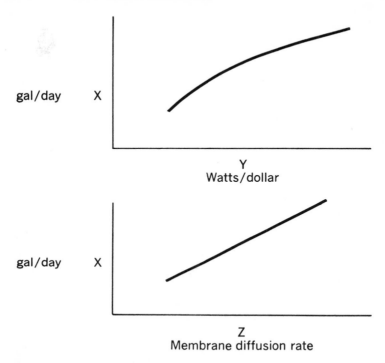

Example: Desalinization of Ocean Water

Figure V–9. Parameter Dependent Trend.

tion plants, but no one is confident of predicting the separate parameters as time-dependent trends.

The picturing of parameter-dependent trends is full of problems. In the first place, partial and contingent dependency is poorly represented graphically. For instance, the rule of combination of the partial effects of y and z on x is not necessarily that implied by the chart, namely, addition. There may be complex relations between diffusion rate and power in specific design applications because of such things as induced potentials. On the other hand, if x, y, and z, are graphed together in a three-dimensional pictorial to account for this specific-design interaction, then the general non-specific design direction of effects may be obscured. The specific functionally-related curves are basic to systems design, whereas the trends are the engineeringly imprecise but directionally-correct information for planning. The engineer cannot use what is useful to the planner and the planner cannot use what is useful to the engineer.

The problem here is not trivial. It bears on the whole issue of the feasibility of forecasting in terms of time and probability. Almost all forecasting, if taken into serious detail, involves parameter-dependent trends as elemental pieces. Time as an independent variable takes on increasingly the role of a modulus and not real time. Again, the correspondence between real and psychological probabilities in predicting R&D products is called into question. With little physical basis for making probability estimates should the available physical elements be combined or should an over-all estimate of probability be made by the forecaster? If the latter makes more sense, the forecaster's projections in probability terms can be logically combined by planners who are not predictors but who deal with even larger aggregates and who need to know their probabilities.

Figure V–10 shows performance characteristics of micro-

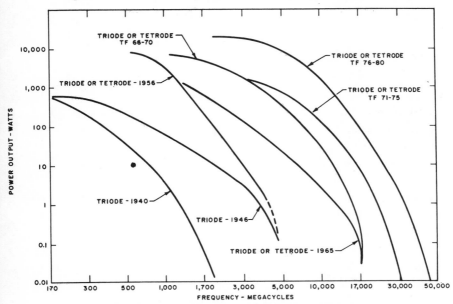

Figure V–10. Progress in Capacities of a Microwave
Tube (Source: Army Long Range
Technological Forecast).

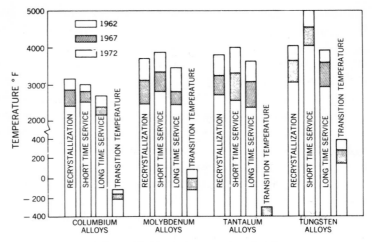

Figure V–11. Refractory Metal Alloys
(Source: Aerospace Industries Forecast).

wave tubes over the past 25 years and as projected through the next 15 years. The trend of a critical parameter may also be presented in bar graph, as shown in Figure V–11.

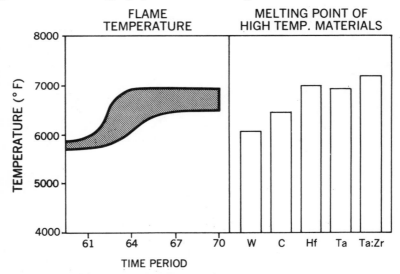

Figure V–12. Projected Propellant Flame Temperature
(Source: Aerospace Industries Forecast).

The projection of a critical parameter in terms of other constraining parameters is shown in Figure V–12. In order to resist the intense temperatures, high pressures, shear forces, corrosion, and erosion of exhaust gases, the uncooled nozzle on the solid-propelled rocket has, of necessity, been undesirably heavy. The flame temperature in 1960 exhaust products ranges between 5,700°F and 5,900°F (Figure V–12). As of the time of the preparation of the forecast, these temperatures were soon expected to exceed 6,300°F, and would approach 7,000°F by 1970, requiring the development of nozzles whose underlying principle of functioning is other than heat-sink methods, since the highly refractory metals, hafnium, tantalum, and tantalum-zirconium alloys, have melting points around 7,000°F.

Forecast of Functional Capabilities

A forecast of projected functional capabilities in terms of the technical state-of-the-art is shown in Figure V–13. The advantages of combined sensors for tracking became obvious because each is most effective in a given portion of the trajectory. For

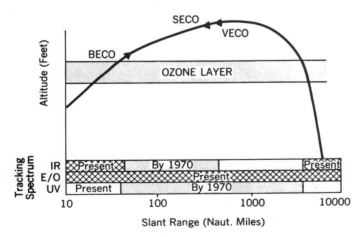

Figure V–13. Typical ICBM Trajectory Showing Optical Tracking Capabilities in Various Spectral Regions (Source: Air Force Technology for Tomorrow).

example, infrared is probably the most used and generally cost efficient sensor for air or space-borne use in tracking a missile through its powered phase and upon re-entry. Ultraviolet is extremely effective for detection and tracing in the powered or mid-course portion of the trajectory, but only from a space platform when the target is above the O_3 layer. Electro-optical techniques are usable in any part of the trajectory if the target is self- or solar-illuminated. Active electro-optical techniques, i.e., incorporating a laser transmitter for illumination of the target will provide tracking capabilities under more varied conditions.

Performance requirements for certain technologies as a result of related system developments can be identified as in Figure V–14. Interference control specifications will have to be expanded to meet the critical requirements of the aerospace age. Frequency coverage of interference measurements and analysis of conducted and radiated electrical energy will have to be extended downward to d.c. and upward to the infrared, visible, and ultraviolet spectra, as shown in Figure V–14.

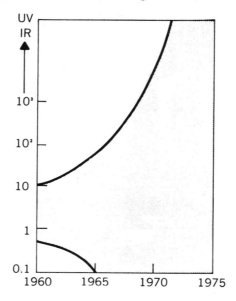

Figure V–14. Expanding Frequency Coverage for Vulnerability Reduction (Source: Army Long Range Technological Forecast).

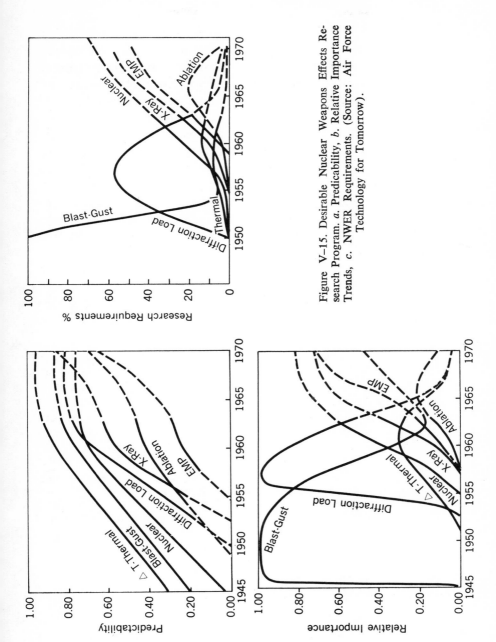

Figure V-15. Desirable Nuclear Weapons Effects Research Program. *a.* Predicability, *b.* Relative Importance Trends, *c.* NWER Requirements. (Source: Air Force Technology for Tomorrow).

In some areas of investigation it becomes necessary to define requirements for research and development in the several elements of the area under consideration. It is possible to project the state-of-the-art in the various disciplinary areas and to estimate their relative importance during the forecast period in terms of operational requirements. From these two trends, it is possible to establish research requirements and associated resource (personnel, funding) needs during the period under examination. For example, Figure V–15c looked to defining a desirable nuclear weapons effects research program for the projection of aircraft and air crew in 1962 and following years assuming an extended moratorium on atmospheric nuclear weapons effects tests. Figure V–15b, indicating relative research requirements (RR), combines relative importance (RI) from Figure V–15c and predictability (P) from Figure V–15a in terms of percent of total requirements as follows:

$$RR = \frac{RI \times (1 - P)}{RI \times (1 - P)} \times 100$$

It should be clear from the foregoing examples that graphics form the most potent tool the forecaster has at his disposal to tell his story. Words, numbers, and esoteric formulae may cause the decision-maker to gasp, but a graph immediately gives him a perspective and facile grasp of all interrelationships involved.

REFERENCES

V–1. "On the Epistemology of the Inexact Sciences," by O. Helmer and N. Rescher, *Management Science* 6 (1959, pp. 47).
V–2. *Energy Input to the United States, 1800–2060: History and Forecast,* J. C. Fisher, Report 66 TMP–26, General Electric Company, Santa Barbara, California, 1966.

The cost of development is far greater than the cost of research, and if a big development gets off on the wrong foot, the price is terribly high. —F. R. KAPPEL

CHAPTER VI

PROBLEMS AND PITFALLS

WHEN A CORPORATION decides to utilize a technological forecast as an input to planning decisions, the administrators are faced with some very fundamental questions. What do we ask for? How is it accomplished? Who should be assigned the task? How can we insure a useful product? Or as one questioning manager put it, "How much time will it take from productive work?"

A primary consideration that affects all of these questions is the forecast content. The prescription for the contents can determine its over-all utility. During 1968 the U.S. Navy prepared and published its first technological forecast. The Navy's product covered three different types of forecasts, comprising over six hundred individual forecasts prepared by twenty-three separate R&D activities. The format used by the Navy required a complete assessment of each field of technology as well as a forecast of the state-of-the-art. In retrospect this work did present some experiences that can contribute to the learning process of management and the technical communities. It will be used in this chapter as a vehicle for a discussion of the practical problems and pitfalls that can develop in the preparation of technological forecasts.

The Forecast—Something for Everyone?

To insure that a technology forecast is useful to technical, operational, and management personnel, the Navy required that each forecast be . . . "the prediction, with a stated level of confidence, of the anticipated occurrence of a technological achievement, within a given time frame with a specified level of support" (VI–1) . . . Supporting information was required for all fore-

115

casts. Each forecast comprised five categories. The categories included all aspects of the technology under examination: the history of its application, the implications of the forecast, and the areas of application. The following paragraphs discuss these five major categories and their requisite contents from corporate and military viewpoints:

— *Background:* This section identifies the organizational goals and other objectives to which the fields of technology being forecast can contribute. It discusses the present fields of application of the technology in areas of interest to the organization. A description of the significant factors influencing past developments and those factors which would tend to emphasize or de-emphasize further developments are included.

For the Navy forecast, the fields of technology were related to military operational objectives. This work was facilitated by the existence of Navy quantitative development goals and identified each technological area forecast with one or more of these goals.

— *Present Status:* Here, the field of technology's current state-of-the-art is described quantitatively. The inherent advantages or disadvantages (safety, stability, etc.) are listed, and a description of existing or potentially troublesome technological barriers or gaps are included. Also, this section describes the efforts made by competitors to utilize the technology and how these efforts have affected their share of market. One example of technology utilization with a marketable difference is the varied approaches to the construction of television sets. The hand-wired and printed circuit technologies are each advertised as having greater advantages than the other.

The military planner must consider the technological advantages, disadvantages, and susceptibility to counter actions by potential aggressors. This involves quantitative statements of current status of a nation compared with its potential adversaries, and identification of gaps where technological advances over present barriers would present clear advantages.

— *Forecasts:* The forecast consists of a projection of the state-of-the-art as a function of time and cost with an indicated level of confidence. Only relevant and accurately identified, pacing technological parameters are projected. (An example of a technological pacing parameter is illustrated in Figure V–7 and discussed on page 104 of Chapter V.) These parameters might be strength, weight, specific impulse, shaft horsepower, per unit volume, or any parameters that typify the advance of the technology areas. The discussion of the pacing parameter is quantitative and is directed to the effects of changes in complexity, cost, performance and other factors that might alleviate or cause limitations. Charts and graphs are used to clarify projections and enhance communication. Adequate supporting data is an essential requirement for preparation of a valid forecast.

— *Product Implications:* This section describes the effect, on the corporation, of the technological advances projected in the forecast. The corporate or product goals discussed in the *Background* section are quantitatively related to the forecast. Factors affecting manpower requirements, training, effectiveness, or operating efficiency are described. Graphic techniques are used where applicable. The implications of new products, market share, profits, and economics of scale are discussed quantitatively.

In military forecasts, this section would discuss the implications to operating forces. The operating environment would be discussed in terms of threat accommodation parameters such as target range, target accuracy, operating speed, and operating depth. For instance, if Figure V–7 (the projection of the technology of air cushion vehicles) were expressed in operational terms, the illustration could represent, say, captured air bubble aircraft carriers with an operational parameter of speed indicated in knots. Of course, this is a purely hypothetical example selected to show how a technology could be exploited and defined in terms that are meaningful to the user—in this case, the Navy.

— *References and Associated Activities:* The publications from which authoritative direction was elicited are cited. A list of the technical documents in the field which add credibility (hence utility) to the forecast is included. The corporate divisions and competitors who have contributed or have interest in this technological area are included. Also, government activities, universities, consultants and their point of contact are listed. The Navy forecast requires its contributors to identify all laboratory reports. The Reference section includes other applicable references with the names of the contributory activities.

The factual content of the forecasts is quite extensive. For each technological field, a history of its application, projections of the state-of-the-art, relative corporate goals, marketing information, possible new applications, and present shortcoming are essential parts of the package. It is this breadth of the technological assessment that allows the forecast to be beneficial to a diverse audience. The manager, technical expert, systems analyst, and marketing expert each can use the forecast as an aid in planning. In contrast, if the content of the forecast was just a state-of-the-art projection of a technological area without background, present status, and operational implications, its usefulness would probably be limited to the technical community.

Recognizing a technological forecast designed for wide utilization will require the variety of information indicated in the five categories, and we gain an appreciation of the nature and extent of the effort involved. The actual mechanics of conducting such a task must be directed by the talents and training of the specific individuals involved. No attempt to prescribe an all encompassing step-by-step procedure to avoid pitfalls will (or can) be made, but a discussion of what appears to be the inherent problems of such an undertaking and an indication of some solutions that were found to be applicable in preparing the Navy forecast are presented here.

The broad area forecast concepts of "something for everyone" may best be summarized by an analogy as illustrated in Figure VI–1. One input results in two distinct outputs, whose applications are vastly different. The first, dairy products, could be considered as the primary output. The second, fertilizer, a by-product of the operation. The end item paying for the input is the dairy products industry; however, the fertilizer application will assist in growing more crops, which in turn serves to increase the input. For military purposes, the primary reason to pursue technology is to provide weapons systems for national defense.

1. INPUT   **2. OUTPUT**

3. APPLICATION

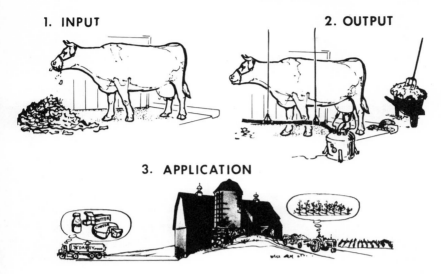

Figure VI–1.

The secondary output is an increased bank of technological knowledge aiding in further systems development. The cycle may be perceived from vastly different viewpoints, indicating the necessity for any forecasting effort to have a communications common denominator. The establishment of such a reference plane is accomplished through the art of structuring.

Structuring—The Key to Understanding

Perhaps the most important factor to consider in directing or preparing a forecast is the problem of structuring. In technological forecasting, the aspects of structuring permeate all levels of effort. It begins when management states the areas in which forecasts are to be prepared. (Here we assume that the implementation of a technological forecasting program would attempt to assess a broad corporate technological base.) The manner in which the various fields of technology are defined will affect the type of forecasts prepared, their content, and the over-all effect of policy and goals of the corporation.

Structuring, as used here, is the art of putting one's mind and

communications in order. It is the attempt to describe the mutually exclusive and collectively exhaustive sets that define the
breadth and depth of the forecasting effort. Stated another way,
a good technological forecast structure will be a good definition
of the technological areas to be forecast. As an example of the
nature of structuring, consider the hierarchy of the various factors that can be used to describe food for human consumption.
A conventional arrangement may begin with the categories of
fruit, vegetable, meat, etc. These major categories are then
broken into their parts, and these parts are further broken into
their parts. Fruit could be divided into apples, oranges, bananas,
etc. Apples, in turn, can be structured into Red Delicious, Wine-
sap, Jonathan, etc. The structure, to have high utility, must be
as complete as possible. In general, the first few items fall into
place quite easily, then as completeness is approached the task
is much more demanding as the inevitable rearrangements occur
and the search for all encompassing terminology is conducted.

When attempting to define a structure to accommodate an
area to be forecast, it is convenient to view the corporate product
(or groups of products) as a system or systems. This system
view simply means the product is viewed as being composed of
separable items that are fully integrated in their contribution to
the product. The task is to take each product, separate it (men-
tally of course) into its components, look for commonality across
product components, and request a forecast for each component.
As an example, an automobile can be viewed as being composed
of a transmission, engine, body, and so on. Any structuring
problem in the example appears to be one of fineness of division,
which might be considered trivial in such a well defined product. This would be true if the problem in hand were so well
constrained.

Here, the main object is to prepare a forecast. This implies
that concern is directed toward the future. The dependence upon
present day configurations of products becomes uncertain, and
complexity is added to the forecasting task as we move our forecasting further into the future.

The Navy forecast covered operating capabilities twenty

years ahead. During such a lengthy period supporting technologies can change drastically.

The problem of future uncertainty is not insurmountable, but
it does complicate forecasting. It will require the corporate product to be viewed as a system in a broader sense than just its
physical components. It should be visualized in terms of the
functions necessary to accomplish the product objectives while
the product is in operation in its environment. The fundamental
premise of the functional approach is: "components may come
and go, but basic functions remain and need to be satisfied." This
look at system functions in an operational environment is sometimes referred to as the systems approach. In prior times it was
probably regarded as part of competence. As an example of the
difference between the views one can take, let's return to the
automobile. The individual who views the auto as an integration
of components such as the engine, steering, brakes and so on is
indeed thinking "systems." There are many variations available
within this framework to accomplish the desired product performance. However, the individual who views the auto as one
part of a transportation system, composed of propulsion, guidance, and control, and so on is thinking functionally. Long-range
forecasting requires functional thinking.

The distinction between components and functions is a relative matter. Words such as function, component, and system
are multi-level. One man's system is another man's sub-system
or one man's function is another's system. Functions, as used
here for technological forecasting, are the product requirements
independent of technological approach. (For example, a function could be defined as a market share increase, and attainment
need not be tied to any particular product or products. As a military illustration one could define a neutralization function to be
achieved without specifying the particular weapons required.)
Thinking functionally for the structuring of the major portion of
the forecast areas won't solve all problems. It will, by taking that
first big step, help avoid many dead ends and much wheel-
spinning.

One should be aware of some side effects of this process.

Structuring of the type discussed here can set the framework for creative contributions to end products. It won't guarantee creativity; however, it will provide a field for development. A good functional structure will point out gaps or holes and will tend to insure completeness of product coverage. Further, everyone will be looking at the corporate product from a common but individually different view. This in itself may be worth the forecasting effort. Another effect will be a definite need to state explicitly and quantitatively the corporate operational objectives. A valid structure cannot be obtained without a clear understanding of the objectives. Product functional structuring may also force consideration of the company's future direction. As an example, if a group is required to think functionally about house refrigerators and house air-conditioners, it will not be too long until the consideration of house refrigeration as a corporate product could arise. It is not a small effort to determine whether the company should be going in this direction in the future. Creativity and explicit product (or corporate) goals seem to be the type of activity that any corporation would encourage. The fact is, many establishments do not have a formalized procedure to handle such demands. The result can be over-all frustration for both the manager and the technical innovators.

A Rose by Any Other Name

A fairly logical argument can be made for structuring a product as if it consisted of a series of functions operating as a total system within a described environment. The extension of this concept to the actual forecast may not be as straightforward. As a matter of fact, strict adherence to a set of functions may artificially constrain the broad view inherent in a forecast. In general, much of this concern can be alleviated when one addresses the question of "what is technology?"

A general consensus of the scientific, technical, and management communities will agree that solid state electronics, lasers, and hydrodynamics are fields of technology. Also, communications, automatic data processing, and ship hull design are regarded as fields of technology. We are faced with the chicken/egg problem when considering that solid state electronics can contribute to automatic data processing, but there is no functional relationship—just one of several techniques. This suggests the functional area forecasts should be complemented with other forecasts. These are forecasts of technologies that in one way or another contribute across several functions. They are multipurpose technologies and can be described as support technologies. As an example, an automobile functional forecast would be complemented by forecasts in areas such as organic materials and materials fabrication. The support technologies should, as a minimum, cover: (1) areas that can constitute the physical end product, (2) the activities necessary to produce the product, and (3) the *total* environment in which the product operates (human, natural, competitive . . .).

To summarize the thoughts on the identification and definition of technological areas to be forecast, there are two complementary approaches. One is the functional structure based upon the corporate product(s). These are forecasts of scientific applications to specific corporate problem areas. The other approach is the preparation of forecasts in technology areas that support product development and use. These tend to be forecasts of scientific/engineering areas such as materials, hydrodynamics, acoustics, and so on. For a complete assessment of technology impact upon the corporation both are required. When defining the technology areas of interest to a corporation, it is important to consider the ramifications of the various ways it can be done. Two illustrations of structuring are shown in Figure VI–2. Note that one major category is concerned with support for product engineering. This is composed of the multi-purpose technologies that support products developed under either structure. Note also the structures in the illustrations are the type that might be developed by a production-oriented manager. A research engineer would probably view the corporation as being in the energy conversion business and proceed from there. Both views are nec-

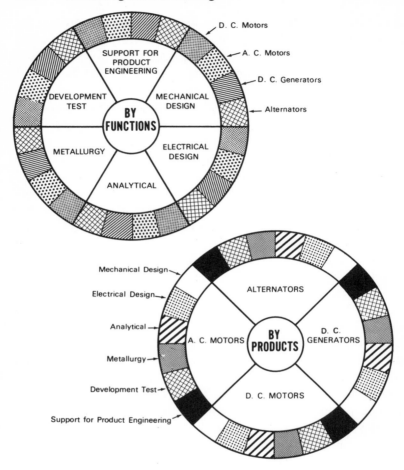

Figure VI–2. Two Different R&D Structures.

essary to develop a common structure. For conflicting views, as in this example, corporate goals would be the modifier between the views.

With an understanding of what areas are to be forecast, the question of the type of forecast can be addressed. The depth of penetration into each technological area will be variable. Also, no one person or group of people has or should have a peer's license in identifying technology areas of interest to the corporation. These considerations can be accommodated by allowing different types of forecasts to be prepared.

The corporate goals indicate a certain area for operations and a forecast should be prepared for each functional area identified by the structuring of the product. This insures the corporate strategy (as it is visualized at present) is covered. The functional area forecasts will tend to be normative (need oriented) forecasts. They should provide a reasonable indication of the corporate technological capabilities in the product field. Further, to insure completeness and because functional forecasts are product oriented, additional forecasts should be solicited for technological areas that could support several functions or that could have an effect on the over-all corporate operations. These forecasts would tend to be exploratory in nature.

Both the functional area and support forecasts should be at a broad level. For simplicity, this type of forecast can be identified as a *Broad Area Forecast*. The definition of the areas to be forecast should be a joint effort between management and technical departments. Any one breakout will not satisfy everyone, but each should be able to interpret the final framework in terms of their area of responsibility.

A second type of forecast should be included to allow excursions in depth into each functional or support area as need dictates, and also as a forum to express new product ideas. These *In-Depth Forecasts* can be considered as avenues for spontaneous efforts of technological opportunities, as well as part of any over-all program of forecasting.

Sell Science!

The forecast presentation will, to a large extent, be governed by the methodology used to project the field of technology. The methods used to forecast the future state-of-the-art are generally categorized as: intuitive, growth analogy, trend extrapolation, and trend correlation. Within each of these categories there are several techniques (VI–2). See Chapter V for a discussion of these techniques. The "a picture is worth a thousand words" guidance is especially valid in presenting a technology forecast. By intent, the forecast will be reviewed (and interpreted) by people with diverse needs and background. The forecaster should present the projection of the state-of-the-art and product implications in a graphic display if at all possible. (See Chapter V.) Further, the forecaster should use the display to convey as much qualification as is deemed necessary and to bring attention to significant points. For example, consider the Navy forecast requirement to express the forecast as a level of confidence. The requirement can be used by a forecaster to insure his forecast is interpreted as a projection to an area—not a point. Figure VI–3 indicates how confidence limits about a "best-estimate" (spread of value at a given time) can be displayed to portray the approximate nature of the projection where time is critical. Figure VI–4 is a way to indicate confidence of time (spread of time for a given value) where the value is critical. Display techniques can be used to guard against misinterpretation or to crystallize concepts. For instance, a planner wants to know how fast a train could travel in the year 1975. The forecaster would present the projection as shown in Figure VI–3 with the pacing parameter, operating speed, given as a spread (say 175 to 200

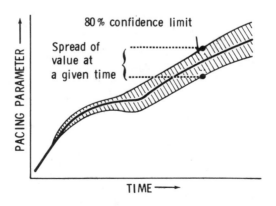

Figure VI–3. Level of Confidence
Shown Where *Time* Is a
Critical Parameter.

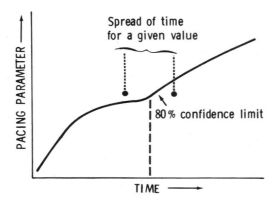

Figure VI–4. Level of Confidence
Shown Where *Value of the Pacing
Parameter* Is the Critical Factor.

miles per hour). If on the other hand the planner wanted to
know when he could operate at 200 mph, the forecast would
be given as a spread of time (say 1974 to 1976) for the operating speed as in Figure VI–4.

At some point in time the top management of a corporation
will want to review the technological forecast. It would be a
waste of time to submit all sections of all forecasts. It would be
wiser to present to top management the portion of the forecast
which will be useful in making decisions at the corporate level.
For this, a separate summary should be prepared. The summary
should cover new ideas and an assessment of what corporate
goals can be met. This is a different view than the technical
community would desire. However, the needs of top management
are reasonably covered in the *Product Implications* section of
the forecast. If the section is prepared with the top management
review in mind, the executive summary can be composed entirely
of the *Product Implications* section.

Who Me?

Having covered what a forecast should contain, the areas to
be forecast, and the various types of forecasts available to serve

the corporate needs, our attention can turn to who should do it. It is doubtful that a general request will generate a stampede of volunteers. The reaction of the technical community is likely to be unenthusiastic. The initial response of many technical people in laboratories to a request for technological forecasts could be described as . . . militant pessimism (VI–3). However, after preparing the forecasts, many found it to be a useful experience. It appears that a considerable portion of the "conversion" was due mainly to the recognition that technological forecasting is really a formalization of what is done (or should be done) in the natural process of technical planning.

At present, there appear to be two approaches on the question of *who* should prepare the forecast. One is, the forecast should be prepared by a technical expert in the field. The other is the forecast should be prepared by a product-oriented technical staff (generalists) or operations research staff. Both approaches were used in preparing the Navy forecast, with most activities using the "technical expert" approach. Several activities used technical experts to prepare the forecast with assistance from an operations research group to determine *Operational Implications* (Product Implications).

Referring to the five categories of the forecast content discussed previously, it should be observed that the information desired covers a broad range. Corporate goals are discussed in the *Background* with the entire *Product Implications* section devoted to a discussion of the effect of advances in technology on the corporate operations. At the other end of the spectrum, the *Present Status* and *Forecast* sections require rather detailed discussions of the technology area. If any one type of person prepares the forecast, it is likely to make severe demands on his depth and breadth of knowledge.

This demand was reflected in the results of the Navy's forecast. Figure VI–5 shows the relationship between the five sections of the forecast and desired quality. Quality was measured as actual content versus requested content. As indicated in the figure, the relative quantitative quality of the *Background, Present Status,* and *References* was more than adequate. The *Forecast*

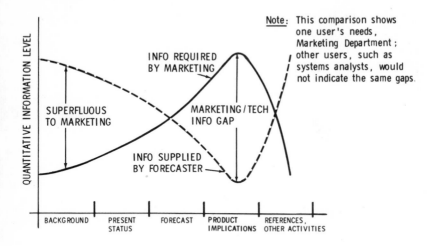

Figure VI–5. Forecast Sections: Comparing
Outputs and Inputs.

section drops off from the desired quantitative (not quantity) level of the specific user with the *Product Implications* section low enough to require additional effort beyond the first submission of most forecasts. It is apparent the individual technical experts encounter difficulty in translating their technical expertise into *Product Implications* terms.

On the basis of the Navy experience and consideration of the extent of information required to prepare a technology assessment type of forecast it appears the preparation may require the joint effort of two distinct types of people. One, a technological area expert to be primarily concerned with the *Present Status* and *Forecast* sections. The other, a system analyst (O.R., Generalist, . . .) to assist in the *Background* and *Product Implications* section. A joint effort of the two can have some beneficial side effects. A communication problem always seems to exist between people in general as can be seen with children in Figure VI–6 or managers and the technical community, as illustrated in Figure VI–7. The joint effort can help open a dialogue between the two groups to help to insure over-all utility.

Figure VI–6. Two Children Playing in the Same Room with Same Toys—Not Two Children Playing Together.

The task of anyone preparing a forecast can be lightened by a good, clear statement of specific and quantitative corporate or product goals. The Navy's recently published "Exploratory Development Goals" provided the product goals for the Navy Technological Forecast. The goals allow the forecast to be related directly to the needs, resulting in a normative forecast. Although a normative forecast has many advantages, it does have one distinct disadvantage. If the goals change (or are misstated, or misinterpreted), the forecast may have minimal utility or be entirely misleading. A reasonable compromise is to have the actual forecast of the state-of-the-art (the *Forecast* section) exploratory to the greatest extent possible. All specific quantitative goal orientation should be placed in the *Product Implications* section.

Just as the goals can influence the forecast, so can the forecaster (VI–4). There should be an effort on the part of the forecaster to be as objective as possible. "Axe-grinding" either

Figure VI–7. Two Men Talking to Themselves—Not to Each Other.
No Real Dialogue.

by commission or omission should be avoided. The forecast should predict what is probable and possible, not what one wants or doesn't want. This concern is exemplified in the scientists' responsibility to society in the area of weaponry. From a management view, the scientist should "be on tap—not on top" in policy decisions. When preparing a forecast, the forecaster should consider what is feasible, not the social implications. However, once the forecast is objectively prepared, avenues should be open for the scientist to express his social views.

Quantification—The Key to Utility

The *Forecast* and *Product Implications* sections are the heart of the technology assessment type of technological forecast. The first indicates, within the stated probability limits, the growth of the technology. The latter is a projection of the effect of this growth on the corporation. It should not take a great deal of persuasion to convince most people that a forecast increases in utility according to the degree with which it is quantified. A statement such as . . . "commercial aircraft will fly higher, faster, and carry more passengers than at present . . ." does not contain information of great value. Whereas, the statement "Commercial aircraft will be capable of speeds of Mach 3 at altitudes of 70,000 feet while carrying up to 400 passengers . . ." contains information that can be used by a diverse audience.

It may appear simple and straightforward to state the need for, and obtain, quantification of forecasts. Experience has indicated otherwise. One reason quantification of the forecast is difficult is because the pacing parameter(s) to quantify is usually not apparent. The forecaster should spend a considerable portion of the time allowed for the task identifying the pacing (key) parameters of the technology. Pacing parameter identification may require a tradeoff study between all major technology parameters. In general, it is not a simple task. When the pacing parameters are not identified, a technique used by some forecasters is to project many parameters. Going the extreme in this

"IN ITS PRESENT STATE, AND EVEN CONSIDERING THE IMPROVEMENTS POSSIBLE WHEN ADOPTING THE HIGHER TEMPERATURES PROPOSED FOR THE IMMEDIATE FUTURE, THE GAS TURBINE COULD HARDLY BE CONSIDERED A FEASIBLE APPLICATION TO AIRPLANES MAINLY BECAUSE OF THE DIFFICULTY IN COMPLYING WITH THE STRINGENT WEIGHT REQUIREMENTS IMPOSED BY AERONAUTICS.

"THE PRESENT INTERNAL-COMBUSTION-ENGINE EQUIPMENT USED IN AIRPLANES WEIGHS ABOUT 1.1 POUNDS PER HORSEPOWER, AND TO APPROACH SUCH A FIGURE WITH A GAS TURBINE SEEMS BEYOND THE REALM OF POSSIBILITY WITH EXISTING MATERIALS. THE MINIMUM WEIGHT FOR GAS TURBINES EVEN WHEN TAKING ADVANTAGE OF HIGHER TEMPERATURES APPEARS TO BE APPROXIMATELY 13 TO 15 POUNDS PER HORSEPOWER."

THE COMMITTEE ON GAS TURBINES
appointed by
THE NATIONAL ACADEMY OF SCIENCES
June 10, 1940

direction and overpowering the reader with data will severely limit the forecast's usefulness. Another factor influencing quantitative discussions is the natural reluctance of the technical community to state a precise number in a forecast when there is doubt about over-all accuracy of the projection. Any quantitative discussion, or any forecast, is expressed as a prediction with a *level of confidence*. This qualification must be kept in mind by both the user and the forecaster.

Hindsight into Foresight

Many technological forecasts have been prepared by government and industry. An area of concern is their utilization. One issue is whether the preparation of the forecast will be self-fulfilling. Will the forecast, consciously or unconsciously, be used to guide·development? We do not know of any correlation studies that indicate they are or are not. Certainly there have been forecasts stating certain things could not be done which did not stop others from doing them. This can be seen from Dr. Th. von Karman's committee on gas turbines (see page 133). On the other hand, Figure VI–8 is a representation of weight trends of certain types of air vehicles which was prepared in 1945. A technical reviewer in 1967 indicated the curve is still valid for present fighter aircraft. The curve was contained in the von Karman Army study conducted by an august group of scientists (see opposite) to indicate new developments in the future. Because of the high stature of the group who prepared the report, it may have been self-fulfilling. The general feeling toward self-fulfillment of technological forecasts is if the forecast was prepared by a laureate in the field, the chances for self-fulfillment increase; if the forecast is prepared by an individual who has equal competence but little recognition in the technology area, the chances decrease.

Another issue concerns the development of forecasting methodology to insure a reasonable degree of credibility. There have been some forecasts which were completely out of phase with

AAF SCIENTIFIC ADVISORY GROUP

Dr. Th. von Karman
Director

Colonel F. E. Glantzberg
Deputy Director, Military

Dr. H. L. Dryden
Deputy Director, Scientific

Lt Col G. T. McHugh, Executive
Capt C. H. Jackson, Jr., Secretary

CONSULTANTS

Dr. C. W. Bray
Dr. L. A. DuBridge
Dr. Pol Duwez
Dr. G. Gamow
Dr. I. A. Getting
Dr. L. P. Hammett
Dr. W. S. Hunter
Dr. I. P. Krick
Dr. D. P. MacDougall
Dr. G. A. Morton
Dr. N. M. Newmark
Dr. W. H. Pickering
Dr. E. M. Purcell
Dr. G. B. Schubauer
Dr. W. R. Sears

Dr. A. J. Stosick
Dr. W. J. Sweeney
Dr. H. S. Tsien
Dr. G. E. Valley
Dr. F. L. Wattendorf
Dr. F. Zwicky
Dr. V. K. Zworykin
Colonel D. N. Yates
Colonel W. R. Lovelace II
Lt Col A. P. Gagge
Lt Col F. W. Williams
Major T. F. Walkowicz
Capt C. N. Hasert
Mr. M. Alperin
Mr. I. L. Ashkenas
Mr. G. S. Schairer

LAYOUT & ILLUSTRATION

Capt M. Miller
Capt T. E. Daley

APPENDIX B

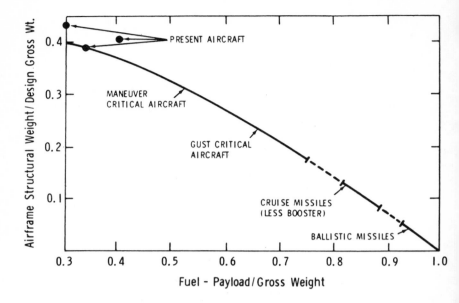

Figure VI–8. Source: "Towards New Horizons," A Report to the General of the Army, H. H. Arnold by Th. von Karman, Director—AAF Scientific Advisory Group, 1945. (Comment: Chart appears correct for fighter aircraft this date, November 1967).

actual developments. We can assume forecasts of this type will continue. However, if the forecasting is approached in an objective scientific manner, one can place a reasonable degree of confidence in the forecast. Figures VI–9 through VI–12 are curves showing predictions made in forecasts that were prepared in 1961. It will be noted from the evaluations appearing under each, relative to their predictive quality over the ensuing eight years, that forecasts can fall wide or short of the mark, as well as be unerringly valid predictions. However, the point to be drawn is that the predictions at the time they were made were feasible, but this was no guarantee that the progress *would* transpire. It is critical that a *need* exists to encourage such progress; in those cases where the predictions fell short, it was evident that need had not materialized in the subsequent years.

The preparation of a technological forecast is not a single-shot affair. It should be considered a continuing effort. Each forecast should be reviewed periodically and updated as required. A specific time period cannot be stated for all forecasts. It will depend upon the dynamic nature of the area. Any updating procedure should include a reassessment of the areas to be forecast to insure compatibility with current needs.

Finally, there seems to be an issue over whether one should attempt to forecast technology at all. It is a relatively new field where military and industry have expanded in a hasty and haphazard fashion. Consequently, technological forecasting bears

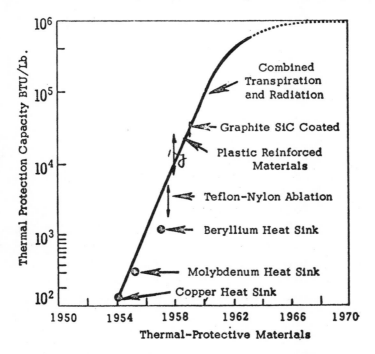

Figure VI–9. "Requirements changed and thermal protection became a less controlling factor." (Source: Technology for Tomorrow. USAF, 1961).

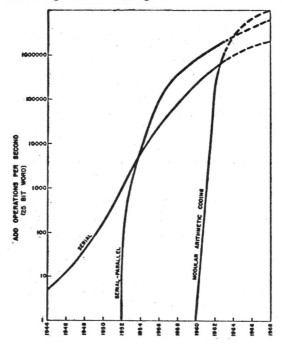

Figure VI–10. "Reasonable." (Source: Technology for
Tomorrow. USAF, 1961).

close scrutiny if for no other reason than it may not warrant the
load on the time of the people required to prepare them. Critical
to the entire issue is the need and utility of forecasting. As to the
need, decisions are made that require an assessment of technology whether a forecast exists or not. As was indicated previously,
a forecast is nothiñg more than a formalized scientific procedure
of activities that are normally utilized either in a fragmented
manner or informally in making decisions concerning the future
state-of-the-art of technology. As to the utility, this is a function
of the over-all effort. If a valid, objective, quantitative forecast
is available it will be used. Quantification and objectivity can be
attempted. Validity cannot be guaranteed, but face validity can
be approached by iterative updating. Actual validity can never
be proven because of self-fulfillment. Technological forecasting

is not a panacea, but neither is it useless. It is, like other systematic analyses, an attempt to quantify to the extent possible the state of technology. As such, it can aid in decisions that might not be made as well if the forecast did not exist.

The various types of problems discussed here should crystallize several important points about technological forecasting. First, there is no cheap and quick way of producing a technological forecast. There are many factors to consider. The forecast effort should be planned and conducted with entire corporate operations in mind. Second, a technological forecast should serve a wide audience. It is not worth the investment if it cannot or is not used. The forecast content should be as broad an assessment of technology as is practicable within corporate goals. Finally, a

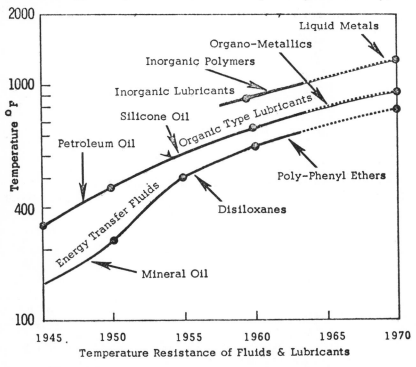

Figure VI–11. "Good." (Source: Technology for Tomorrow. USAF, 1961).

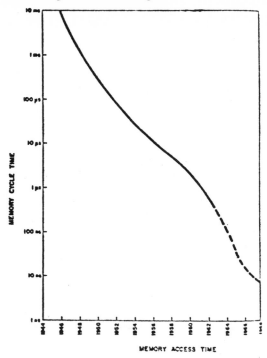

Figure VI–12. "Too Optimistic." (Source: Technology for Tomorrow. USAF, 1961).

comprehensive forecasting effort is not possible without the backing of *all* levels of management. An objective technological forecast can provide a valuable input to the future direction of the corporation—an area of vital importance to all levels of the corporation.

REFERENCES

VI–1. Cetron, M. J. *et al., A Proposal for a Navy Technological Forecast— Part I, Summary Report;* Headquarters Naval Material Command, Washington, D.C., May, 1966.

VI–2. Cetron, M. J. and Weiser, A. L., "Technological Change, Technological Forecasting and Planning R&D—A View from the R&D Manager's Desk," *The George Washington Law Review—Technology Assessment and the Law,* Vol. 36, No. 5, Washington, D.C., p. 1091.

VI–3. Cetron, M. J. and Monahan, T. I., "An Evaluation and Appraisal of Various Approaches to Technological Forecasting," *Technological Forecasting for Industry and Government,* ed. J. F. Bright; Prentice-Hall, Englewood Cliffs, N.J., 1968.

VI–4. Cetron, M. J. and Mahinske, E. B., "The Value of Technological Forecasting for the Research and Development Manager," *Futures;* Iliffe Science and Technology Publication Ltd., London, England, Sept. 1968, Vol. 1, No. 1.

To make a right decision here one requires, in addition to judgment, of course, a particularly clear, unblemished crystal ball, and a rabbit's foot of proven efficacy.

—C. G. Suits

CHAPTER VII

THE DELPHIC METHODOLOGY

A LIVELY CONTROVERSY has developed regarding the use, methodology, and validity of various technological forecasting techniques. High interest has centered upon intuitive forecasting methods and, in particular, the DELPHIC approach. It is generally assumed that the DELPHI technique is merely one method of technological forecasting. Indeed, this is true—but, since it combines the forecasting with the perceived wants or needs of the participants (VII–1), it is really more than a technological forecast.

The usual forecast attempts to predict what *could* be— DELPHI tries to predict what *will* be. DELPHI could be described as an elegant method for developing a consensus (VII–2). It is a polling technique employed for the systematic solicitation of expert opinion. DELPHI bears deeper investigation because it is directed toward the prediction of the future as it will develop in a situation influenced by many factors beyond the control of the company or agency making the forecast. Its methodology includes the polling of experts representing the controlling factors and from the ensuing data develops a consensus which can be used in planning. Its advantage consists in the systematic treatment of data that includes the experts' intuitive assessment of related imponderables.

This chapter will examine the Naval Supply Systems Command (NAVSUP) use of a variation of the DELPHI approach, SEER (System for Event Evaluation and Review), to produce a technological forecast of what is expected to occur in the information-processing industry for submission to the over-all Navy Technological Forecast. Since any single organization will have only very limited influence on the future decisions and out-

145

comes in an industry, a technique that incorporates the consensus of opinions of the participant experts should be of inestimable value in planning for the user's allocation of research and development resources, as well as other future-oriented requirements.

Deciding on a Technique

Preparations for the NAVSUP technological forecast in the field of information-processing led to a study of intuitive methods and resulted in the utilization of a variation on the DELPHI approach. This research and experience is described and evaluated here.

When NAVSUP became interested in the DELPHI approach, it was decided to thoroughly investigate this technique's potential for producing user-oriented forecasts. After reviewing the DELPHI literature, meetings were held with Dr. Helmer of RAND Corporation and with Dr. H. Q. North and Mr. D. L. Pyke of TRW, Incorporated, in order to discuss the problems and pitfalls of DELPHI. TRW was in the process of evaluating "Probe I" (VII–3), an attempt to employ the DELPHI method in an industrial environment. These conversations concerned the modification to DELPHI that TRW was contemplating in its effort to make "Probe II," a follow up study, more user-oriented. The essence of these modifications can be found in a presentation Dr. North made to the NATO Defense Research Group (VII–4).

As research progressed, questions raised concerning DELPHI were becoming more concrete. Prior to formalizing these questions and amorphous doubts, an effort was made to obtain a firmer basis in conduct and employment of user-oriented forecasts. This research led to the study of articles, books, and technical papers listed in the bibliography.

During this period much soul-searching transpired which resulted in a list of the shortcomings in the current DELPHI methodology. This list was validated through conversations with experienced former panel members. The major drawbacks in this list include:

— Panel members dislike beginning with a blank piece of paper. A set of sample projections would improve the panel member's understanding of his task and stimulate patterns of thought.

— The extensive number of interactions required by the DELPHI process results in a heavy investment of time. The panelist is prone to resent this imposition.

— After the several rounds, the panelist may be faced with evaluating projections in areas totally outside his area of expertise. Several former panelists indicated much indignation over being asked to play the role of "expert" and being forced to give a layman's view under the guise of expert opinion.

— A lack of goal orientation leaves the questions: When has the information been refined enough? When do we stop the iteration process?

— Efforts to determine event feasibility and desirability are barely addressed.

— Most importantly, no effort is made to: (a) determine event interrelationships; (b) prepare "menus" of alternative short-, mid-, and long-range goals; or (c) identify the supporting events desirable and necessary to make these goals achievable.

— The basic design of such a technique precludes the (hopefully empathetic) give-and-take potentially possible in face-to-face confrontation.

NAVSUP decided to develop a modified DELPHI technique (SEER) and test it in a project for the purpose of forecasting information-processing technology. This approach was designed to take advantage of DELPHI's strong points and avoid its weaknesses.

A Fifteen-Year Forecast of Information-Processing Technology—The SEER Technique

As previously noted, many governmental agencies and a number of large corporations are attempting to predict their future operating environment. The Navy has made such a study to develop estimates of future potential capabilities in information-processing technology. Although the long-range future is addressed, the 1968–1983 time frame was stressed. Predicting technical advance is dependent upon many unknown variables, and at first glance such predictions may appear to be futile. In this regard, the forecast in question is designed to evaluate the probability and general significance of possible future developments.

The product of this study is a 15-year forecast of information-processing capabilities available to satisfy user requirements. These forecasts were designed to:

• Highlight unexploited current capabilities.

• Identify gaps and/or deficiencies in the present information processing state-of-the-art.

• Enable the establishment of long-range capabilities and standardization goals.

• Facilitate R&D planning and resource allocation through the identification of alternative short-, mid-, and long-range goals and the supporting events desirable and necessary to make these goals achievable.

It was recognized that many elements of the Department of the Navy are concerned with the processing of data and would benefit substantially from the availability of detailed technological forecasts concerning the direction of the information-processing industry. Therefore, areas of study and analysis included data storage and processing equipment, visual display devices, data reduction and reproduction techniques, remote interrogation, audio, video, and facsimile transmission and receiving equipment. The results of these investigations were intended for use in projecting technological potentials for satisfaction of anticipated user needs over five-, ten-, and fifteen-year time frames.

The SEER forecasting technique is a combination of the more desirable elements of several existing techniques: (1) intuitive (consensus and individual forecasting), (2) trend extrapolation (simple extrapolation, curve fitting, and curve fitting with judgment modification), (3) trend correlation analysis (precursor events and correlation), and (4) normative approach

TABLE VII–1
SEER CONTRIBUTORS

Government

Advanced Research Projects Agency
Atomic Energy Commission
Department of the Air Force, Rome Air Development Center
Department of the Navy, Office of the Special Assistant to the Secretary
    of the Navy
Federal Communications Commission
General Services Administration, National Archives and Record Services
National Security Agency
Office of the Director of Defense, Research and Engineering
Social Security Administration

Academic

Carnegie-Mellon University
Case Western University
Duke University
The George Washington University
Massachusetts Institute of Technology
University of California, Lawrence Radiation Laboratory
University of California, Los Angeles
University of Illinois
University of Pennsylvania, The Moore School of Electrical Engineering

Industrial

Adage, Inc.
Addressograph-Multigraph Corp.
Alden Electronic and Impulse Recording Equipment Co., Inc.
American Telephone and Telegraph
Amp, Inc.
Ampex Corp.
Astrodata Corp.
Auerbach Corp.
Beta Instrument Corp.
The Bunker-Ramo Corp.
Burroughs Corp.
Calma Co.
Carson Labs.
Comcor, Inc.
Computer Associates, Inc.
Computer Command & Control Co.
Computer Industries Co.
Computer Sciences Corp.
Consolidated Electrodynamics Corp.

TABLE VII–1
SEER CONTRIBUTORS—Continued

Industrial—Continued

Control Data Corp.
Control Data—Rabinow
Core Memories, Inc.
Dasa Corp.
Datmec (Div. of Hewlett Packard)
Data Disc, Inc.
Data Products Corp.
Digitronics Corp.
Eastman Kodak
Electronic Assoc., Inc.
Electro-Mechanical Res., Inc.
Fabri-Tek, Inc.
Farrington Corp.
Ferrox Cube Corp.
Frieden
General Electric Co.
General Inst. Corp. (Div. of Magna Head)
General Precision, Inc.
Hobbs Associates
Honeywell, EDP Div.
Honeywell, 3C Div.
Hewlett Packard
Houston Fearless Corp.
Hughes Aircraft
Informatics
Information Displays, Inc.
International Business Machines Corp.
Itek
ITT Data Systems
ITT Gilfilan, Inc.
Kennedy Co.
Leasco Data Systems, Inc.
Litton Industries
Magnavox
McDonnell Douglas
Memory Technology
Micromation Technology Corp.
Milgo Electronic Corp.
3M Co.
Mohawk-Data Sciences Corp.
National Cash Register
National Microfilm Association
Philco-Ford Corp.

TABLE VII–1
SEER CONTRIBUTORS—Continued

Industrial—Continued

Potter Inst. Co., Inc.
Radiation, Inc.
Raytheon Computer
RCA, EDP Div.
Rixon Elec., Inc.
Sanders Assoc., Inc.
Stromberg-Carlson
Synnoetic Systems
Systems Applications and Software
System Development Corp.
Tally Corp.
Tally/Dartex
Tasker
Teletype Corp.
Univac
Uptime Corp.
Western Union
Xerox Corp.
Yerks-Wolf Associates, Inc.

(goal-oriented). The influence of TRW, Incorporated's, experience on "Probe I" (VII–5) is readily apparent.

SEER was made up of two phases or rounds. In Round 1 of the forecast described, industry was asked to provide a data base. Approximately 85 innovative firms producing both hardware and software were contacted. (See Table VII–1.) They were asked to select several top-level experts to participate in evaluation of a pre-prepared list of potential events. This list was developed through a literature search (VII–6) and a series of primary interviews of users and producers from government, industry, and academia. Several of these sample events appear in Figure VII–1.

The evaluators were usually product planners, research and development engineers, and/or operational engineers. Each of these participants was asked to add and evaluate additional events related to *his* area of expertise; he was also permitted to perform similarly in sub-categories of technology of tangential

POTPOURRI OF EVENTS FROM DATA BANK

EVENTS	USER DESIRABILITY			PRODUCER FEASIBILITY			PROBABLE TIMING		
	Needed Desperately	Desirable	Undesirable but Possible	Highly Feasible	Likely	Unlikely but Possible	Year by which the probability is x that the event will have occurred.		
							x=.20	x=.50	x=.90
Breakthrough in long-range weather and sea state forecasting for Naval forces at sea. Forecasts are now limited to 2 to 3 days, automated weather forecasts for 15 and 30 days of conditions at sea is sorely needed for fleet planning operations, ship routing, and training.	X				X		72	76	85
LSI (Large-Scale Integrated) circuits may make small computers so inexpensive that each scientist would have one on his desk.		X			X		75	80	85
Large memories (perhaps hierarchies of memory) will be shared by many computers.		X			X		71	73	75
Low error rate—human operated, remote keyboards, used with self-checking numeric systems will be used in parts ordering, inventorying, etc. in conjunction with central computer systems and DDD communications (digital duplex division).	X			X			70	72	75
There will be greater standardization of data systems and procedures in order to use standard software and programs in conventional type business operations.		X		X			72	75	80
Digitized voice/analog transmission between central offices and switching centers to facilitate time-division multiplexing, encryption and switching.	X				X		71	74	78

Figure VII–1.

interest. These evaluations were made utilizing the following three parameters:

• *User Desirability*—He was asked to consider the need to make the results of a given event available as a usable product.

• *Producer Feasibility*—He was asked to consider the technical, economic, and commercial feasibility of converting the event into a usable product.

• *Probable Timing*—He was asked to project a series of three dates for each event: a date of *"reasonable chance,"* ($p = 0.2$), a *"most likely"* date ($p = 0.5$), and an *"almost certain"* date ($p = 0.9$).

Thus, Round I was basically an application of intuitive techniques; yet it was designed to permit the participant to base his comments upon more formal technological forecasts such as trend extrapolation, trend correlation analysis, etc. Figure VII–2 shows a trend extrapolation for computer technology.

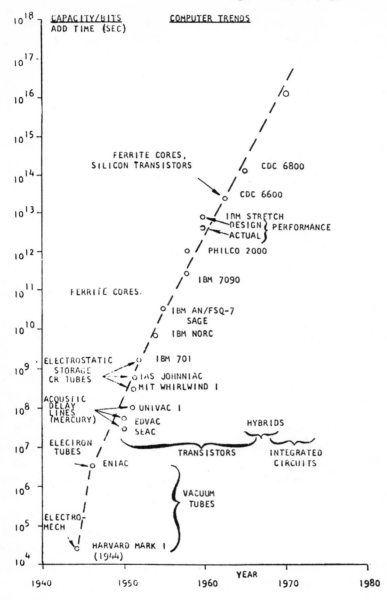

Figure VII–2. Source: The Year 2000, by Kahn and Wiener.

Two approaches were used to view information-processing: (1) *functionally* (hardware and software) and (2) *system-oriented*.

The *functional* approach was divided into 12 categories:
- Pattern Recognition
- Circuits and Modules
- Computers and Calculators
- Data Communications Equipment
- Graphic Data Systems and Devices
- Media Converters
- Memory Systems and Magnetic Recorders
- Peripherals
- Microforms and Related Equipments
- Facsimile and Reproduction Equipment
- Long Distance Communications
- Software

The *systems-oriented* approach was divided into three categories:
- Systems and Applications
- Computer Organization
- Standards

Inputs from Round I participants were gathered during the early summer months of 1968 and converted into the Round I Data Bank. Some of the more representative examples have been drawn from this document and appear as Figure VII–3.

Round II attempted to refine and extend the Round I results. It involved an attempt to interpret event significance in relation to the total information-processing environment in which the Navy would have to operate in the future. Round II served three functions: (1) a reevaluation and expansion of the data base; (2) a delineation of the interactions among the events forecasted; and (3) an extension of the state-of-the-art in technological forecasting. During this Round, a group of outstanding individuals in the field of information-processing was asked to evaluate the Round I data base to refine and augment the data base, to identify events of importance, and to determine possible interrelationships between events.

SAMPLE EVENTS

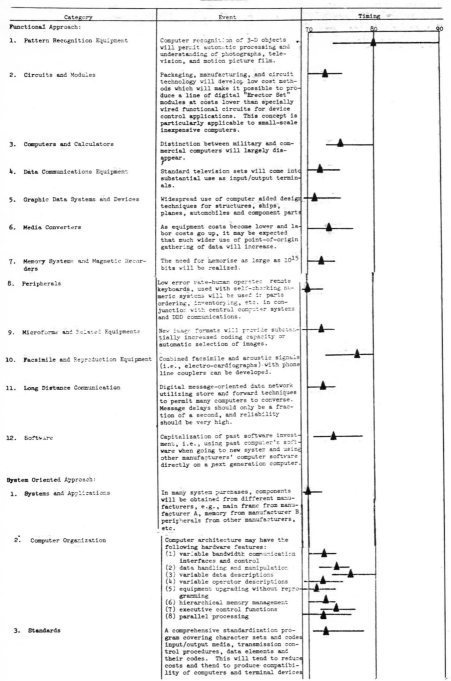

Category	Event	Timing
Functional Approach:		70 80 90
1. Pattern Recognition Equipment	Computer recognition of 3-D objects will permit automatic processing and understanding of photographs, television, and motion picture film.	
2. Circuits and Modules	Packaging, manufacturing, and circuit technology will develop low cost methods which will make it possible to produce a line of digital "Erector Set" modules at costs lower than specially wired functional circuits for device control applications. This concept is particularly applicable to small-scale inexpensive computers.	
3. Computers and Calculators	Distinction between military and commercial computers will largely disappear.	
4. Data Communications Equipment	Standard television sets will come into substantial use as input/output terminals.	
5. Graphic Data Systems and Devices	Widespread use of computer aided design techniques for structures, ships, planes, automobiles and component parts	
6. Media Converters	As equipment costs become lower and labor costs go up, it may be expected that much wider use of point-of-origin gathering of data will increase.	
7. Memory Systems and Magnetic Recorders	The need for memories as large as 10^{15} bits will be realized.	
8. Peripherals	Low error rate-human operated remote keyboards, used with self-checking numeric systems will be used in parts ordering, inventorying, etc. in conjunction with central computer systems and DDD communications.	
9. Microforms and Related Equipments	New image formats will provide substantially increased coding capacity or automatic selection of images.	
10. Facsimile and Reproduction Equipment	Combined facsimile and acoustic signals (i.e., electro-cardiographs) with phone line couplers can be developed.	
11. Long Distance Communication	Digital message-oriented data network utilizing store and forward techniques to permit many computers to converse. Message delays should only be a fraction of a second, and reliability should be very high.	
12. Software	Capitalization of past software investment, i.e., using past computer's software when going to new system and using other manufacturers' computer software directly on a next generation computer.	
System Oriented Approach:		
1. Systems and Applications	In many system purchases, components will be obtained from different manufacturers, e.g., main frame from manufacturer A, memory from manufacturer B, peripherals from other manufacturers, etc.	
2. Computer Organization	Computer architecture may have the following hardware features: (1) variable bandwidth communication interfaces and control (2) data handling and manipulation (3) variable data descriptions (4) variable operator descriptions (5) equipment upgrading without reprogramming (6) hierarchical memory management (7) executive control functions (8) parallel processing	
3. Standards	A comprehensive standardization program covering character sets and codes input/output media, transmission control procedures, data elements and their codes. This will tend to reduce costs and thend to produce compatibility of computers and terminal devices	

Figure VII–3. Computer Trends.

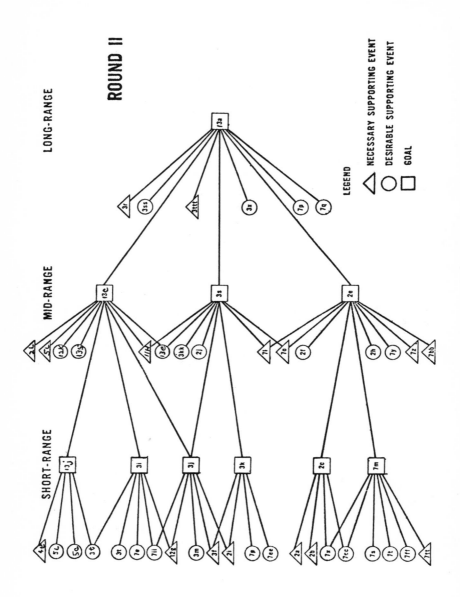

Figure VII–4.

Block Identifier	Event
13a	An international technical data system will be in operation with access by individual scientist through desk top devices.
13c	Development of machine-processable languages, capable of representing and simulating the combined action of hardware and software systems at whatever level is desired, from logic elements through modules and more complex units.
21	The one-hundred-fold increase in the use of large scale integrated circuit technology on a truly integrated basis.
11h	Research identifying technical and cultural linguistic communities within a natural language, with a view to simplifying man-machine intercommunication by specifying the linguistic environment.
51	An inexpensive alphanumeric terminal (with limited graphic capability) will revolutionize this field at about $1K per terminal.
12k	User will have his choice of performing many functions either in the hardware or as programmed in the software.
13s	Hardware and software purchases will be divorced.
13e	With the advent of time-sharing, interpreters will assume greater importance in systems, and provide simpler processing of variability.
13j	A major increase in the use of computers for simulation is predicted facilitated by major change in the use of peripheral equipment.
4e	I/O data communication terminals will become more versatile at higher speeds and lower costs by sharing common control electronics within geographical clusters.
3t	Very cheap special purpose computers to solve specific data processing problems in standardized ways will be available.
5c	A flat TV tube providing reduced glare, will be available on the market at reduced cost.

This group was made up of forty-eight representatives of government, industry, and the academic world. Each of these experts had been assigned one or more categories for consideration. Assignments were made to consider each expert's area(s) of expertise; representation was assured from government, industry, and academia in each specialty. A careful attempt was made to balance the attitudes of participants to mollify "ax grinding" tendencies.

Round II was a direct application of the normative approach. It should be stressed that Round I was an attempt to provide a data base, whereas, Round II was an attempt to refine, extend, and structure the data base to enhance the value of this forecast for planning and system design personnel.

After receiving the inputs from the panel of Round II experts, a refined list of potential events was produced. This list was used to develop a "menu" of alternative potential short-, mid-, and long-range goals; and identify supporting events which might be desirable or even necessary to make these goals achievable. Something of a "reverse PERT" (Program Evaluation and Review Technique) display technique was used to document alternative pathways from the current state-of-the-art to where it could be in the future. An example of the display model technique used is shown in Figure VII–4. The number/letter combinations identify events by category and item as they appear in the ordered event list.

Diagnosis and Prognosis

Seven shortcomings to the DELPHI technique (as currently described) were enumerated above. SEER addressed itself to the satisfactory handling of six of these shortcomings, specifically:

— A set of sample potential events was developed from interviews and secondary sources. This set of sample events was structured into technological sub-categories of information-processing and provided a starting point for Round I participants. In addition, these events served as control questions used to validate participant response.

— The study design provided for two iterations. Each round involved a different set of participants. A participant was not asked to comment a second time unless a response was so divergent with those of his contemporaries that it might be deemed as representing a potential breakthrough or simply an error. The first panel consisted of people working in the information-processing industry, while the second consisted of top experts drawn from industry, government, and academia.

— Each panelist was assigned work in those sub-categories in which he currently worked. He was permitted to comment on and add events to other sub-categories where he had tangential interest. More weight was given to a panelist's comments in his area of expertise and proportionately less to comments in those sub-categories outside his normal work situation.

— Specifically, two rounds were established as the finish of the DELPHI phase of this study. The panelists participating in both rounds were informed of the study plan prior to their involvement.

— Event desirability (from the user's point of view) was specifically addressed. Each event (whether originating in the sample, Round I or Round II) had received this same type of evaluation.

— Round II included an effort to identify major events and supporting events. Each Round II panelist segregated these supporting events into two categories: desirable and necessary. This process had permitted an identification of a "menu" of potential short-, mid-, and long-range goals in information-processing technology, as well as alternative pathways (through supporting events) to make these goals achievable.

It is felt that the effort was successful to an appreciable degree in overcoming the first six shortcomings. However, the basic thesis of DELPHI and any of its mutations (e.g., TRW's "Probe" or NAVSUP's SEER) precludes the direct answering of the seventh drawback. The potential spur to idea generation made possible by personal contact is a valuable element lost in the trade-off for anonymity. Perhaps the best answer is to follow

SEER's Round II with a series of seminar discussions between Round II panel members, utilizing the Round II data bank as a point of departure. Such a face-to-face confrontation would permit the accrual of almost all potential advantages SEER currently offers, with the added benefit of a fully-prepared, well-structured panel series. Consideration is currently being given to such a follow-up effort.

In conclusion, it can be stated that positive results were achieved by the use of the SEER technique. It permitted the forecasting organization to utilize the information being generated by an industry in which it had little influence and no control over trends. The application of SEER has identified alternatives in a sufficiently clear and complete manner to facilitate executive decision-making. NAVSUP planning, as influenced by technological developments in the area of information-processing, is being modified based on the SEER forecast. New resource allocations will be affected by the results of the study.

REFERENCES

VII–1. Cetron, Marvin J. and Weiser, Alan, "Technological Change, Technological Forecasting and Planning R&D—A View from the R&D Manager's Desk," *The George Washington Law Review—Technology Assessment and the Law,* July 1968, Vol. 36, No. 5, pp. 1079–1104.

VII–2. Cetron, Marvin J., "Using Technological Forecasts," *Science and Technology,* July 1968, No. 79, pp. 57–63.

VII–3. TRW Systems, *A Probe of TRW's Future,* North, Harper, Q., 5 July 1966.

VII–4. North, Harper Q., "Technological Forecasting in Industry." A presentation during a Seminar to the NATO Defense Research Group, Teddington, Middlesex, England, 12 November 1968.

If you do not expect to be in business five years from now, there is no need for expenditures for scientific research.

—G. GUY SUITS

CHAPTER VIII

PUTTING FORECASTS TO WORK:
RESOURCE ALLOCATION

GOVERNMENT AND INDUSTRY are developing many new ways to forecast future technical developments, but the payoff comes when these projections are incorporated as part of the R&D planning process. This is done on two levels: when deciding on future work in a specific development project and when assigning priorities to the over-all R&D effort. Systems being developed in the Navy and other branches of the federal government are able to integrate technological forecasts with data on future needs, probabilities of success, and potential funding levels. The computerized result is a complete ranking of all on-going and potential projects according to their over-all worth. But care must be taken to insure that the computer printout retains its role as a servant and not a ruler of managers.

One of many Normative (goal-oriented) Technological Forecasting Techniques currently being examined by the Navy will be discussed in this chapter by exploring the structure of project selection decision problems in the context of the information and organization environment of the R&D manager and by exploring characteristics of the R&D process which are relevant to the design and implementation of management systems for planning and controlling resource allocation among various R&D projects.

Background

Over the past five years, both government and industry have become actively interested with the potential of technological forecasting as an aid in planning R&D budgets. As laboratories expanded and budgets grew, managers found that many of the

163

traditional ways of allocating their resources of men and money seemed inadequate. But most attempts to build better allocation systems foundered on two basic questions: Which research areas are most likely to be the source of significant technical breakthroughs? Which breakthroughs are most likely to bring an important new development?

The realization that technological forecasting methods could help answer these questions was catching hold slowly when many R&D planners were rudely shaken by a new reality: a leveling-off or even a cutback in most government-sponsored research efforts. With NASA's post-Apollo projects whittled back, the United States DOD research budgets cut extensively, and other usually expanding budgets on a shorter rein, the need to make hard choices in funding became more critical than ever. Now many planners were turning to technological forecasting to help them make their difficult selections. However, the critical questions which arose were not on how Technological Forecasting could be made, but how Technological Forecastings once made could be integrated into R&D planning efforts. Accordingly, helpful hints for planners grappling with their own problem of using technological forecasts in allocation problems will be presented (VIII–1, –2).

The foundation underlying technological forecasting is the tenet that individual R&D events are susceptible to influence. The times at which they occur—if they can occur at all—can be modulated significantly by regulating the resources allocated to them. Another basic tenet of technological forecasting is the belief that many futures are possible and that the paths toward these futures can be *mapped* (VIII–3).

In use, a technological forecast can be looked at from two vantage points. One, in the present, gives the forecast user a view which shows the path that technological progress will probably take if it is not consciously influenced. In addition, the user will see critical branch points in the road—the situation where alternative futures are possible. He will also gain a greater understanding of the price of admission to those branching paths.

The second vantage point is in the future. The user selects or postulates a technical situation he desires. Looking backward from the point, he can then discern the obstacles that must be overcome to achieve the result he wants. Once again, he is brought up against the hard realities of what he must do to achieve a desired result. As one user has said: "The process substitutes forecasting for 'forecrastination'."

Putting Forecasts to Work

In most cases, a manager does not have a total system to work with. Instead, he has the results of trend extrapolations or other regular technological forecasting projections. How does he use these data? While there are many approaches, the following is one which the Navy Department is examining to determine which techniques can best help decide which R&D projects to fund.

We begin with a technical planning flow chart (Figure VIII–1) that shows the "shredding out" of all the bits and pieces that comprise the makeup of a new vehicle. Assume that we have a technological forecast for each and every parameter of the shred-out. The forecasts, at each level of the breakdown, are the probable paths that various technologies will take. Armed with this type of data, a meaningful discourse can ensue between the user and producer. For a given set of operational requirements and performance characteristics called for by the user, the technical planners can respond with data that tell the user by what alternative means his needs can be satisfied, and when he can expect these to be accomplished. Many of the trade-offs—between steam, diesel, and nuclear energy, for example—become clear.

Operations officers, however, are not usually quite so acquiescent in accepting what a planner sees ahead. When faced with a military threat, or an anticipated threat, they want an effective answer to that threat by a specified date. The same holds true if they wish to create a new force of their own. In these situations,

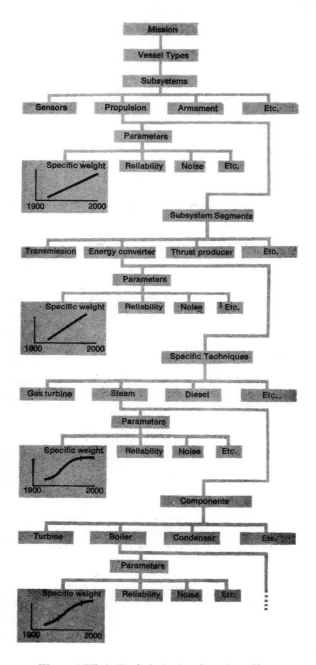

Figure VIII–1. Technical Planning Flow Chart.

planners are taking a vantage point at some time in the future and are trying to discover if they will have the technology they need by that time.

Quite likely an examination of the technological forecasts to that point in time will reveal that the users are not likely to get what they want. Now, this is useful information in itself, and represents an approach that is not yet widely used in industry.

However, this view of the technological forecasting task is not the only one. There is the question of which path we should take to achieve a desired result. By deciding on our needs in the future and looking at the forecasts, we can spot the principal obstacles standing in our way, and the magnitude of those obstacles. The inference is clear: If the given goal is to be achieved in a given time, the efforts must be applied in the areas containing the major obstacles. Or, we can settle for something less with clear knowledge of what that something less will be. Often, this analysis will show that two or more paths may be taken to achieve the needed or acceptable capabilities. The point here is that an environment of flexible choice is engendered—choices of which the user was not previously aware. A truly comprehensive technological forecast is backed up not only by material and data which were used in generating the specific forecasts but also by supplementary analysis of various sub-factors that could influence each technological forecast. Forecasts like these help indicate the future posture of an enemy or competitor. While you don't know what he *will* do, you at least have a better idea of what he *could* or *could not* do.

Mechanics of Decision-Making

Now let's turn to an example and see how a specific decision can be analyzed, based on the forecasting techniques utilized at the Annapolis Division of the Naval Ships Research and Development Center (VIII–4). Forecasts for ship propulsion systems are given in terms of specific weight, reliability, noise, etc. The next level of consideration takes us into the area of subsystem segments—transmission, energy converter, thrust producer, etc.

Each of these key into an associated set of parameters which, in turn, key into specific forecasts. In this fashion, we can work our way down the chart (Figure VIII–1), eventually going into any degree of detail we wish.

This information is used for very practical decisions. Marine gas turbines, for example, have a tremendous potential for development. The possibilities for high-power, lightweight, compact power plants are unmatched in any other type of unit. These characteristics are particularly vital for powering new-concept vessels such as hydrofoils and air-cushion craft. In the last few years, there has been a rapid growth in the horsepower capacity of gas turbine units. Engines as large as 43,000 horsepower have been built, and units exceeding 50,000 horsepower are projected. This growth trend will probably continue but at a lesser rate as limitations of mechanical, thermal and ducting size are approached. However, much larger power outputs will be built by using multiple gas generators to drive a single turbine engine. Power outputs as high as 150,000 horsepower have already been attained by this method. The R&D manager's problem is to decide which aspects of turbine development are most critical.

The development trends for the specific weight, volume, and fuel consumption for a simple cycle gas turbine are shown in the graphs (Figure VIII–2). In all of these the trend correlation (lead-follow relationship) was used in the study. Aircraft gas-turbine technology has been the leader not only because of the greater aircraft speed payoff, but also because the marine environment led to problems of corrosion. Now that materials and other problems are being overcome, the curves are coming together—the aircraft experience gives some indication of what can be expected in future naval turbines.

As shown in the efficiency graph in Figure VIII–2, the compressor, combustion, and turbine efficiency have reached a plateau according to a growth-analogy study. Any future improvement will be limited. Consequently, these component efficiencies will have an insignificant effect on future engine characteristics. Recent improvements, moreover, have resulted from an increase in the compressor-pressure ratio. But any further increase will

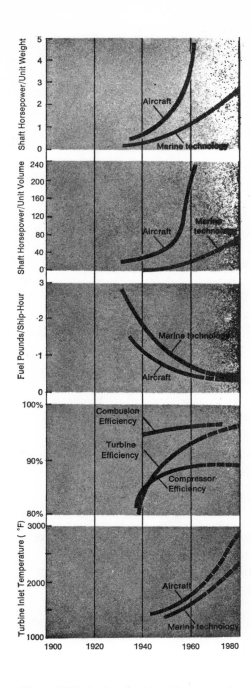

Figure VIII–2. Gas Turbine Characteristics.

be small. Because of improvements in blade loading, compressors are now designed to an optimum pressure ratio determined by turbo inlet temperature. And this blade loading, which has enabled engines to obtain higher pressures with fewer stages, appears to be approaching a limit.

This combination of forecasts shows that the addition of more heat energy within the same basic engine configuration—the major contributing factor to recent engine improvement—is likely to be the key factor in future improvement. Extrapolation of the curve to temperatures in excess of 2500° F is based on laboratory tests in which operating temperatures as high as 4000° F have been achieved—another trend correlation forecast.

As a result of this forecasting approach we now know where our R&D efforts should be concentrated. These are the high payoffs:

— Cooling of turbine blades and other components in high-temperature ambients. This will allow higher turbine inlet temperatures.

— New materials and protective coatings for these high-ambient components. This will increase high-temperature capabilities by increasing resistance to high-temperature oxidation and sulfidation. An increased resistance to thermal fatigue and creep is also required.

— Improved materials, designs, and fabrication techniques for regenerative gas turbines to reduce their cost, weight, and bulk.

— Further application and adaptation of aircraft gas turbines and technologies to ships.

— Attempts to improve efficiency of combustion, compressor, and turbine.

— Attempts to increase significantly the blade loading or compressor-pressure ratio if accompanied by major design changes.

The Over-All Picture

Up to this point we have been discussing the technological forecasting needed for one problem in a laboratory. But any organization has many such problems (VIII–5). Here the question becomes one of allocation of resources of men, money, and materials. The evaluation scene therefore shifts from the technical specialist to the department manager, the head of research, and the over-all planners. The forecast data must be fitted into their over-all planning approach if it is to be really useful.

When management problems are simple, a decision-maker can examine the various factors he must consider with relative ease. One man, such as the hermit in a cave, the individual homeowner, the small businessman, or the teacher in a one-room school, may be able to interrelate all of the necessary information and succeed in his endeavors.

As the management scope becomes larger and the complexity of problems increases, more and different factors must be considered to reach a decision. Soon, staff and management procedures are needed to assist in all phases of management. Eventually, the point is reached where any one decision affects many facets of the operation; all efforts become interrelated to an alarming degree.

Increasing complexities are particularly true with programs or projects which must operate within a fixed government or corporation resource ceiling. Choices must be made on alternative approaches, specifically, which efforts should proceed and which should be dropped or delayed. Since numerous efforts are interrelated in time, resources required, purpose and possible technical transfer one to another, choices must be made with consideration of the total effect. Whether he be a manufacturer, a service industry director, government administrator, or university professor, every manager seeks the greatest payoff for resource investments.

What alternatives does a manager have for developing resource allocation approaches? The resource allocation problem is usually too big to keep in one man's head and often inputs come from levels completely outside of his control. Hundreds of inputs can be involved when the alternatives are examined in depth.

A familiar resource allocation approach is termed the *squeaking wheel* process. One can cut resources from every area (one can be sophisticated and cut some areas more than others) then wait and see which area complains the most. On the basis of the loudest and most insistent squeaking, the manager can then restore some of the resources previously withdrawn until he reaches his ceiling budget.

Another common approach develops the minimum noise level and results in fewer squeaks by allocating this year's resources in just about the same manner as last year. The budget perturbations are minimized and the status quo maintained. If this *level funding* approach is continued very long within a rapidly changing technological field, the company, group, or government agency will end up in serious trouble.

An effortless version of the preservation of management security approach of resource allocation seeks to perpetuate the *Glorious Past*. Last year, or the year before, or perhaps several years ago, a division or organization had a very successful project, therefore why not fund the unit for the next five years on any projects that they advocate? The premise is "once successful, always successful." This method really means that no analysis should be made of the proposed project or its usefulness; instead, projects will be assigned resources solely upon the basis of past record of an individual or organization.

Still another way to allocate resources is called the *white charger* technique. Here the various departments come dashing in to top management with multi-color graphs, handouts, and well-rehearsed presentations. If they impress the decision-maker, they are rewarded with increased resources. Often the best speaker or the last man to brief the boss wins the treasure (VIII–6).

Finally, consider the *committee approach,* which frees the manager from resource allocation decisions. The committees tell the manager to increase, decrease, or leave all allocations as they are. A common danger is that the committee may not have enough actual experience in the organization or sufficient information upon which to base its recommendations. If the committee is ad hoc or from outside the organization, the members can also avoid responsibility in not having to live through the risky process of implementing their recommendations.

Obviously, the described allocation methods are neither scientific nor objective, though they are utilized quite extensively. These naive approaches point up the need of the manager and his staff for an aid to bring information into a form upon which judgment may be applied. It is a common experience for an organization to have numerous reports on specific technical subjects which recommend increased resources for the particular area. But the direct use of this data only compounds the manager's problem when he tries to allocate resources among the many technical areas. If he is operating under a fixed budget ceiling, to increase funding for one technical area requires that either one or more technical areas must be correspondingly decreased.

Technological Resource Allocation System

A more sophisticated alternative approach involves the use of staff or specialists in operations research. Information they assemble can be used to significantly assist managerial judgment. This is the point where quantitative evaluation techniques enter the picture. Each major aspect of a program can be examined, first separately and then as it is interrelated to competing factors. Items such as timeliness, cost utility or payoff, confidence level or risk, personnel, facilities, etc., can be evaluated by specialists in each field and the total picture made available as a basis for decision. Greater payoff areas can be identified and problems can be highlighted. Inputs can be accurately recorded, made clearly visible and analyzed for assisting the final decision.

The use of quantitative techniques permits input factors and possible outcome to be reexamined readily and different managerial emphasis applied. The manager can still hedge his "allocation selections" by allocating resources through such criteria as increased resources to previously successful groups, backing a high-risk effort—i.e., a high cost project with slim chances of success which might yield gigantic results. The decision-maker can incorporate any desired additional criteria—such as the politics of selection, competitive factors, or technological barriers.

The question now becomes one of allocation of the resources

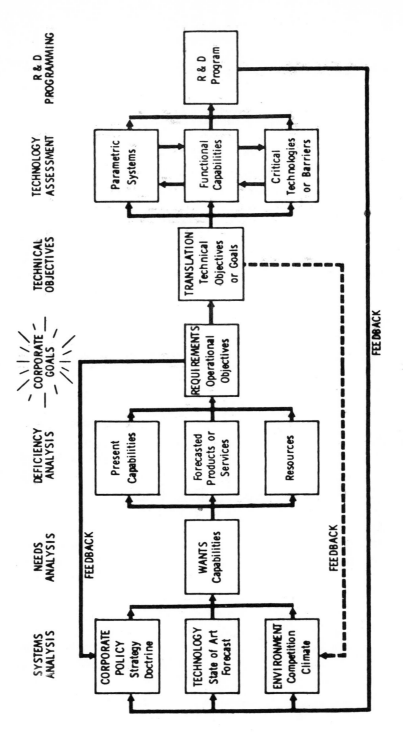

Figure VIII-3. Long Range R&D Planning.

of men, money, and materials. Figure VIII–3, the long-range planning diagram, which is really a broad allocation diagram, shows the interactions of numerous managers from the technical specialist to the department manager, the head of research, and the corporate planners. The data must be fitted into an over-all planning approach if it is to be really useful. Corporate goals are the main topic and occupy the central position in the chart. In order to establish corporate goals, the preliminary steps of systems analysis, needs analysis, and deficiency analysis must be accomplished. After the goals and technical objectives are established, technology assessment and R&D Programming take place to complete the R&D resources allocation process. Each of these steps will be explained in greater depth.

System Analysis

Corporate policy must be considered and involves philosophic and strategy questions, including these: Shall I be the industry leader? Shall I keep abreast of the industry technically and see if a major market develops? In the over-all environment, competitors' actions must be followed closely, but there are other factors such as interest rates, business expectation, economic forecasts, etc. to be identified (VIII–7). Figure VIII–3, viewed as the corporate planning chart, shows a recommended organization of considerations.

The technology forecasting element acts as a catalyst in setting and implementing over-all corporate goals. At present only a handful of the largest corporations are really utilizing their full corporate technical potential. The next question is how to relate the technological forecasts with appraisal in this total picture. A discussion of the numerous appraisal methods would be a long story in itself. For example, all systems employed by the Department of Defense utilize three major factors in the appraisal or normative forecasting process: military utility, technical feasibility, and financial acceptability. Each of these factors is amenable to quantification and can be fitted into a model which compares the value of each component project or system. Due to the complexity of the analysis, it is necessary to program the job on a computer to get usable information quickly. It must be remembered, however, that these computer processes are simply a tool to aid the decision-maker; the machine merely arranges the material in accordance with his instructions so that he can quickly focus his attention on those areas which require his special knowledge and judgment.

The environment (competition, climate) also must be considered, and include such questions as: Who are the competitors? What unique skills, products, or finances do these competitors possess? What is the industry-wide climate? Will the industry demand continue to expand rapidly, will there be a sudden drop in demand, or will a leveling of demand be expected. The factors considered under the systems analysis allow the needs (wants) as well as the unique or strong capabilities of the firm to be identified.

Need Analysis

Analysis of the wants or desirable areas of growth for the firm is equally as important as defining the areas where no growth or decline is expected.

The national or international economy provides the broadest scope for analysis of the needs for the firm's products or services. The stage of development in the country, the requirements from related industries, the availability and cost of capital and governmental controls may all require attention for the process of determining what the firm "wants" to do.

The industry share-of-the-market for the firm relates directly to its volume. That is, in an industry of rapid growth the individual firm may grow while remaining constant relative to its competitors. Conversely, the share-of-the-market may need to be greatly increased to remain at a level stage in a declining industry.

Finally, the desire of the firm and of the individual groups within the firm can be assessed. However, these desires may not be attainable within the capability of the firm. Thus, the wants need to be balanced against the firm's capabilities.

Deficiency Analysis

After the wants of the organization have been established, the capabilities available must be delineated in order that areas of deficiency can be identified. Ordinarily, the present capabilities of an organization will be known, but often effort is required by management to obtain a comprehensive statement of its technological capabilities in terms of men, money, and machines. Because we are dealing with futures, the products and services such as new manufacturing methods, new materials, and advanced skills that are forecasted to be available must also be carefully identified. Other resources available to the organization will also be important information. Skills or manufacturing processes or equipment, etc. may exist that could be available from outside the organization when and if required.

By identifying and analyzing the present capabilities, forecasted products and services along with other resources available, the deficiencies and excesses will become evident. The analysis now permits management to focus upon realistic corporate goals.

Corporate Goals

The most important phase of the resource allocation system may now be brought into focus—the corporate goals (objectives). These goals may be viewed by top management from the wants (desires or needs) of the organization which have been carefully considered for feasibility against the present or potential capabilities of the organization. Several passes through the analysis described above usually are required before acceptable goals are achieved by top management.

These corporate goals will be translated into requirements for performance of the organization, or as operational objectives.

Technical Objectives

The idea of applying quantitative approaches to resource allocation has too long been suspect by management. Currently, both industry and government are seeking tangible improvements in the results from use of available resources. Economy drives and/or cost/benefit analyses have resulted in pared budgets with the need more critical than ever to make hard choices among alternative programs. The application of objective measurements to resource assignments has too long been classified as visionary and impractical.

For example, how does a corporation decide whether its allocation this year for research and technology is adequate? And how does it decide the right balance between the research and development of manufacturing projects?

A prime example of lack of quantitative data exists in the area of assessing technological effort. Querying the scientist or engineer and requesting a justification of his selection of a program or a task (including projected benefits to a mission or product-oriented organization) has often been construed as an assault against the scientific professionals' prestige and prerogatives. Today, scientists and engineers are beginning to realize that they are accepted at the highest organization levels and that one of the signs of this ascendancy is their high visibility and responsibility to the interrogation of criteria and rational judgments. The technical manager's intuition can no longer be accepted as infallible and beyond managerial review (VIII–8).

Several project evaluation and selection techniques have as their basis a belief in the efficacy and acceptance of Bayesian statistics and theories of probability (VIII–9). Bayesians believe that it is correct to quantify feelings about uncertainty in terms of subjectively assessed numerical probabilities. Thus, assessments are made of probabilities for events that determine the profitability or utility of alternative actions open to the decision-maker.

For example, there is a necessity to assess the criterion of whether a piece of research is technically feasible (technological forecasts) or what is the probability that it will be successfully accomplished (level of confidence criterion). Bayesian theory believes that it is possible for an "expert" in the field being assessed to assign a figure of merit or "subjective" probability number that the event will actually occur. This theory states that on this very subject matter an expert can assign a "subjective" probability number from a scale, for example, between 0 and 10. Men of considerable experience in a field usually have no difficulty in utilizing a Bayesian probability scale. In a like manner, other criteria, such as the utility of the research to the objectives of the organization, or relevance to desired priority systems or corporation products, are assessed (criterion of utility).

The use of Bayesian subjective probabilities makes feasible the incorporation into the decision process, in a formal and visible way, many of the subjective and objective criteria and variables previously taken into account by the decision-maker informally and without visibility.

The probability assignment, a number between 0 and 10 to each facet, factor, criterion, or parameter inherent to a rational decision, reflects the degree of belief held by the individual expert(s) that the above objective will be met.

Thus the experience, knowledge of the subject, and judgment of the various experts are summarized by the subjective probabilities that they assign against the respective criteria. The final or top decision-maker then has a clear view of the alternatives and can use the results of the probability assignments of the different experts. A computer can be used to summarize the choices or probabilities of the experts. The computer can also be used to determine "consequences" if the probability assignments are changed or if the final decision-maker adds new information or weighting factors, etc.

Advocates of allocation and selection procedures are accused of assuming that the myriad of quantitative estimates of scientific relevance, importance, feasibility, and the like should and can be collected and manipulated (VIII–10). Apparently, the academic community also believes in the above assumption. For example, in the field of education, the university admission policy is based on a "myriad of quantitative estimates."

Mr. Robert Freshman, one of the U.S. Air Force Laboratory planners who was previously a professional educator, relates the following example (VIII–11): High school students are admitted to universities based on the quantitative judgments of teacher grades as the key criterion. These teachers grade about

5 subjects a year, for 4 years of high school—thus, 20 teacher judgments. Different teachers, different subjects, different tests, different subject matter taken in high schools throughout the nation, are fused into one. Teacher opinions on how to grade, biases and prejudgments, oral recitations, grades or nonstandardized, unstructured subject matter and tests are all injected into the above conglomeration to form the individual teacher's final grade in one subject.

High school grades for the four years are averaged to come up with one number—the high school average—the *magic number* which has great influence in college admission. More miraculous is that there is a good, positive correlation between this magic number and success in college. It is recognized that this "quantitative estimate" of many judgments is the best single criterion or indicator of success in *college;* but again it is just an aid to the decision-maker. The personal interview, college boards, or extra curricular activities also affect his judgment prior to making a final decision.

Opinions and judgments can be and should be weighed by every decision-maker in his final decision. Several quantitative techniques gather and summarize the opinions and judgments to enable the final decision-maker (like the university dean of admissions utilizing teacher judgments) to visualize and weigh, as one input to his decision, the judgments of numerous people on diverse factors.

Two main points on quantitative decision making should be emphasized:

— The quantitative management techniques discussed do not make decisions, but provide a basis of information upon which decisions can be made.

— A validity check cannot be made since once the resources are allocated, the plan becomes self-fulfilling.

Subsystem Analysis or Technology Assessment

Assessment of technology or subsystem analysis is employed to answer the question: which, when and how many resources should be allocated among the alternative projects: Since the topic is multi-faceted it is necessary to draw information from a variety of sources including operations research, project selection techniques, and technological forecasting.

Technology assessment is not official jargon. The expression "assessment of technology" is not found listed in the table of contents or indexes of texts on management. Nor is it identified and found in the general literature of management or in official planning, programming and policy documents of the government agencies.

Assessment is commonly considered to mean "setting a value to." Assessment of technology, then, means setting a value to technology. Technologies include areas of special knowledge such as gas turbines, diesels, thermionics, thermoelectrics, fuel cells, and energy conversion as opposed to the areas of science which include items such as alloy theory, surface physics, cryogenics, and magnetism. The kinds or measures of value attributed to technologies will be discussed later. Also, it can be demonstrated that the nature of the assessment of technology depends on who assesses, why the assessment is performed, and the nature of the technology, itself.

How is Technology Assessed?

One simple technique of assessing technology may be described by the following example. To assess the value of two baskets of fruit with contents as listed in Table VIII–1, first assess or determine the value of the baskets in one of many respects such as weight (a critical criteria for submarines), volume (a critical criteria for space craft), calories (a critical criteria for weight-watchers), and cost (a critical criteria for budgeteers). For this example, assessment can be readily done

TABLE VIII–1

Basket #1	Fruit Cost (¢/unit)	Basket #2
5 apples	10	10 apples
8 oranges	20	2 oranges
6 bananas	30	9 bananas

in terms of financial cost with monetary cost values assigned to the individual items as follows:

$$10 \text{ cents per apple}$$
$$20 \text{ cents per orange}$$
$$30 \text{ cents per banana}$$

$$\begin{aligned} \text{Value } (\#1) &= (5 \times 10) + (8 \times 20) + (6 \times 30) \\ &= 50 + 160 + 180 \\ &= \$3.90 \end{aligned}$$

$$\begin{aligned} \text{Value } (\#2) &= (10 \times 10) + (2 \times 20) + (9 \times 30) \\ &= 100 + 40 + 270 \\ &= \$4.10 \end{aligned}$$

The analogy is made by having the baskets of fruit represent technologies, the fruits to represent characteristics of parameters of the technologies, and the cost values of the fruit to represent their "relative importance factors." The value for each basket can be represented by the formula:

$$\text{Value} = \text{summation of}$$
$$(\text{relative importance factor}) \times (\text{criteria or parameter})$$

This illustration introduces the terms "importance factors" and "parameters" and demonstrates (assuming that the analogy is valid) that the parameters, while different from each other, provide measures of technology that can be taken collectively to determine a single numerical value which can be compared to a similarly derived value of another technology. Note again that the assessment could have been made for the purpose of comparing other importance factors—values of weight, volume, calories, etc. It is easy to see that the selection of the relative importance factors is dependent upon the parameters (kinds of fruit, in the example), and upon the purpose of the assessment. This latter dependency will be discussed further in addressing the question: Why (or for what purpose) assess technology? Please note that the above example does not add together apples and oranges, rather importance factors have been constructed so as to cancel the different units of fruit in the multiplications, and does add like units of cost associated with each different fruit.

Another hypothetical example of technological assessment is provided by Keith Ellingsworth of the Annapolis Division of the Naval Ship Research and Development Center, Division Planning Office (VIII–12). This one is not in the form of an analogy nor is it trivial. It concerns the design of a boat for river warfare use in Vietnam. The design has proceeded to the point where a choice must be made between two parameters of two boats, as illustrated in Table VIII–2.

TABLE VIII–2

Boat #1	Importance Factor	Boat #2
25 K		20 K
80 db		50 db

The two boats respectively have speeds (knots) and noise levels (decibels) of 25K, 80db and 20K, 50db. Here it appears difficult to assign relative importance factors, but there are methods which can be used. In this case a mission analysis can allow us to determine the relative importance factors. Imagine the boat patrolling a river "looking" up and down the river with its radar. Its mission is to prevent enemy junks from crossing the river. The more noise the boat makes, the further up the river the enemy can hear the boat. The farther away the boat can be heard, the more time the enemy has to escape by crossing the river or by ducking back into a shallow creek where our boat can't go, and the faster our boat must be to catch the enemy. It is simply a matter of physics and geometry to determine, say for a given boat noise, the speed required to achieve a stated level of mission effectiveness. The results of a mission analysis might be stated as for every 16 decibels of noise, 4 knots of speed are required in order to be able to intercept those junks up to a mile away and in the middle two-thirds (width) of the river. In other words, 4 decibels of noise are equivalent to 1 knot of speed, and these are the relative importance factors needed.

TABLE VIII–3

Boat #1	Importance Factors (db/kts)	Boat #2
25 K	4	20 K
80 db	1	50 db

The boat is then selected as illustrated in Table VIII–3. Calculations of value from data follows:

$$V\,(\#1) = (25 \times 4) - (80 \times 1) = 20$$
$$V\,(\#2) = (20 \times 4) - (50 \times 1) = 30$$

Note that speed adds to the boat's value, noise subtracts. The above assessment indicates the choice of Boat #2. It's a slower boat, but its reduced noise makes it more effective by the criteria established. This sort of assessment might be done to determine operational capabilities, to determine design criteria, or in resource allocation determine the appropriate levels of effort in the two technological areas of boat power and noise reduction.

Who Assesses Technology and Why—Or for What Purpose?

Intuitively, nearly everyone assesses technology at some time, for some purpose, and to some degree of sophistication. The "man on the street" for example may essentially assess the aggregates of the technologies of color versus black and white television. He may consider the collective value of parameters such as cost, picture quality, repair frequency, and pressure from his wife in order to choose which, if either, to buy. That nearly everyone has different values was pointed out by William D. Guth and Renato Tagiuri which emphasized the following points (VIII–13):

—The personal values that businessmen and others have can be usefully classified as theoretical, economic, aesthetic, social, political, and religious.

— The values that are most important to an executive have profound influence on his strategic decisions.

— Managers and employees often are unaware of the values they possess and also tend to misjudge the values of others.

— The executive who will take steps to better understand his own values and other men's values can gain an important advantage in developing workable and well-supported policies.

Earlier it was stated that the assessment of technology depends on who assesses, why the assessment is undertaken, and on the nature of technology itself. A hypothetical situation which provides some illustration of the range of assessors, and how assessment might vary over this range is provided in the following example. This example also illustrates one of the difficulties in assessing technology which results from variations of people and purposes involved.

Consider the technology of batteries and three of its parameters: volume, cost, and time between recharging. A broad range of assessors might be the following in the situations described.

Technology

Involvement	Situation
User	LT USN: Commanding Officer of a boat, which contains batteries; drifting on a Vietnamese river on night patrol.
R&D Manager	Chief of Naval Development; responsible for Navy's total Exploratory Development Program (Applied Research) considering each year's fiscal budget.
Boat Designer	Naval Architect, Naval Ship Systems Command, designing a boat for use in Vietnam.
R&D Engineer	Project engineer; working in a Navy R&D lab to improve the general performance of batteries.

These four people might assess battery technology using the same quantitative techniques, where 10 is the highest value that may be assigned and 0 the lowest, as shown in Table VIII–4.

Table VIII–4 shows the relative importance factors that the four persons might assign to the parameters based on intuition. The differences shown by the variations of relative importance

TABLE VIII–4
TECHNOLOGY: BATTERIES

Parameter	User	Manager	Designer	Engineer
Volume	3	2	10	8
Cost	0	10	2	2
Time between Recharging	10	2	4	1

are possibly true, while perhaps exaggerated. The importance factors were chosen considering the following rationalizations.

The boat operator's life depends to a large extent on his boat. He's probably very concerned when, in the situation described, he must start-up his *loud* engines to charge the batteries. He therefore considers the necessity and the time between recharging very important. He's probably not too concerned with the volume of the batteries so long as they don't infringe significantly on ammo storage space. He probably doesn't care what the batteries cost, much less the cost of the battery R&D effort.

The R&D manager is likely to place more importance on cost and less importance on individual performance characteristics. This is probably due to his responsibility for a large number of R&D programs and proposed programs involving many different parameters of many different technologies and the common element among these is cost.

The boat designer is concerned with the over-all performance of the boat. He must assure that all components required fit onto the boat, and he therefore considers volume relatively more important than cost or time between recharging.

The project engineer is concerned with many characteristics of batteries; he is concerned with the improvement of batteries in general. It is not particularly required of him that he produce a profit. Therefore he may not be particularly cost conscious. It is not required of him, perhaps, that he produce the smallest possible boat battery, and therefore he places less importance on volume than the boat designer does.

The above considerations suggest that the selection by a person of relative importance factors for parameters describing a technology is highly influenced by the environment in which the person is involved. Key expressions taken from the above for the persons described are:

User: life, Vietnamese river (warfare)

Manager: total R&D program; command

Designer: performance of boat (system made up of many technologies); engineering center

R&D: many characteristics of one technology; laboratory

A difficulty in assessing technology, illustrated above, is the problem of obtaining and maintaining an alignment of relative importance factors between the users of technologies and those responsible for improving the capabilities of technologies.

In the *hypothetical* example, the R&D engineer may not have been aware of the degree of importance of a particular parameter to a particular user. In other words, an R&D engineer may not recognize the need for a particular technological improvement. The importance of such need-recognitions as it contributes to the successful development of weapon systems is well illustrated by the comprehensive technology source study Project HINDSIGHT conducted by Col. Raymond Isenson and Dr. Chalmers Sherwin of the Department of Defense (VIII–14).

R&D Programming

To reiterate three factors used by the U.S. Department of Defense to evaluate systems programs are "military utility," "technical feasibility," and "financial acceptability." These factors are also important when planners evelute research and development. However, it is necessary to quantize these factors so that they may be compared for different Research and Development programs.

One of the simpler techniques being investigated by the Navy utilizes Appraisal Sheet No. 1 (see Figure VIII–4) which addresses the problems of military utility. Military utility with respect to development atmosphere is a measure of R&D work

APPRAISAL SHEET NO. I

VALUE TO NAVAL WARFARE

Column I - Categories General Operational Requirements (GORs)	Column 2 Impact of Task Contributions										Column 3 Value to Individual Category
	1.0	.9	.8	.7	.6	.5	.4	.3	.2	.1	
31 - STRIKE WARFARE											
6 - Airborne Attack											
3 - Surface Attack											
5 - Submarine Attack											
4 - Amphibious Assault											
7 - Sea Based Strategic Deterrence											
3 - Airborne Anti-Air Warfare											
3 - Surface Anti-Air Warfare											
31 - ANTISUBMARINE WARFARE											
5 - Airborne ASW				✓							3.5
4 - Surface ASW						✓					2.0
5 - Submarine ASW						✓					2.5
10 - Undersea Surveillance							✓				3.0
2 - Mining											
3 - Mine Countermeasures											
2 - ASW Ancillary Support									✓		0.4
23 - COMMAND SUPPORT											
3 - Command and Control											
4 - Naval Communications											
4 - Electronic Warfare											
1 - Navigation											
4 - Ocean Surveillance											
5 - Reconnaissance & Intelligence											
1 - Environmental Systems											
1 - Special Warfare											
15 - OPERATIONAL SUPPORT											
2 - Logistics											
4 - Personnel											
2 - Astronautics											
2 - Aviation Support											
2 - Ship Support											
2 - Ordnance Support											
1 - NBC Defense											

4. TOTAL VALUE TO NAVAL WARFARE = $\boxed{11.4}$

Scale of Definitions for "Impact of Task Contribution" (Column 2):

Points - Descriptors

1.0   Creation of radically new mission concepts (meets overriding critical need)
 .7   Revolutionary extension of capabilities
 .4   Incremental or marginal improvement of capabilities
 .2   Increase in economy

Figure VIII–4. Value to Naval Warfare—Appraisal Sheet No. 1.

in terms of its usefulness in meeting U.S. Navy's General Operational Requirements (GOR). To be useful, hardware or information must provide a new or improved capability in the shortest possible time after its need is recognized. Thus, military utility is made up of three interdependent criteria: value to naval warfare, responsiveness, and timeliness. In this condensed version, we will consider "value to naval warfare."

This criterion considers the extent of the contribution of a task area objective (TAO), a unit of work, in terms of its inherent value as well as its military operational value. The importance of a task is measured by its relative impact on any individual naval warfare category as well as the number of categories receiving a contribution from the task objective. This is done by multiplying the assigned value of the warfare category by the impact value of the contribution to arrive at a value for each individual category. The sum of these values will determine the value of the task area objective.

Note: The figures of merit, or point values assigned to each naval warfare category (Column 1) are dummy figures; they were assigned for this example only. The actual total number of points assigned these 29 naval categories is equal to 100, and they are assigned for test purposes on the basis of the importance of each of these categories in the 1975 and 1980 time frame since this is when most of the Navy's current exploratory development work will find its way into the Fleet. The operational users provided the test figures based on the present world situation and their estimates of the most probable future situations.

When the warfare area specialist filled in Column 2, the impact of the task area objective contributions, he considered the descriptors at the bottom of the page (Scale of Definitions). In some cases the 4 descriptors do not adequately describe the contribution; in those cases he interpolates between these numbers.

The credibility of the ratings of technical feasibility and the probability of success increase if they are rated by personnel who have the necessary technical expertise and competence, as they can best judge these factors on the basis of the ability and ex-

APPRAISAL SHEET NO. 2

Probability of Success

☐ 80 - 100% Chance of Meeting TAO

☑ 30 - 80% Chance of Meeting TAO

☐ 0 - 30% Change of Meeting TAO

Number of Different Concurrent Approaches

☐ 1   ☐ 3   ☐ 5   ☐ 7   ☐ 9

☐ 2   ☑ 4   ☐ 6   ☐ 8   ☐ 10 or more

Sacred Cow?   Who Says?

S-1 ☐ President   S-5 ☐ JCS (Joint Chiefs of Staff)

S-2 ☐ Congress

S-3 ☐ DOD (Department of Defense)   S-6 ☐ CNO (Chief of Naval Operations)

S-4 ☐ ASN (R&D) (Assistant Secretary of Navy for Research and Development)   S-7 ☐ CND (Chief of Naval Development)

S-8 ☐ Other _____

Appraisal Summary

No. of GOR's ___5___

Value (V) ___11.4___

Probability of Success (P_s) ___0.9375___

Expected Value (EV) ___11.4 x 0.9375 = 10.7___

Optimum Funding ___$2 million___

Desirability Index (D) ___5.35___

Figure VIII–5. Probability of Success—Appraisal Sheet No. 2.

perience of the individuals and/or organizations carrying on the development efforts under consideration.

The top half of Appraisal Sheet No. 2 (see Figure VIII–5) solicits the opinion of the technical specialist regarding the probability of achieving the total task area objective that is being undertaken. It considers whether the task could be successfully accomplished from a scientific and technical feasibility point of view. Technical risk also takes into consideration the degree of confidence or prediction that the remaining portion of the total task objective can be attained. The degree of confidence or prediction that the remaining portion of the total task objective can be attained usually assesses the factors of the present state-of-the-art, either implicit or explicit. This technical appraisal is naturally based on technical forecasts and includes time factors and resource levels, as well as the competence of the investigating team.

Therefore, the technical specialist checks the box that best describes his opinion regarding the task area objective being evaluated, as well as the number of different concurrent approaches being taken which are also a measure of probability of success.

The area called "sacred cow?" and "who says?" was also considered in what we call the "management environment." This section solicits opinions on the acceptability of the effort in the management structure. Here, the evaluator is asked to give what he believes to be "the Washington environment" considerations concerning this effort, and he checks the applicable box.

The bottom of Appraisal Sheet No. 2 is then analyzed. The total program is calculated by Value, Expected Value, and Desirability Index for three funding levels, by the computer. The inputs for military utility come from Appraisal Sheet No. 1.

For example: Suppose the proposed task area objective (TAO), or R&D effort, is to devise a system able to detect submerged submarines a given distance away from a sensor, say 20 miles. We shall consider the criterion "Value to Naval Warfare." Of the 29 naval General Operational Requirements shown in Column 1 of Appraisal Sheet No. 1, the TAO would be of value and contribute only to five GOR's: Airborne ASW, Surface ASW, Submarine ASW, Undersea ASW, and ASW Ancillary Support.

With respect to airborne ASW, the success of the R&D venture in this hypothetical example is considered a "revolutionary extension of capabilities," and is accorded 0.7 point. At the same time, airborne ASW is said to contribute 5 out of the 100 units assigned to all the GOR's. Thus, the value of the TAO to naval warfare with respect to airborne ASW is $0.7 \times 5 = 3.5$. The other categories can be similarly evaluated for their contributions, and the total value of this TAO to naval warfare is summed at 11.4, as shown on the appraisal sheet.

For our calculation of the Probability of Success (P_s) in meeting the TAO, we use the probability chart shown on Table VIII–5. In this chart, n is the number of concurrent approaches used to accomplish the TAO, and C is a number arbitrarily assigned to the chances of succeeding in a given approach. We use:

$$80–100\% \text{ chance of success: } C = 0.8$$
$$30–\ 80\% \text{ chance of success: } C = 0.5$$
$$0–\ 30\% \text{ chance of success: } C = 0.2$$

We assume that all approaches n have the same chance of success, and therefore the same value of C. If each n were to have a different C, a more involved calculation would have been necessary.

The number assigned to the probability of one approach failing is then $(1 - C)$.

The number assigned to the probability of n approaches failing is $(1 - C)^n$

Further, if we assume that at least one of the approaches taken will succeed, then the number assigned to the probability of success P_s is $1 - (1 - C)^n$.

This figure for P_s is filled in on Appraisal Sheet No. 2 under the Probability of Success column.

Example: On an Appraisal Sheet No. 2, we might have had 4 approaches $(n = 4)$ with a 30–80% chance of meeting TAO $(C - 0.5)$. Then the number corresponding to the probability

TABLE VIII–5
TABULATION OF P_s

C			
n	0.8	0.5	0.2
1	0.80000	0.50000	0.20000
2	0.96000	0.75000	0.36000
3	0.99200	0.87500	0.48800
4	0.99840	0.93750	0.59040
5	0.99968	0.96875	0.67230
6	0.99993	0.98438	0.73786
7	0.99997	0.99219	0.79029
8	0.99999	0.99609	0.83223
9	0.99999	0.99805	0.86578
10	0.99999	0.99902	0.89263

of success is 0.93750 or 93.75%. From our previous example we calculated the total value of a given TAO to be 11.4. Therefore, the expected value is $11.4 \times 0.9375 = 10.7$.

The preceding has been a discussion of concurrent approaches. If the task area were made up of phased or sequential operations, these probabilities would be handled in a different manner.

Three funding levels are utilized in the "concurrent" approach: the actual/optimum, maximum, and minimum.

The actual/optimum consists of the latest approved fiscal data. For each subsequent year, funds are entered based on what is estimated as necessary to achieve the completion date if the task area is supported at an optimum rate. An optimum rate is one which permits aggressive prosecution using orderly developmental procedures—not a crash program.

The maximum consists of what could effectively be expended in advancing task area completion date. Maximum funding is the upper limit in which unlimited resources are assigned in order to accelerate the accomplishment of a task area.

The minimum consists of what could be effectively utilized to maintain continuity of effort and some progress toward fulfilling the task area objective. Minimum funding is the threshold limit below which it would not be feasible to continue further efforts in the task area.

The simplified formula is:

$$\text{VALUE } (V) \times \text{PROB OF SUCCESS } (P_s) = \text{EXPECTED VALUE } (EV)$$

$$\frac{\text{EXPECTED VALUE } (EV)}{\text{FUNDING LEVEL } (C)} = \text{DESIRABILITY INDEX } (D)$$

Finishing up the analysis of the rating sheet, "GORs" represent the number of general operational requirements affected by the project; "P_s," as previously stated, is read off a probability chart; and the optimum funding level is determined according to the resources needed to complete the project in the time span of the study. The final desirability index numbers now provide a way to compare a great multitude of current and proposed R&D projects. By carrying out similar evaluations on the basis of responsiveness to expected needs, the timeliness of the projects, and other criteria, it is possible to combine all the information about the project and come up with its "total warfare value."

The end results of a research and development planning effort like this are computer printouts (Figures VIII–6, –7) which rank every project according to its value in the over-all program. In the Navy, this comes to over 700 separate R&D projects. It would be a mistake, however, to think that the impressive-looking computer printouts are taking over the final decision-making job. Most of those who design and work with information systems like the one described, fully realize that technological forecasts and quantitative estimates of project value are no more or less than a planning tool—and only one of many that a manager must use in making final decisions. Thirty other techniques that are available are shown in Chapter IX.

Opinions

There are differing opinions as to the applications of these techniques, but they fall into one of three categories:
1. The unbeliever,
2. The strong advocate, and
3. The non-commital.

N A V R A T   P R O G R A M   E V A L U A T I O N   R E P O R T
(RANKING OF 6324P012   BY TOTAL WARFARE VALUE MH. (ETROR 6YTPC)

TASK AREA NUMBER	TITLE	SC	EXP. VALUE	MAX	CUM	FINANCING OPT	FINANCING CUM	MIN	CUM	RANKING*
WF1151175﹦1 "FO190101	(U)SPACE SYSTEMS ENGINEERING		20.446875	300	300	300	300	300	300	2/.3
XFU322200﹦1 "FO19020n	(U)COMMUNICATIONS SATELLITE SUPPORT		22.050000	2000	2300	1375	1675	1000	1300	25.2.
WFU32227﹦1 "FO190101	(U)SATELLITE COMMUNICATIONS		10.350000	350	2650	350	2025	0	1300	21.8
WF1255277﹦1 "FO190202	(U)SATELLITE OCEANOGRAPHIC DATA COLLECTION		9.375000	900	3550	700	2725	150	1450	12.5
WF12551752 "FO190202	(U)SOLAR RADIATION MONITORING SATELLITE		8.000370	3000	6550	2800	5525	1200	2650	11.9
WFU323397﹦1 "FO190101	(U)SATELLITE NAVIGATION			2250	8800	2250	7775	0	2650	10.2
WF1255517﹦1 "FO190202	(U)METEOROLOGICAL SATELLITE DATA READOUT		8.750000	600	9400	200	7975	150	2800	10.0
WF021127﹦1 "FO190103	(U)ADVANCED TECHNIQUES FOR SPACE OBJECT DETECTION AND IDENTIFICATION		2.800000	850	10250	850	8825	0	2800	5.6
WF0211175﹦2 "FO190202	(U)OCEAN SURVEILLANCE SYSTEMS ANALYSIS			5500	15750	5000	13825	4000	6800	4.8
WFU531175﹦1 "FO190102	(U)SATELLITE INTERCEPTER SYSTEMS ANALYSIS			500	16250	500	14325	200	7000	1.0
WFU533727﹦1 "FO190103	(U)ASTRO-DEFENSE THREAT STUDIES			300	16550	200	14525	100	7100	1.0

Figure VIII–6. Example: Computer Printout Ranked by Warfare Value and Expected Value.

860801260001
C

NAVMAT PROGRAM EVALUATION REPORT
(RANKING BY OPT DESIRABILITY)

TASK AREA NUMBER	TITLE	SC	MAX	CUM	OPT	CUM	MIN	CUM	RANKING*
					F U N D I N G				
SF08452002	(U)ACOUSTICAL SILENCING (INTERNAL SHIPS SYSTEMS)	S6	320	320	220	220	185	185	.266477
SF08452004	(U)ACOUSTICAL SILENCING, SHIP ISOLATION DEVICES	S6	535	855	435	655	333	518	.181034
XF10532001	(U)TEST EQUIPMENT	S3	2400	3255	1300	1955	770	1288	.124614
SF08452005	(U)ACOUSTICAL SILENCING, HULL VIBRATION AND RADIATION	S6	955	4210	680	2635	610	1898	.093750
SF02132001	(U)DIRECT VIEW IMAGE INTENSIFIER TECHNIQUES	S4	400	4610	300	2935	65	1963	.080000
SF08452001	(U)SHIP SILENCING MEASUREMENTS, ANALYSIS AND PROBLEM DEFINITION	S6	1360	5970	1095	4030	860	2823	.072602
WF02132001	(U)IMAGING RECONNAISSANCE SENSOR DEVELOPMENT	S3	1000	6970	750	4780	200	3023	.056666
HF08412002	(U)DEEP RESEARCH VEHICLE PROGRAM	S6	1700	8670	1510	6290	1180	4203	.048344
SF01121003	(U)DOMES AND SELF NOISE	S6	600	9270	550	6840	540	4743	.041236
XF10545001	(U)ADVANCED ACTIVE DEVICES AND TECHNIQUES	S3	4000	13270	2600	9440	2000	6743	.039711
PF11521004	(U)IMPROVED NAVY STAFFING CRITERIA	S6	500	13770	500	9940	253	6996	.036400
SF01121007	(U)SYSTEM ANALYSIS AND ENGINEERING	S6	1000	14770	850	10790	500	7496	.037058
SF08452003	(U)ACOUSTICAL SILENCING, EXTERNAL SHIP SYSTEM	S6	1920	16690	1735	12525	1412	8908	.033789
TF10531001	(U)CARGO MOVEMENT AND DISTRIBUTION	S6	700	17390	550	13075	300	9208	.018039
SF01121004	(U)TRANSDUCERS AND ACOUSTIC POWER GENERATORS	S6	4500	21890	4009	17084	2700	11908	.011785
SF01121002	(U)SONAR SIGNAL PROCESSING AND CLASSIFICATION	S6	7000	28890	6520	23604	5800	17708	.007246
SF01121001	(U)UNDERWATER SOUND PROPAGATION	S6	6400	35290	6000	29604	4800	22508	.005250
SF09443004	(U)NUCLEAR PROPULSION PLANT MATERIALS DEVELOPMENT	S4	1100	36390	1100	30704	0	22508	
SF09443001	(U)NUCLEAR PROPULSION PLANT TECHNOLOGY	S4	1000	37390	1000	31704	0	22508	
SF09442003	(U)SURFACE SHIP REFUELING EQUIPMENT AND PROCEDURES DEVELOPMENT	S4	2200	39590	2200	33904	0	22508	

Figure VIII-7. Example: Computer Printout Ranked by Desirability.

However, the developers of these techniques have been greatly concerned over the apparent resistance to implementing the techniques.

An illustration of the unbeliever may best be shown in a quote from Professor Edward B. Roberts of MIT. "Although a number of industrial firms are striving to improve their R&D funding decisions, the Defense Department under McNamara is the first major organization to react definitively to this folklore approach. And the reaction is a somewhat characteristic over-reaction that produces a decision-making system that promises to be even more cumbersome, less realistic, and more ironclad in appearance than . . . The outputs thus derived emerge from the computer with the same factual appearance as does a payroll tabulation. Upon such illusory bases will fundamental research funds be allotted, if present DOD trends hold sway" (VIII–15).

An example of one of the supporters and potential users of this appraisal information came from Captain Edmund Mahinske, USN, when he stated in a management memo: "A planning appraisal system which operates on task area proposals . . . is a crucial necessity to our attempts to derive our program on a basis of *relatively* unimpeachable logic. . . . Remember our goal is to *improve* our management of the program *not* to perpetuate the 'control we now exercise' " (VIII–16).

COL Buck, Technical Director of the Air Force Flight Dynamics Laboratory at Wright-Patterson AF Base, has used a computerized quantitative resource allocation system as an aid in planning his R&D program for three years. Perhaps the best answer to this question was given when we asked COL Buck how he used the quantitative technique and he answered, "Very carefully."

We must agree with Professor Roberts. If one had to choose between any machine and the human brain, he would select the brain. This is because the brain has a marvelous feed-back system that learns from experience. The mind also has an uncanny way of pulling out the salient factors and rejecting useless information. But it is wrong to say that one must select intuitive experience over analysis or minds over machines, really they are *not* alternatives, they complement each other. If the two are used together the results are far better than if either is used individually.

One of the best quotes pertinent to these matters comes from Paul Sturm, Assistant Director of Plans and Policy, Office of Director of Defense Research and Engineering. He said:

"Attempts to quantify the unquantifiable, in the interests of satisfying the demands of an unyielding methodology, is a potentially stifling practice that could cause irreparable damage to our technological supremacy and the consequent ability to defend ourselves during the challenging decades ahead. The prudent course lies between those two extremes" (VIII–17).

Conclusions

It is necessary to be aware of many of the omissions and weaknesses of these quantitative selection or resource allocation techniques. It should be stressed again that they were not intended to yield decision, but rather information which would facilitate decision. Indeed, these techniques are merely thinking structures to force methodical, meticulous consideration of all the factors involved in resource allocation. *Data* plus *analysis* yields *information. Information* plus *judgment* yields *decisions.*

Data + Analysis = Information
Information + Judgment = Decision

A close look at a few "facts" concerning the quantitative resource allocation methods shows these approaches to be merely experimental management techniques. The fact that a computer or an adding machine may be used to facilitate data handling should in no way obscure the basic fact that human subjective inputs are the foundation of these systems. Accurate human calculation, as opposed to use of a computer for the calculations of all the interrelationships considered would not alter the basic principles of these management tools in any respect. Yet, it is often heard that quantitative measurements cannot be applied to management processes because human judgment cannot be forsaken and machines cannot replace the seasoned experience expertise of the manager (VIII–18).

The real concern should be directed toward using the collective judgment of technical staffs (technological forecasts) and decision-makers in such a manner that logically sound decisions are made, greater payoff is achieved for the resources committed, and that less, not more, valuable scientific and engineering time is expended. To make an incorrect decision is understandable, but to make a decision and not really know the basis for the judgment is unforgivable. The area of good resource allocation certainly must have advanced beyond this point; oherwise, a pair of dice could replace the decision-maker.

Case Studies

Appendices A and B which appear at the end of these chapters provide additional examples of structuring the resource allocation problem and typical attacks on mounting efforts in given areas of endeavor. Appendix A depicts the situation where a company having certain corporate goals must make a selection among many alternatives open to it in advancing into the fuel cell business. In Appendix B, Dr. E. B. Roberts, in his analysis therein, presents an opposing view to the material presented in these chapters. In a sense, he poses a challenge to forecasters and allocators and otherwise establishes a body of conscience to their efforts.

REFERENCES

VIII– 1. Cetron, M. J., R. Isenson, J. Johnson, A. B. Nutt and H. Wells, *Quantitative Methods for Technological Resource Management;* accepted for publication by MIT Press, Cambridge, Mass., in the spring of 1969.

VIII– 2. Cetron, M. J., J. Martino and L. Roepcke, "The Selections of R&D Program Content—Survey of Quantitative Methods," *IEEE Transactions on Engineering Management*, Vol. EM–14, No. 1, March 1967, pp. 4–12.

VIII– 3. Cetron, M. J. and A. L. Weiser, "Technological Change, Technological Forecasting and Planning R&D—A View from the R&D Manager's Desk," *George Washington Law Review* (Technology

Assessment and the Law), Vol. 35, No. 5, George Washington University, Washington, D.C., July 1968.

VIII– 4. Smith, D. F. and F. A. Hansen, "Long Range Research and Development Planning," (MEL 395/66) Naval Ship R&D Center, Annapolis, Md., 1966.

VIII– 5. Nutt, A. B., "An Approach to Research and Development Effectiveness," *IEEE Transactions on Engineering Management,* September 1965, pp. 103–112.

VIII– 6. Cetron, M. J., P. H. Caulfield and R. D. Freshman, "Facts and Folklore in R&D Management Revisited," submitted to *Management Science* (TIMS) for publication in the winter of 1969.

VIII– 7. Ansoff, H. I. and J. M. Stewart, "Strategies for a Technology-Based Business," *Harvard Business Review*, Cambridge, Mass., Nov.-Dec. 1967, pp. 71–83.

VIII– 8. *Ibid.* 6 *supra.*

VIII– 9. *Ibid.* 1, 2 and 5 *supra.*

VIII–10. Roberts, E. B., "Facts and Folklore in R&D Management," *Industrial Management Review,* Sloan School of Management, Cambridge, Mass., spring 1967.

VIII–11. *Ibid.* 6 *supra.*

VIII–12. Ellingsworth, K., "Technology Assessment," an unpublished masters paper in R&D Management, American University, Washington, D.C., June 1968.

VIII–13. Guth, W. D. and R. Tagiuri, "Personal Values and Corporate Strategy," *Harvard Business Review,* Cambridge, Mass., Sept.-Oct. 1965.

VIII–14. Isenson, R. S. and C. W. Sherwin, *Project Hindsight* (Interim Report), Office of the Director of Defense Research and Engineering, CSTI (AD 642 400), Springfield, Va., June 30, 1966 (revised, Oct. 13, 1966).

VIII–15. Roberts, Edward B., "Facts and Folklore in Research and Development Management," *Industrial Management Review*, May 1967.

VIII–16. Mahinske, Edmund B., Hq. Naval Material Command, "Memorandum on Exploratory Development Planning Appraisal System," November 22, 1966.

VIII–17. Strum, Paul J., "Problem Mongers, Solution Mongers and Weapon System Effectiveness," *Defense Industry Bulletin,* July 1966.

VIII–18. *Ibid.* 10 *supra.*

Golden Rule: He who hath the gold maketh the rule. —ANONYMOUS

CHAPTER IX

SURVEY OF QUANTITATIVE METHODS

THIS CHAPTER provides a summary of a number of known techniques for quantitative evaluation of R&D projects. Successful application of quantitative methods to problems such as inventories, queueing, transportation, and other problems requiring decisions on resource allocation or scheduling, has at least made it conceivable to raise the question of whether comparable quantitative evaluation methods could also be applied to research and development projects. The advent of the computer has made such applications appear feasible, where the R&D efforts are large in number. The desired outputs from such quantitative methods would be an evaluation of a prescribed selection of projects, or better yet, a procedure for scheduling projects or allocating resources among competing projects.

Interest in such quantitative methods, especially within the Department of Defense, has become quite high within the past few years. As a result of this interest, a survey of methods, both completed and on-going, which have been devised in industry and in the government, has been conducted. These methods have been evaluated against a fixed set of factors.

Features of the Methods

The various methods uncovered in this survey took into account various items of information about the R&D projects to be evaluated, and provided various items of information as output from the evaluation. A total of 15 different features were found which could describe the items of input and output of the various methods. No single method possessed all the features. The various features are described in some detail below:

— *Utility Measure:* Does the method take into account some measure of the utility or value of success of a particular R&D project? This measure may be share of a market, profitability, some measure of military worth, etc.

— *Probability of Success:* Does the method explicitly take into account an estimate of the probability of success of each individual R&D project?

— *Orthogonality of Criteria:* Are the criteria used by the method mutually exclusive (orthogonal), rather than being highly correlated or having a high degree of overlap?

— *Sensitivity:* Has the sensitivity of the output to small changes in the input been checked? A high degree of sensitivity to small variations in input is undesirable, since the output then becomes unstable in the presence of minor perturbations in the input.

— *Rejected Alternatives Retention:* When a project is rejected for funding, is it retained for later consideration in the event of a budget increase or other adjustment, rather than being rejected completely?

— *Classification Structure:* Does the method provide a structural relationship between the R&D project and a hierarchy of higher-level goals of the organization?

— *Time:* Does the method take into account scheduling requirements, or provide scheduling information as an output?

— *Strategies:* Does the method permit the user to take into account several possible scenarios, world environments, market situations, etc.?

— *System Cross Support:* Does the method give a system development credit for support which it provides to another system development?

— *Technology Cross Support:* Does the method give a project for advancement of technology credit for support which it provides to the advancement of other technologies?

— *Graphical Display:* Is the output amenable to presentation in some graphical form which gives the user a condensed picture of the evaluation of various projects?

— *Flagging:* Does the method flag problem areas, to bring them to the attention of the responsible management?

— *Optimization Criteria:* What criterion for optimization does the method use, and what constraints are considered? All methods used either a composite score from a number of factors, to obtain a ranking, or used some form of maximum (discounted) net value.

— *Constraints:* Constraints considered by the methods were budget, skills available, facilities available, competitor efforts, and raw materials available.

— *Computerized:* Is the method implemented in a computer program, and is it a linear program or a dynamic program? Those marked as computerized are known to the authors to have been programmed for some machine. It should be noted that most of the techniques could be computerized if desired.

Ease of Use

Each method was evaluated according to several criteria bearing on ease of use. The criteria considered are described below:

— *Data Requirements:* While in general the more data a method uses as input, the more information it provides as output, nevertheless, the ease of use is affected by the amount of data required. Two factors enter into the amount of data required: the level of organization at which data is obtained, i.e., individual work unit, subsystem, system, etc.; and the amount of data required on each effort on which data is gathered.

— *Manual:* Is manual operation of the method possible or reasonable to consider?

— *Computer Program:* If a computer is required, has the method been programmed for some computer?

— *Running Time:* If the method has been programmed, what is the running time for one cycle of evaluation or allocation?

— Updating: What is the ease of updating the system to take into account new information, whether the new information is developed periodically or new items come in on an unscheduled basis?

— Proficiency Level: What level of proficiency is required of the operator (not the manager who is using the output)? Can it be handled by a clerk? Does it require a skilled technician? Does it require a degreed professional?

— Outside Help: Is help or information required from persons outside the R&D organization, in evaluating goals set by others, environments not under control of the R&D organization, etc.?

Area of Applicability

Few of the systems appeared to be applicable throughout the entire R&D spectrum. Some were more applicable to one portion of the spectrum than to others. The methods are rated as being applicable to research, to exploratory development, to advanced development, or to engineering development.

Description of Methods

Each method surveyed is described briefly below. The methods are identified with the name or names of the originators, unless some acronym or title has been used to designate the method. (The first ten descriptions were taken from the Baker-Pound article "R&D Project Selection: Where We Stand," printed in IEEE Transactions on Engineering Management, vol. EM–11, no. 4, December 1964.)

— Mottley-Newton, 1959: "A decision theory approach. Project proposals are rated with respect to a number of evaluation criteria. An over-all score is computed and used to rank the alternatives. Selection criteria are considered with respect to constraints including research budget, risk, and over-all program balance."

— Gargiulo et al., 1961: "A decision theory approach.

Project proposals are rated with respect to a number of evaluation criteria. An over-all score is computed and used to rank the alternatives. Constraints such as research budget, skills available, facilities available, and competitor efforts in the area are considered."

— *Pound, 1964:* "A decision theory approach. Project proposals are rated with respect to a number of weighted selection objectives. An over-all score is computed and used to rank the alternatives. The budget constraint is considered."

— *Sobelman, 1958:* "An operations research approach. For each alternative project, estimates are made of average value per year, economic life, average development cost per year and development time. Selection is accomplished by maximizing discounted net value, perhaps subject to constraints."

— *Freeman, 1960:* "An operations research approach. For each alternative project, an estimate is made of the probability distribution of net value. Selection is accomplished by maximizing expected discounted net value subject to constraints on the total budget, facilities, and personnel. A linear programming formulation is used."

— *Asher, 1962:* "An operations research approach. For each alternative project, estimates are made of the discounted net value of the project and probability of success. Selection is accomplished by maximizing expected discounted net value subject to constraints on the man hours available and on the raw materials available. The optimal manpower allocation is indicated by the result. A linear programming formulation is used."

— *Hess, 1962:* "An operations research approach. For each alternative project, estimates are made of the discounted gross value as of several points in time. Probabilities of success are also estimated. Selection is accomplished by maximizing expected discounted net value subject to a budget constraint for the first period. The optimal allocation to each project is indicated for each period. A dynamic programming formulation is used."

— *Dean-Sengupto, 1962:* "An economic analysis and operations research approach. The optimal research budget is first determined. Then for each alternative project, estimates are made of the discounted net value and the probability of technical and commercial success. Selection is accomplished by maximizing expected discounted net value subject to a budget constraint. A linear programming formulation is suggested."

— *Disman, 1962:* "An economic analysis approach. For each alternative project, an estimate is made of the discounted net value (not including R&D costs). This estimate, perhaps modified by a probability of technical and/or commercial success is considered to be the maximum expenditure justified. The ratio of the maximum expenditure justified to estimated project cost is an index of the desirability of the project."

— *Cramer-Smith, 1964:* "An economic analysis and operations research approach. An application of portfolio selection and utility theory to the problem of research project selection. For each alternative project, estimates are made of net values and probabilities of occurrence. Utility curves are also obtained. Projects may be ranked on the basis of expected value or expected utility. Lack of project independence is also mentioned."

— *Esch, "PATTERN," 1963:* Combination decision theory approach and operations research approach. Project PATTERN is a continuing, large-scale, corporate effort to assign quantitative, relative values to the importance of conducting R&D on the various technology deficiencies which now stand in the way of the achievement of the national security objectives for the decade from 1968 to 1978. The model considers national survival, threat force structure, capability, prestige, cost effectiveness, requirements, scientific implications, feasibility, effort, risk, capability improvement, and operational advantages. This technique is the first full-scale application of the heuristic "relevance tree" concept developed in 1958 by H. Wells in his Ohio State University Master's thesis.

— *Blum, 1963:* A mathematical treatment leading to a methodology of ranking R&D events in the project by their cost, risk, time, and value. The methodology sequences the efforts by a version of the DOD and NASA PERT-cost technique.

— *Bakanas, 1964:* A model to aid in the selection of applied research and development tasks for inclusion in a long-range R&D program. The model consists of a structure relating the conceptional elements of the R&D program; formats for delineating the characteristics of the conceptional elements; mathematical relations between the expected program value and military priority, probability of task success, task cost, and program cost; and a rank-ordering procedure to select a program of maximum expected value. A computer program aids in formulating the R&D program.

— *Dean, 1964:* An operations research approach. Mathematical models consider the relevant resource variables, non-controllable variables, parameters, and constraints that are responsive to corporate goals and yield solutions for allocating technical resources to projects. The scoring model permits determination of important factors in a profitability model.

— *Hill-Roepcke, 1964:* An operations research approach. A mathematical model considering the military value of the objective for technology, the technical probability of success, the expected value of the individual efforts, and a method to select the optimum program from many such efforts.

— *Nutt, 1965:* An operations research approach. A deterministic model which quantifies the value or technical payoff of each research task. The model developed considers the world environment; the Air Force missions; future weapons systems configurations; laboratory technical objectives; and the timeliness, complexity, and scope of each research effort. The result consists of recommended funding levels of efficient tasks along with suggested tasks for close scrutiny or possible elimination. A modified linear program.

— *Cetron, "PROFILE," 1965:* Decision theory approach designed to aid in exploring (a) the total structure of project selection decision problems in the context of the R&D manager, and (b) R&D processes which are relevant to the design and implementation of management systems for planning, appraising, and controlling resource allocation among various projects. PROFILE's nine quantified criteria (value to warfare, task responsiveness, timeliness, long range plan, probability of success, technological transfer, manpower facilities, and funding) are used in developing a task "Profile" as well as in determining the military utility, the technical feasibility, and the application of resources for each project.

— *Rosen & Saunder, 1965:* An operations research approach. A modification of Hess' dynamic programming approach by discussing it in the context of different optimization criteria for obtaining optimum expenditure patterns. The optimization criteria are: expected profit; total expected output; life expected output; and a minimum fixed percent return on nondiscounted expenditure.

— *Sacco, 1965:* An operations research approach. A refinement to the Hill-Roepeke model that permitted dynamic programming to be used and thus achieving a more nearly optimum R&D program.

— *Albertini, 1965:* An operations research approach. A methodology for the evaluation and selection of research and development tasks directed toward the determination of material development objectives. A mathematical choice model to assist management in the synthesis of pertinent information for the purpose of selection, within applicable constraints, of a maximum expected value program of research and development effort. Specifications, in the form of flow charts, are included for the computerization of the model.

— *Berman, 1965:* An economic analysis and decision tree approach. The approach considers the incremental cost of the project in R&D resources, the incremental production and operating and manning costs on introducing the new technology, and the incremental military value of the technology.

— *Sobin-Gordon, 1965:* A comparative method which will analyze alternative applications of resource allocation techniques and attempt to evaluate the value of these techniques against various frames of reference. The analytical method thus developed (basically using ordinal values converted to relative value made up of interdependence of different proposals, definiteness of applications, capability values, probability of success, and military utility) will be used to optimize the selected principles of resource allocation in the dynamic multiple project environment. Linear programming will be used. Principal application to laboratory selection of efforts.

— *Albertini, 1965:* An operations research approach to synthesize information pertinent to the planning process for the purpose of determining which long-range technical plan tasks to recommend for funding. This technique begins with given major barrier problem areas (MBPA's), operations on these MBPA's using the following criteria: expected technical value, annual cost of a configuration, annual monetary quota cost of a configuration. A computer program helps formulate the recommended R&D program.

— *Cetron, "QUEST," 1966:* An operations research approach. QUEST utilizes a double set of matrices, consisting of the sciences, technologies, and missions, developed with the "technology" parameter common to both. By having "figures of utility" assigned to each mission and by determining the value of the contribution of each technological area to each mission, a cumulative quantified value for each technological area is then related to each scientific area and the relevant impact of each of the scientific disciplines is identified with each technological area.

— *Dean-Hauser, 1966:* An economic analysis and operations research approach. An application of project selection under constrained resource conditions. By using mathematical models, computer programs, and available information concerning costs, uncertainties, and military values, it is possible to obtain optimum solutions. The Case study has developed a mathematical model for handling the large number of alternatives through the use of a series of simpler computerized methods, where the results of one stage are used in the succeeding stage. A dynamic programming formulation is used.

— *Belt, 1966:* A decision theory approach based on quantified subjective judgments on the predicted value of a successful laboratory project outcome, the likelihood of success of the project in terms of its technological achievability, the specific plan of attack, and the suitability of the proposed performers of the work, and the predicted cost. This technique stops short of producing a single numerical rating of project value, but gives the decision maker the opportunity to select from a group of alternative projects.

— *De L'Estoile, 1966:* A decision theory approach. This refined rating scheme uses a formula including four factors: military utility, probability of technical success, possibility of realization in France, and direct and indirect economic impact (including the cross support to the civilian sector of the economy). This total system, because of the large number of projects involved, will be computerized in 1967.

— *Martino et al., 1967:* An operations research approach. Factors taken into account are importance of military missions, criticality of technological effort to mission, and level of technology required. Funds are allocated among technical projects on the basis of maximum marginal payoff per dollar, within a budget total.

— *Caulfield-Freshman, 1967:* A decision theory approach. Development project proposals are rated with respect to a number of weighted selection categories. These six categories consist of progress of program, military utility, technical risk, resources, management environment, and technological transfer; an over-all score is computed and used to rank the alternatives. This technique is used to develop a task "Profile" which serves as an aid in the allocation of resources.

Comparison of Methods

The various methods are compared as to features, ease of use criteria, and area of applicability in Figures IX–1, –2, and –3, respectively. The various methods and features, criteria, or areas are displayed in matrix form. An entry of X in the matrix indicates that the method has the feature, satisfies the criterion, or is applicable to that area. For level of information or data required, the methods are coded L for little or none, M for

	Utility Measure	Prob. of Success	Orthog. Criteria	Sensitivity	Retain Rej. Alt.	Class Struc.	Time	Strateg.	Sys. Cross Support	Tech. Cross Support	Graph. Displ.	Flag	Optimiz.* Criteria	Constraints**	Computerized
1. Mottley–Newton, 1959	X	X	X	X			X	X	X	X			1	1, 6, 7	X
2. Gargiulo et al., 1961	X	X	X				X		X	X			1	1, 2, 3, 4	
3. Pound, 1964	X	X				X							7	L	
4. Sobelman, 1958	X	X	X				X						7		
5. Freeman, 1960	X	X	X				X						7	2, 3	X
6. Asher, 1962	X	X					X						7	2, 5	X
7. Hess, 1962	X	X			X	X							7	1	X
8. Dean–Sengupta, 1962	X	X	X		X	X							7	1	
9. Disman, 1962	X	X											7		
10. Cramer–Smith, 1964	X	X	X	X	X	X	X	X	X				7	1	
11. Esch, "PATTERN," 1963	X	X	X		X	X							1, 2		X
12. Blum, 1963	X	X	X	X	X	X							6	6	
13. Bakanas, 1964	X	X	X	X	X	X							3		
14. Dean, 1964	X	X	X	X	X	X							4	1, 6	X
15. Hill–Roepcke, 1964	X	X	X	X	X	X	X	X	X	X	X		2	1, 6, 7	X
16. Nutt, 1965	X	X	X	X	X	X	X	X	X	X	X		1, 2, 3	1, 2, 3	X
17. Cetron, "PROFILE," 1965	X	X	X		X	X	X			X		X	1, 2	1, 2	X
18. Rosen–Saunder, 1965	X	X				X							3, 3, 4, 7	1	
19. Sacco, 1965	X	X				X							3, 3		
20. Albertini, 1965	X	X		X	X	X	X	X	X	X	X		2	1, 6, 7	X
21. Berman, 1965	X	X				X							5		
22. Sobin–Gordon, 1965	X	X	X	X	X	X							1	1, 2, 3, 7	X
23. Albertini, 1965	X	X	X	X	X	X	X	X		X	X	X		1, 6, 7	X
24. Wells, 1966	X	X	X		X	X						X	2	1, 7	X
25. Cetron, "QUEST", 1966	X	X		X	X	X	X	X	X			X	1, 2	1, 7	X
26. Dean–Hauser, 1966	X	X			X	X			X	X		X	3		X
27. Belt, 1966	X	X				X				X					
28. De l'Estoile, 1966	X	X	X	X	X	X	X	X	X	X	X	X	3		X
29. Marino et al., 1967	X	X			X	X	X	X					3	4, 7	
30. Caulfield–Freshman, 1967	X	X			X	X	X		X	X	X		1, 2, 3	1, 7	

* Optimization Criteria
1. Ordinal Ranking
2. Expected Value
3. Cost-Benefit
4. Profitability
5. Incremental Costs
6. Composite Score
7. Discounted Net Value

** Constraints
1. Budget
2. Skills Available
3. Facilities Available
4. Competitor Efforts
5. Raw Materials Available
6. Risk
7. Program Balance

Figure IX–1. Features of the Methods.

	Data Req'ts	Manual Oper'n Poss.	Comp. Prog. Avail.	Comp. Run Time	Diffic. of Updating	Operator Profic. Level	Need for Outside Help
1. Mottley–Newton, 1959	L	X	X		L	T	L
2. Gargiulo et al., 1961	M	X				T	L
3. Pound, 1964	C	X				T	L
4. Sobelman, 1958	M	X					
5. Freeman, 1960	C	X				T	
6. Asher, 1962	C		X			T	
7. Hess, 1962	C		X			T	
8. Dean–Sengupta, 1962	C					T	
9. Disman, 1962	C						M
10. Cramer–Smith, 1964	M	X					M
11. Esch, "PATTERN," 1963	C		X	C	C	P	C
12. Blum, 1963	M	X			L	T	
13. Bakanas, 1964	C		X	M	L	T	
14. Dean, 1964	M	X			L	P	L
15. Hill, Roepcke, 1964	C			M	L	T	L
16. Nutt, 1965	C		X	L	L	P	C
17. Cetron, "PROFILE," 1965	L	X			L	P	M
18. Rosen–Saunder, 1965	C		X			T	
19. Sacco, 1965	C			L	L	P	L
20. Albertini, 1965	C		X	M	L	T	
21. Berman, 1965	C			C	L	T	
22. Sobin–Gordon, 1965	M		X	M	L	P	L
23. Albertini, 1965	C		X	M	L	T	L
24. Wells, 1966	M		X	L	L	P	C
25. Cetron, "QUEST," 1966	C	X			M	P	C
26. Dean–Hauser, 1966	C		X	L	L	P	L
27. Belt, 1966	M	X			M	P	L
28. De l'Estoile, 1966	C		X	C	C	P	C
29. Martino et al., 1967	C	X			M	P	C
30. Caulfield–Freshman, 1967	C	X			M	P	C

Symbol Keys

Computer Running Time
L —little
M —moderate
C —considerable
Difficulty of Updating
L —low
M —moderate
C —considerable

Need for outside help
L —little or none
M —moderate
C —considerable
Operator Proficiency
C —clerk
T —technician
P —degreed professional

Figure IX–2. Ease of Use.

	Rsch.	Expl. Devel.	Adv. Devel.	Engr. Devel.
1. Mottley–Newton, 1959	X	X	X	
2. Gargiulo et al., 1961		X	X	X
3. Pound, 1964		X	X	
4. Sobelman, 1958			X	
5. Freeman, 1960				X
6. Asher, 1962			X	X
7. Hess, 1962				X
8. Dean–Sengupta, 1962				X
9. Disman, 1962		X²	X	X
10. Cramer–Smith, 1964	X			
11. Esch. "PATTERN," 1963		X	X	X
12. Blum, 1963		X	X	X
13. Bakanas, 1964		X	X	
14. Dean, 1964		X	X	X
15. Hill–Roepcke, 1964		X	X	
16. Nutt, 1965		X	X	
17. Cetron, "PROFILE," 1965		X	X	
18. Rosen–Saunder, 1965				X
19. Sacco, 1965		X	X	
20. Albertini, 1965		X	X	
21. Berman, 1965		X	X	X
22. Sobin–Gordon, 1965	X	X	X	
23. Albertini, 1965	X			
24. Wells, 1966			X	X
25. Cetron, "QUEST," 1966	X	X		
26. Dean–Hauser, 1966		X	X	X
27. Belt, 1966		X	X	
28. De l'Estoile, 1966		X	X	X
29. Martino et al., 1967	X	X		
30. Caulfield–Freshman, 1967			X	

Figure IX–3. R&D Areas of Applicability.

moderate amount, and C for considerable amount. These evaluations are subjective, of course, but will provide some guidance as to the ease of use.

Summary

Several methods for appraisal of R&D programs have been evaluated against a set of criteria. The capabilities and limitations of each of the methods have been indicated. Each method, within its capabilities and limitations, can provide assistance to the management of an R&D enterprise in appraising the worth of its R&D effort. In particular, the use of quantitative methods tends to eliminate bias, provide a degree of consistency, and force managers to render their judgments more explicit in evaluating R&D programs. While some of the techniques described lack certain features, these usually can be added with some modification if desired.

The value of any of the appraisal methods is further limited by two factors:

a) the validity of input information supplied by the laboratory workers and management staff;

b) the effective support and use of the system by higher management. If management supports a method, and makes proper use of it, and furthermore insures that the input information is as valid as humanly possible, the methods can provide a very valuable tool for improving the management of an R&D organization.

Considering the limitations of the methods described, there is clearly much room for further refinement and improvement of quantitative methods for appraisal of R&D programs. However, even in the absence of these refined methods, the spectrum of existing methods can provide the R&D manager with considerable assistance in appraising his program.

APPENDICES

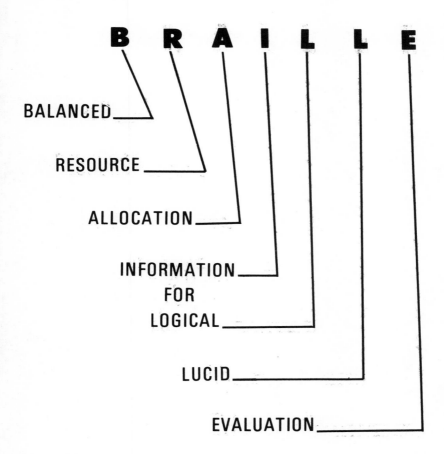

B BALANCED

R RESOURCE

A ALLOCATION

I INFORMATION
FOR
L LOGICAL

L LUCID

E EVALUATION

APPENDIX A

BRAILLE: A CASE STUDY
TO GET A "FEEL" FOR A CORPORATE RESEARCH
AND DEVELOPMENT PROGRAM

IN VARIOUS INDUSTRIES, particularly the dynamic and very competitive ones, Technological Forecasting (TF) has already become an accepted tool of management. TFs have proved to be most useful in guiding a corporation's R&D effort provided that the Forecasting outputs are properly integrated (A–1) into the company's over-all planning structure and meaningfully related to the corporate objectives. The most accurate forecast does not mean much, however, unless it is utilized and eventually influences action.

The Forecasting as such should be the primary concern of various technical specialists or even marketing production staff where appropriate. But the weighing of probabilities, at which point in time and with which level of confidence a certain technological or scientific goal might be achieved, is a task solely for the experts in the R&D department who by virtue of their expertise, competence, experience and over-all knowledge of a given field can alone provide the proper outputs. It is normally here that the Forecasting process stops and this for a number of reasons: An over-all plan within the company is not available or has not been made, company objectives are lacking, experienced transfer personnel capable of relating scientific outputs to technological needs (coupling) and marketing goals are missing, or middle management simply does not know how to utilize the Forecast.

In my contacts with various planning organizations, both in private industry and government, I have encountered an additional barrier to the utilization of technological forecasts which is perhaps the single most important reason why TFs are not used more broadly and that is, that most planning models, incorporating project selection and resources allo-

219

cation features, make use of R&D appraisal methods which are too complex, require too many data and are too time consuming and too costly to operate, yet often simple, practical models are frowned upon and not used either. All of these "resistances against introduction" seem to fit into one or two categories: either the forecast and planning procedures are too philosophical and complicated and cannot be utilized in the "real world" or they are too "simple minded," in a way not impressive enough, to be considered seriously by the decision-makers. In this latter case, the technical management feels that all that they are doing is manipulating quantitative subjective judgments as if this were technological data. I agree that this might be so, but at least such approaches structure and make visible our thinking and can greatly assist in the planning, evaluation and decision-making processes.

The literature is full of examples of appraisal techniques (A–2) that got no further than the journals they were published in for the reasons indicated above.

I wish to present here a simple but practical model, time proven and tested, which contains the basic elements necessary to arrive at meaningful decisions, does not require a model 360 computer, yet can easily expand in scope and sophistication should this be desired. This simple approach to corporate planning has been utilized by a number of small companies, various government agencies (who employ "utility" in place of "profits"), academic institutions and by the Technological Forecasting Institute, Inc., New York, New York.

For my exercise I have chosen the "Mighty Charge Corporation," a fictitious company producing various power sources.

Assume that the company has a working capital of $600,000 and with a turn-over of five times a year makes a 30% profit ($900,000 — net profit after taxes = $450,000) and has an annual R&D budget of $90,000. The company employs about 500 people and produces primary (nonrechargeable) batteries: MnO_2/Zn, mercury dry cells, etc., and secondary (rechargeable) batteries: Ni/Cd, Ag/Zn and lead-acid types.

Motivated by a desire to have both short and long term growth potential the company now plans to manufacture fuel cells (H_2/O_2, CH_4/O_2, NH_3/O_2 or some such system), and is seriously considering establishing a capability in direct thermal converters, thermo-electric, thermoionic and MHD machines. Though the company is small, management "thinks modern" as evidenced by an integrated though inexpensive planning procedure.

I am assuming that the board of directors has agreed on a number of company objectives and determined their merit, that is their relative contribution to the over-all objectives. (There may be more than the ones listed here. They are only representative samples.*)

---

* The assumptions and corporate objectives presented in this case are used for illustrative purposes in order to demonstrate the methodology and feasibility of the procedures. Figures used here were specifically changed from those of a real working concern because I wanted to prevent any similarity or associa-

Product ① (Primary Batteries) VALUE SHEET

Figure of Merit	Column I — Corporate Objectives	1.0	.9	.8	.7	.6	.5	.4	.3	.2	.1	Column III — Value to Individual Category
						Column II — Impact of Product Contribution						
12	1. Low volume, high margin									x		2.4
15	2. 10% share of total market							x				6.0
18	3. 12-15% annual growth rate								x			5.4
14	4. High versatility										x	1.4
10	5. 5 years to reach maximum profits									x		2.0
12	6. Not more than 25% Government business									x		2.4
19	7. Cash flow 6% of investment							x				7.6

Total Value (V) to Corporation   27.2

Scale of Definitions for "Impact of Product Contribution" (Column II):

1.0 Critical line or service (defensive product)

.7 Extension of existing product line(s)

.3 Improvement of current product

221

Product ② (Secondary Batteries) VALUE SHEET

Figure of Merit	Column I Corporate Objectives	Column II Impact of Product Contribution										Column III Value to Individual Category
		1.0	.9	.8	.7	.6	.5	.4	.3	.2	.1	
12	1. Low volume, high margin										x	1.2
15	2. 10% share of total market							x				6.0
18	3. 12-15% annual growth rate							x				7.2
14	4. High versatility								x			2.8
10	5. 5 years to reach maximum profits							x				4.0
12	6. Not more than 25% Government business									x		2.4
19	7. Cash flow 6% of investment									x		3.8

Total Value (V) to Corporation   27.4

Scale of Definitions for "Impact of Product Contribution" (Column II):

1.0 Critical line or service (defensive product)

.7 Extension of existing product line(s)

.3 Improvement of current product

222

Product ③ (Fuel Cells) VALUE SHEET

Figure of Merit	Column I — Corporate Objectives	Column II — Impact of Product Contribution										Column III — Value to Individual Category
		1.0	.9	.8	.7	.6	.5	.4	.3	.2	.1	
12	1. Low volume, high margin	x										12.0
15	2. 10% share of total market						x					7.5
18	3. 12-15% annual growth rate						x					9.0
14	4. High versatility			x								11.2
10	5. 5 years to reach maximum profits										x	1.0
12	6. Not more than 25% Government business			x								9.6
19	7. Cash flow 6% of investment									x		3.8

Total Value (V) to Corporation 54.1

Scale of Definitions for "Impact of Product Contribution" (Column II):

1.0 Critical line or service (defensive product)

.7 Extension of existing product line(s)

.3 Improvement of current product

223

Product ④ (Direct Thermal Conversion) VALUE SHEET

Figure of Merit	Column I Corporate Objectives	Column II — Impact of Product Contribution										Column III Value to Individual Category
		1.0	.9	.8	.7	.6	.5	.4	.3	.2	.1	
12	1. Low volume, high margin										x	1.2
15	2. 10% share of total market									x		3.0
18	3. 12-15% annual growth rate								x			5.4
14	4. High versatility		x									12.6
10	5. 5 years to reach maximum profits										x	1.0
12	6. Not more than 25% Government business									x		2.4
19	7. Cash flow 6% of investment										x	1.9

Total Value (V) to Corporation 27.5

Scale of Definitions for "Impact of Product Contribution" (Column II):

1.0 Critical line or service (defensive product)

.7 Extension of existing product line(s)

.3 Improvement of current product

224

The company wants:

Figure of Merit

12	1. To be in a low volume, high margin business.
15	2. Minimum share of the market, 10%.
18	3. An annual growth rate of 12–15%
	(7–10% over and above present 5% inflation rate).
14	4. To maintain a product of high versatility.
10	5. No more than 5 years to reach maximum profits.
12	6. No more than 25% government business.
19	7. To have a net discounted cash flow value of 6%
——	of investments.
100**	

Now that the necessary assumptions have been made and the objectives have been selected, I can proceed with the evaluation of our proposed R&D program as part of the company's systematic planning effort.

I begin with the VALUE SHEET, where the impact which each of the company's present or future products might make towards achieving the corporate objectives is assessed. The figures of merit (Column I) were already established by the board of directors and assigned on the basis of the relative importance of the various selected corporate objectives. Now a marketing or other non-technical expert evaluates and fills in Column II. He should know the corporate situation thoroughly and when making his evaluation take into consideration the descriptors at the bottom of the Value Sheet (Scale of Definitions). In some cases the three descriptions do not adequately fit the contributions; in those instances he interpolates between the numbers. For example: A new development with respect to product I (primary batteries) in this hypothetical case is considered a bit more important than "an improvement of the current product" when related to contributing toward the "10% share of total market," and is accorded 0.4 point (Column II). The figure of merit of that particular corporate objective had been assigned 15 units out of the available 100. Thus the value to this individual category is $0.4 \times 15 = 6.0$ (Column III). The other categories are similarly evaluated for their contributions and the total value of Product I to the corporation (V) is summed at 27.2. (Of course you may want to expand on the number of definitions when you adapt this model for your own planning purposes.) The expert then proceeds to do the same for the other products under consideration.

We now turn to the APPRAISAL SHEET. The top half of the appraisal sheet solicits the opinion of the technical specialist regarding the probability of achieving the technical objective that is being undertaken.

---

tion to any existing company. Such information as given here, for instance the corporate objectives, is normally proprietary and the examples selected might even be contradictory in a real business environment.
** Conveniently, the total adds up to 100. Any other figure will do, but it should then be normalized (A–3) to 100 for ease of manipulation of the data.

Product: 1 (Primary Batteries)

APPRAISAL SHEET

*Chance of Meeting Technical Objectives
with Level of Confidence* (C)

( )   80—100%

(x)   30— 80%

( )   0— 30%

Number of Different Concurrent Approaches (n)

(x) 1   ( ) 2   ( ) 3   ( ) 4   ( ) 5

( ) 6   ( ) 7   ( ) 8   ( ) 9   ( ) 10 or more

Management Environment

( ) Board of Directors   ( ) V.P. Marketing

( ) President   ( ) V.P. Production

( ) V.P. R&D   ( ) Other

Appraisal Summary

Number of Corporate Objectives: _____

Value (V): _____27.2_____

Probability of Success (Ps): _____0.5_____

Expected Value (EV): _____13.6_____

Funding (F): _____20_____ (in thousands)

Desirability Index (D): _____0.68_____

Product: 2   (Secondary Batteries)

APPRAISAL SHEET

Chance of Meeting Technical Objectives
with Level of Confidence (C)

( )   80—100%

(x)   30— 80%

( )   0— 30%

Number of Different Concurrent Approaches (n)

(x) 1   ( ) 2   ( ) 3   ( ) 4   ( ) 5

( ) 6   ( ) 7   ( ) 8   ( ) 9   ( ) 10 or more

Management Environment

( ) Board of Directors   ( ) V.P. Marketing

( ) President   ( ) V.P. Production

( ) V.P. R&D   ( ) Other

Appraisal Summary

Number of Corporate Objectives: _____

Value (V):   ____27.4____

Probability of Success (Ps): ____0.5____

Expected Value (EV): ____13.7____

Funding (F): ____25____ (in thousands)

Desirability Index (D): ____0.55____

Product: 3   (Fuel Cells)

APPRAISAL SHEET

*Chance of Meeting Technical Objectives
with Level of Confidence* (C)

( )   80—100%

(x)   30— 80%

( )   0— 30%

Number of Different Concurrent Approaches (n)

( ) 1   ( ) 2   (x) 3   ( ) 4   ( ) 5

( ) 6   ( ) 7   ( ) 8   ( ) 9   ( ) 10 or more

Management Environment

( ) Board of Directors   ( ) V.P. Marketing

( ) President   ( ) V.P. Production

( ) V.P. R&D   ( ) Other

Appraisal Summary

Number of Corporate Objectives: _____

Value (V): _____54.1_____

Probability of Success (Ps): _____0.875_____

Expected Value (EV): _____47.3_____

Funding (F): _____80_____ (in thousands)

Desirability Index (D): _____0.59_____

Product: 4   (Direct Thermal Conversion)

APPRAISAL SHEET

Chance of Meeting Technical Objectives
with Level of Confidence (C)

( )   80—100%

( )   30— 80%

(x)   0— 30%

Number of Different Concurrent Approaches (n)

(x) 1   ( ) 2   ( ) 3   ( ) 4   ( ) 5

( ) 6   ( ) 7   ( ) 8   ( ) 9   ( ) 10 or more

Management Environment

( ) Board of Directors   ( ) V.P. Marketing

( ) President   ( ) V.P. Production

( ) V.P. R&D   ( ) Other

Appraisal Summary

Number of Corporate Objectives: _____

Value (V): ____27.5____

Probability of Success (Ps): ____0.2____

Expected Value (EV): ____5.5____

Funding (F): ____30____ (in thousands)

Desirability Index (D): ____0.18____

It considers whether the task could be successfully accomplished from a scientific and technical feasibility point of view. Technical risk also takes into consideration the degree of confidence or prediction that the remaining portion of the total objective can be attained. The degree of confidence or prediction that the remaining portion of the total objective can be attained usually assesses the factors of the present state-of-the-art, either implicit or explicit. This technical appraisal is *naturally based on technical forecasts* and includes time factors and resource levels.

The credibility of the ratings of technical feasibility and the probability of success increase if they are rated by personnel who have the necessary technical expertise and competence, as they can best judge these factors on the basis of the ability and experience of the individuals and/or organizations carrying on the development efforts under consideration. Therefore a technical specialist, preferably an R&D man still working at the bench, now checks the box that best describes his opinion regarding the technical objective that is being evaluated, as well as the number of different concurrent approaches being taken which are also a measure of probability of success.

For illustrative purposes, I have appended a fuel cell forecast. The expert who made this forecast assigned a 30–80% chance of meeting the technical objective, for instance a new hydrocarbon/oxygen fuel cell (Product 3), and he will use three current approaches to achieve this goal. The appropriate spots on the Appraisal Sheet are checked.

The third area, Management Environment, solicits an opinion on the acceptability of the effort in the management structure. Here the evaluator is to give what he believes to be the management considerations concerning this effort and he checks the applicable box.

Then the Appraisal Summary is completed. For our calculation of the probability of success (P_s) of meeting the technical objectives (TO), we use the probability chart shown in Table I.

In this chart, n is the number of concurrent approaches used to accomplish the TO, and C is a number arbitrarily assigned to the chances of succeeding in a given approach. We use:

$$80\text{–}100\% \text{ chance of success: } C = 0.8$$
$$30\text{–} 80\% \text{ chance of success: } C = 0.5$$
$$0\text{–} 3\% \text{ chance of success: } C = 0.2$$

We assume that all approaches n have the same chance of success, and therefore the same value of C.

The number assigned to the probability of one approach failing is then $(1 - C)$.

The number assigned to the probability of all approaches failing is $(1 - C)^n$.

For success in achieving the technological objective, it is only necessary that at least one approach succeed. This failure only occurs if *all* the approaches fail. The chance of failure of any one approach is $1 - C$. The chance that all approaches fail is $(1 - C_1)(1 - C_2)(1 - C_3)$ ... etc. Hence the chance that not all the approaches fail, that is success, is $1 - (1 - C_1)(1 - C_2)(1 - C_3)$ ... etc.

If all the approaches have an equal chance of success, this formula reduces to $1 - (1 - C)^n$ for n approaches.

Example: We have four approaches, n_1 to n_4. The chances of success are:

$$C \text{ of } n_1 \qquad C_1 = 0.5$$
$$C \text{ of } n_2 \qquad C_2 = 0.2$$
$$C \text{ of } n_3 \qquad C_3 = 0.5$$
$$C \text{ of } n_4 \qquad C_4 = 0.8$$

$$P_s = 1 - (0.5)(0.8)(0.5)(0.2) = 0.960$$

For convenience values of P_s for several n have been calculated and are tabulated in Table 1 (all n approaches have equal probability of success).

TABLE I

n	C = 0.8	0.5	0.2
1	0.80000	0.50000	0.20000
2	0.96000	0.75000	0.36000
3	0.99200	0.87500	0.48800
4	0.99840	0.93750	0.59040
5	0.99968	0.96875	0.67230
6	0.99994	0.98438	0.73786
7	0.99999	0.99219	0.79029
8	0.99999	0.99609	0.83223
9	0.99999	0.99805	0.86578
10	0.99999	0.99902	0.89263

Now back to our Appraisal Summary. The probability of success (P_s) is multiplied with the value (V) from the Value Sheet to get the expected value EV. Thus for Product 3 we obtain: $V \times P_s = EV$ or $54.1 \times 0.875 = 47.3$. Completion of this project is estimated to require a funding of $-80,000$ or $F = 80$. The desirability index (D) is then calculated by dividing the expected value (EV) by the funding level (F): $\frac{EV}{F} = D$ or $\frac{47.3}{80} = 0.59$.

We carry out these same calculations for the other products and can then rank our projects according to their desirability index for instance and can use that as a basis for our decisions (or we can use the EV's or other factors for the same purpose).

These techniques are intended, not to yield decisions, but rather to furnish information which will facilitate making decisions. Indeed these techniques are merely thinking structures to force methodical, meticulous analysis. The *data* plus the *analysis* only gave us *information*. It takes this *information* plus *judgment* to render the *decisions*.

In our particular case, corporate management decided to only pursue R&D work for Product 1, 2, and 3, and to drop 4. The research deficit was to be made up by seeking government support for the fuel cell venture.

Conclusions:

Certainly this result is unlike the output of a linear programming model which one might want to utilize if there were more products and R&D programs to be considered, more than 100 let us say, but I wish to stress the point that in my opinion, management decisions should be made by managers and not by a system, not even a highly sophisticated computerized system. There are places where operational research techniques (A–4) are not only desirable but required, but in the case of R&D management, a maximum amount of flexibility must be retained and freedom of decision is the manager's prerogative. This is absolutely essential if the decision-maker is not only to be given responsibility, but also to be held accountable for the work under his control.

FUEL CELL FORECAST*

A. BACKGROUND

A fuel cell is a direct energy converter which produces electrical energy by electrochemically combining a fuel and oxidant. The basic components of a single fuel cell are two electrodes and an electrolyte. Fuel is oxidized at one electrode with the release of elctrons to an external circuit to do useful work. Electrons are returned to the other electrode where the oxidant is reduced. The electrical circuit is completed with the transport of ions across the electrolyte. A practical fuel cell battery consists of a number of these individual cells in an appropriate electrical array, together with the necessary structural supports, fuel, oxidant, electrolyte, coolant and electrical current distribution components.

There are several characteristics of fuel cells which make them attractive for a variety of applications. Some of the unique features are:

—High Efficiency—Fuel cells are not subject to Carnot-cycle limitations and thus are more efficient than other energy conversion systems Over-all thermal efficiencies greater than 50% are presently obtainable.

—Low Noise—Like conventional primary or secondary batteries, fuel cells are inherently quiet because of the lack of moving parts. This makes them attractive for submarine applications.

—High-Overload Capability—Fuel cells can operate at power outputs

---

* This forecast is for illustrative purposes only.

several times the normal rated power for several hours without significantly reducing the lifetime of the system.

B. CURRENT STATUS

The concept of a fuel cell, and the first laboratory demonstration model, date back to the early 19th century. Improvements through research and development in the United States and elsewhere over the past five years have advanced fuel cell technology to the stage where engineering development of power plant systems appears technically and economically feasible for many different applications. The several fuel cells which have reached this state of development use fuels such as hydrocarbons (including alcohols), hydrogen, ammonia, and hydrazine. Oxygen is the common oxidant whether it is supplied from a cryogenic tank, by dissociation of hydrogen peroxide or from atmospheric air. The reliability of such systems has been demonstrated again during the recent perfect flight around the moon by Apollo 8. The spaceship used H_2/O_2 fuel cells as a power source.

Hydrocarbon Fuel Cell Systems—From the standpoint of fuel costs, fuel logistics and ease of handling, fuel cells operating on liquid hydrocarbon fuels are the most attractive for a large number of applications. Systems under development include indirect systems in which the hydrocarbon fuel is reformed to produce hydrogen either in an external reformer or in an internal reformer using the fuel cell excess heat to support the endothermic reforming reaction, and direct systems for the direct electro-chemical oxidation of the hydrocarbon fuel at the fuel cell electrode. An advanced hydrocarbon fuel cell system is shown schematically in Figure 1. The principal subsystems of this power plant are the hydrogen reformer and fuel cell battery. The reformer generates hydrogen from a hydrocarbon fuel. After purification, the hydrogen reacts electrochemically with the oxidant in the fuel cells.

The hydrogen-oxygen (H_2–O_2) fuel cells for this system are more advanced in their development than any other type. The space program provided the major impetus for engineering development of H_2–O_2 fuel

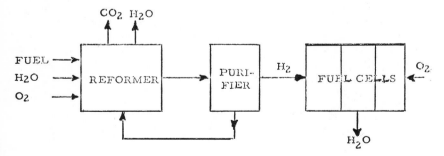

Figure 1.

cells. Naturally, the fuel cell concepts associated with this well-funded effort have more established capabilities. A well-developed technological base has been established by the space programs which will be applicable to many other future developments.

The following paragraphs provide state-of-the-art data on the three principal versions of H_2–O_2 fuel cells are distinguished by the type or condition of the electrolyte employed. These are:

1. Ion-exchange Membrane Electrolytes
2. Free Electrolytes
3. Fixed Electrolytes

1. *Ion-Exchange Membrane System*—The fuel cells for the Gemini space-craft were of the ion-exchange-membrane (IEM) type. These cells con-sisted of an organic cation exchange membrane as the electrolyte with electrodes made of teflon-bonded-platinum deposited on a very thin, fine mesh tantalumpalladium screen. The fuel cell electrode power density was about 28 watts per square foot. Power density for Gemini fuel cell modules was about 0.6 kw per cubic foot at normal rated load and about 1.6 kw per cubic foot at peak overload conditions.

Further improvements in the IEM cell are in the development stage. Reduced-catalyst-loading cells (5 to 10 gm per sq ft) have operated for 3,000 hours and reportedly have polarization characteristics similar to the higher-catalyst-loading cells. Present cell production facilities can pro-duce cells as large as 17 in. by 72 in.; Gemini cells were 8 in. by 8 in. A 1-to-1 polarization characteristics ratio has been demonstrated in a scale-up to an 11 in. by 22 in. electrode.

2. *Free Electrolyte Systems*—There are two main types of free electrolyte fuel cell systems presently in engineering development, i.e., the moderate-temperature, low-pressure, modified-Bacon system and the low-tempera-ture, low-pressure, thin-carbon-electrode system.

a. *Modified-Bacon Cells*—As the power source for the Apollo Com-mand and Service Module, this fuel cell system was the beneficiary of the largest effort that has been expended in fuel cell development. The modi-fied-Bacon cell has the highest efficiency of any known H_2–O_2 fuel cell at a given current density due to the higher operating temperatures.

Unfortunately, these high fuel-cell efficiencies do not come without penalty. To operate at temperatures in the range of 400°F at three or four atmospheres pressure requires about 80% potassium hydroxide (KOH), which is solid at room temperature. Hence, one problem is the start-up and shut-down of modules. Also, the mechanical stresses, due to the unavoidable phase changes during repeated start-up and shut-down may further reduce reliability. Another problem, resulting from operation at these higher temperatures, is cathode corrosion.

b. *Low-Temperature Free-Electrolyte Systems*—Two versions of this system have been under development. The earliest of ·these employed catalyzed, ¼ in. thick, baked carbon electrodes and a 25% KOH electro-lyte. Laboratory-model systems up to 30 kw have been built. The elec-trodes currently used consist of a 0.030 inch nickel plaque to which is applied a carbon layer and 1 to 2 gm of precious metal catalyst per square foot. This system has operated at about 150°F with a circulating 12 Normal KOH electrolyte. The guaranteed performance characteristics of these power plant modules are depicted in Figures 2 and 3.

The compactness of the design and the low electrode cost suggested by the low-catalyst loading are attractive features of the thin-carbon electrode. A circulating electrolyte also has many advantages. The principal ones are:

—Greater latitude in the dynamics of control of termal energy and by-product water removal,
—Better temperature uniformity,
—Thermal energy removal at its origin, and
—Compact module construction.

3. *Fixed Electrolyte Systems*—Several fuel cell systems presently undergoing development use an immobilized, aqueous KOH electrolyte in a

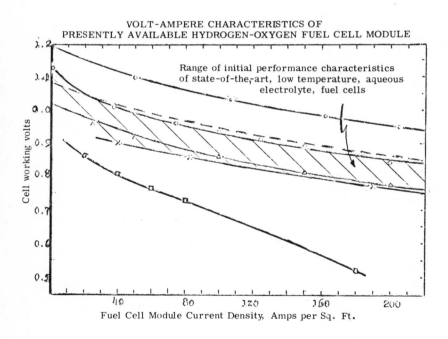

Figure 2.

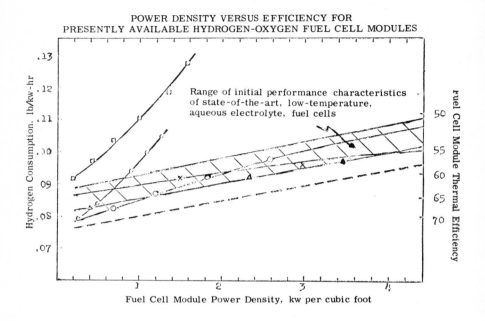

Figure 3.

0.020 to 0.030 in. thick asbestos membrane. The major differences between the systems are the types of electrodes used and the method of by-product water removal. They have been called "static-moisture-systems" because they do not require circulation of the reactant gases. Removal of the by-product water is accomplished by diffusion across the individual-cell hydrogen gas cavity where it is removed from the system.

Improvements over the performance represented in the curves (Figures 2 and 3) have reportedly been achieved in recently delivered 2 kw power plants which operated at 100 amps per sq ft for 1,800 hours to a 10% degradation in terminal voltage. Some of these higher performance plants have used teflon-bonded-platinum screen electrodes.

Another fuel cell which uses an immobilized KOH electrolyte in a thin asbestos membrane is being developed for the use of precious-metal, catalyzed screen electrodes. Catalyst loadings have been nominally 16.5 gm per sq ft cell with platinum as the primary constituent. Product water removal is accomplished by condensation from recirculating reactant gases. Heat removal has been achieved with a circulating coolant or circulating electrolyte.

Development of this fuel cell system is being pursued in several places. Single cell tests have shown power degradation rates of 2 to 3% per 1,000 hours up to present test durations of about 2,000 hours. Power plants in the nominal 1 kw range have been built for industrial customer evaluation.

Performance characteristics of fuel cell modules based on estimates from developmental-model "compact cell" units are also plotted in Figures 2 and 3.

Pilot plant production facilities have been developed for teflon-bonded-platinum screen electrodes which have a catalyst loading of 43 gm per sq ft. These electrodes have been tested at 100°C, 50% KOH in 0.020 in fuel cell asbestos, and atmospheric pressure reactant gases. Polarization data from these tests are plotted in Figure 3. The volt-ampere characteristics of these high-performance electrodes were incorporated into an engineered module configuration which uses physically identical electrodes (in a fixed electrolyte design) to provide an "optimistic" estimate of fuel cell power density and efficiency that might be produced by present technology. The results of this analysis are shown as a dashed line in Figure 3.

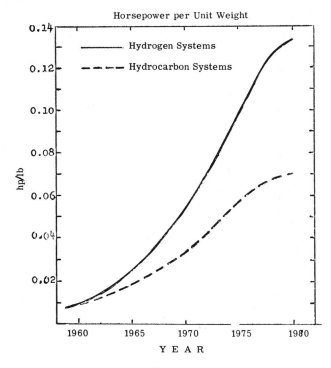

Figure 4.

Performance Summary—The range of initial performance characteristics, in terms of power density and efficiency, for low-temperature, low-
pressure, aqueous electrolyte fuel cells is indicated by a cross-hatched
band in Figures 2 and 3. Rather than attempt to relate a single point of
performance for a specific fuel cell to a given application, it is deemed
more appropriate to consider this range of capabilities as representative
of the technological base from which the development of other fuel cell
power plants must emanate.

Reliability Summary—The performance spectrum of present low-
temperature, H_2–O_2 fuel cells, as depicted in Figures 2 and 3, does not
consider the reliability aspects of the various fuel cell systems operating
at these power densities. A summary of the more pertinent reliability
information available on the various fuel cells is given in the following
paragraphs:

—Thin-Carbon Electrode System—A lifetime of 10,000 hours mean
time before failure (MTBF) is possible for cell modules of 0.375
sq ft thin carbon electrodes based on 50 amps per sq ft. This 8-cell
stack lifetime is being structured into nominal 1 kw modules to provide a quoted module reliability of 0.989 for the 1,000 hour guaranteed performance period.

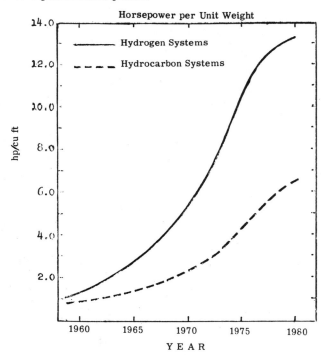

Figure 5.

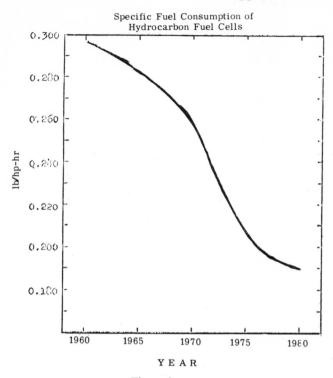

Specific Fuel Consumption of
Hydrocarbon Fuel Cells

Figure 6.

—Fixed Electrolyte Cell—Lifetimes of 2,000 hours have been obtained
on recently built breadboard systems operating at 100 amps per
sq ft. Single cells using the latest 9 mg catalyst per sq cm electrodes
show power degradation rates of 2 to 3% per 1,000 hours up to
the present 1,800 hours on test. A 2.0 kw module using these
electrodes and rated at 19 lb per kw showed no statistically significant degradation in the 100 hours acceptance test.
—Apollo—Production-model 2 kw power plant systems are now
qualified for the Apollo mission power profile of 1,500 hours.
NASA expects the lifetime to be improved to 2,000 hours.
—Ion-Exchange Membrane—Life data available on the Gemini production-model power plants show spacecraft power profile lifetimes ranging from 300 to greater than 1,000 hours.

The above life data summary is, for the most part, based on operation at relatively high current densities (100 amps per sq ft and higher)
that are dictated by a need for low-weight fuel cells in short mission space
applications. Contrast this with missions to 60 days which may be considered for certain other fuel cell applications. If it is assumed that 100
watts per sq ft is the maximum electrode power density required at the

high power operation, then the average power density over a typical 60 day mission is about 15 watts per sq ft. There is no incentive to make the average electrode power density higher by designing for higher power density at peak load because tradeoff studies indicate that the electrode power density should be in this range to achieve minimum total weight and volume. In reliability investigations it was determined that for a constant current density on the cells, the voltage degradation per unit time is proportional to the square of the current density.

One source indicates that their fuel cell voltage degradation rate with time is probably more nearly proportional to current density. Taking the more conservative estimates indicates that operation of fuel cells, in the range of 15 to 25 watts per sq ft, will probably improve the lifetime by a factor of 3 or 4 over the 50 to 100 watts per sq ft operation of current fuel cells.

C. FORECAST OF FUTURE STATE-OF-THE-ART

The projected capabilities of various fuel cell systems are portrayed graphically in Figures 4 through 9. These projected capabilities do not necessarily represent an evolutionary improvement along a time-proven-trend curve, such as the projections for conventional thermal power plant systems. These projections are based largely on engineering judgment and

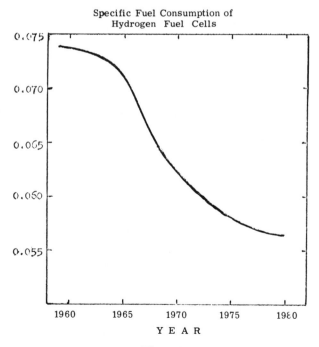

Figure 7.

TYPE LIFE

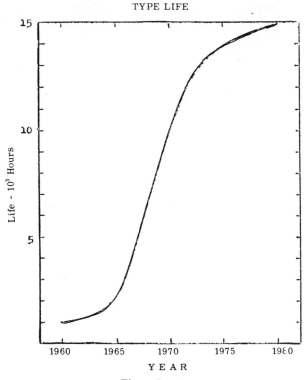

Figure 8.

studies of the limited amount of engineering systems data available in present fuel cell technology. The projected capabilities indicated are believed to be technically feasible if the necessary resources are allocated. Available resources may permit the realization of selected capabilities within the time periods indicated. The chance of meeting the technical objectives outlined is estimated to be 30–80%.

The general pattern and time schedule of development, initial application and evolutionary improvement to provide the capabilities indicated are as follows:

—1966–1970—Exploratory and advanced development of prototype systems using low temperature H_2O_2 fuel cells supplied by hydrocarbon fuel reformers and cyrogenic fuel and oxidant storage systems.
　　　　　—Exploratory development of moderate temperature, direct hydrocarbon oxidation systems.
　　　　　—Research on high and low temperature, direct hydrocarbon oxidation systems.

COSTS

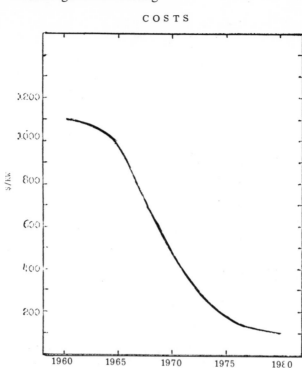

Figure 9.

—1970–1975—Engineering improvement of low temperature indirect
hydrocarbon and cryogenic fuel systems to improve
power density, increase life, and lower cost.
—Initial engineering development and application of
moderate temperature indirect hydrocarbon systems.
—Initial application of low temperature, high pressure
systems.
—Exploratory development of direct hydrocarbon fuel
oxidation systems.
—1975–1980—Engineering improvement of moderate temperature,
low pressure systems and low temperature, high pressure systems.
—Initial application of low and high temperature, direct
hydrocarbon fuel oxidation systems.

REFERENCES
1. Using Technical Forecasts, by M. J. Cetron, Science and Technology, July
1968

2. The Selection of R&D Program Content—Survey of Quantitative Methods, by M. J. Cetron, J. Martino and L. Roepcke, IEEE Transactions on Engineering Management, Vol. EM–14, No. 1, March 1967
3. PROFILE, M. J. Cetron in Technological Forecasting in Perspective by Erich Jantsch, OECD, Paris 1967, pp. 228–229
4. An Evaluation and Appraisal of Various Approaches to Technological Forecasting, M. J. Cetron and T. I. Monhan in Technological Forecasting for Industry on Government, J. R. Bright, Editor, Prentice Hall, Inc., 1968, pp. 144–179

"A new truth does not triumph by convincing its opponents and making them see the light, but rather because its opponents eventually die, and a new generation grows up that is familiar with it." — MAX PLANCK

APPENDIX B

EXPLORATORY AND NORMATIVE TECHNOLOGICAL FORECASTING: A CRITICAL APPRAISAL

DR. EDWARD B. ROBERTS
Associate Professor of Management
Alfred P. Sloan School of Management
Massachusetts Institute of Technology

Abstract

Comparison of the still evolving approaches to "exploratory" and "normative" technological forecasting yields marked contrasts. In particular the simple schemes used by those trying to *predict* the technology of the future look pallid when matched against the sophisticated techniques designed by those who are allocating the resources that will *create* the future. Exploratory technological forecasts are largely based either on aggregates of "genius" forecasts (e.g., the Delphi technique) or on the use of leading indicators and other simple trend-line approaches. The practitioners of economic forecasting, in contrast, long ago recognized the need for multi-variate systems analysis and cause-effect models to develop reliable predictions.

Normative forecasting is at the opposite extreme on the sophistication scale, fully utilizing Bayesian statistics, linear and dynamic programming, and other operations research tools. Here, despite the uniqueness, uncertainty, and lack of uniformity of research and development activities, each of the designers of normative techniques has proposed a single-format wholly quantitative method for resource allocation. Along the dimensions of unjustified standardization and needless complexity, for example, the proposed R&D allocation methods far exceed the general cost-effectiveness approach used by the Department of Defense in its program and system reviews.

For both exploratory and normative purposes, dynamic models of broad technological areas seem worthy of further pursuit. In attempting to develop "pure predictions" the explicit recognition of causal mechanisms offered by this modeling approach seems highly desirable. This feature also has normative utility, provided that the dynamic models are limited in their application to the level of aggregate technological resource

245

allocation and are not carried down to the level of detailed R&D project funding.

On Technological Forecasting

Increased recognition during the present decade of the importance of science and technology to corporate and national existence has produced an intensive search for new methods for managing research and development. The attention being devoted to so-called "technological forecasting" is one manifestation of this concern.

"Technological forecasting," as defined by those claiming to be its practitioners, is actually two fields, joined more by a vision than a reality. On the one hand is "exploratory forecasting," the attempt to predict the technological state-of-the-art that will or might be in the future, or as Cetron puts it, ". . . a prediction with a level of confidence of a technical achievement in a given time frame with a specified level of support."[1] Most laymen assume that all of "forecasting" is this kind of forecasting. The second aspect has been called "normative forecasting"[2] and includes the organized attempts to allocate on a rational basis the money, manpower, and other resources that might effect the creation of tomorrow's technological state-of-the-art. Normative forecasting presumably provides aids to budgetary decisions in the technological area. Still more broadly defined by some of its leading exponents, "normative forecasting" applies to a wide variety of attempts to determine policies and decisions that will influence the effective growth of science and technology, in the corporation, the government agency, or the nation as a whole.

There is no doubt that both kinds of "forecasting" are necessary contributors to the technical planning process. And for the military as well as for most corporations this technical input is a critical ingredient of an overall business plan. Yet only in theory but not in fact have these two components, the exploratory and the normative, been integrated adequately. In his milestone book on the subject, Erich Jantsch expresses the logic of and the need for this integration: *"Exploratory technological forecasting* starts from today's assured basis of knowledge and is oriented towards the future, while *normative technological forecasting* first assesses future goals, needs, desires, missions, etc., and works backward to the present . . . The full potential of technological forecasting is realized only where *exploratory and normative components* are joined in an iterative or, ultimately, in a feedback cycle."[3]

This paper presents a critical appraisal of the field of technological forecasting. The central theme is that the two phases of exploratory and normative approaches are out of step with each other. Exploratory techniques are too naive and do not take advantage of what has been learned about forecasting in non-technical areas. Nor do the exploratory techniques reflect what is known about the influences upon the generation of future technology. Normative techniques in contrast are too complex and mathematically sophisticated and cannot justify their elegance on substantive grounds.

If "the full potential of technological forecasting" is to be realized, a more harmonious relationship must be established between the exploratory and normative parts. Dynamic systems models of broad technological areas, stressing the feedback relations that affect the growth of science and technology, demonstrate promise of providing a basis for that harmony. Such models have already been developed in prototype form, addressed to a number of problems of interest to technological forecasters. Their further development is dependent upon the availability of skilled manpower and necessary funding.

An Appraisal of Exploratory Technological Forecasting

Exploratory technological forecasting includes a variety of techniques for predicting the future state of science and technology. Unfortunately most of the methods are really only variants on simple trend extrapolation procedures, broadly defined, that have limited utility in today's rapidly shifting technological environment. The principal exploratory methods are:

(1) so-called "genius" forecasting, based either on individual wisdom or on a group "genius" forecasting process known as the Delphi technique; and

(2) formal trend extrapolation to either a straight-line fit or an S-shaped expectation.

The formal trend methods include single-curve projections as well as estimations based on the envelope encompassed by the projection of a family of related curves. They also include both the extrapolation of a single time series as well as the projection of lead-lag relationships between two time series, the latter known as "precursive event" forecasting.

INTUITIVE TREND FORECASTS

In theory technological forecasting is not supposed to be able to foretell the "major breakthrough." In fact this is one of few ways in which intuitive hunches or guesses might provide service. Occasionally, but unpredictably, the brilliant scientist (or the perceptive marketeer, or the starry-eyed science fiction writer) may predict the future as different from a mere extension of the past. But more usually individual wisdom-based forecasting works on the rule that "past is prologue." Trend extrapolation thus becomes the simple kind of model that the unaided mind can manipulate intuitively.

With the promotional boost of The RAND Corporation's sponsorship, the hunches of individual "experts" have been coaxed and guided in an iterative group forecasting procedure known as the "Delphi method."[4] This Delphic oracle procedure assumes that collective (and normalized) wisdom is better than individual "guesstimates," although recent behavioral research plus the mythology regarding Delphi itself question this assumption. In using the Delphi approach a panel of experts is solicited for their opinions on the future technology in a specified area. Assembled opinions thus gathered are redistributed to the panel for a series of reassessments during which criticisms and defenses of extreme forecasts are also obtained and communicated. The end result tends to be a more polarized and justified range of future estimates than were originally gathered. Thus the collective "ballpark guesses" of the experts are refined and legitimized. It is interesting to speculate whether a Delphic sampling of the appropriate whiz kids would have predicted an effective intercontinental ballistic missile when Vannevar Bush failed in his prophecy! Would Delphi have done better than Lindemann in his lack of foreseeing the German V-2 rockets? Is there sufficient evidence to believe that the Delphic search for concensus produces more "truthful" forecasts than a comparable assemblage of individual genius forecasts?

Formal Trend Forecasts

Those who lack the wisdom demanded by genius forecasting (perhaps in reality they possess the wisdom needed to appreciate the weaknesses of the intuitive methods!) have adopted formal procedures for translating the events of the past into the predictions of the future. Data on the time-history of some parameter of technological progress (e.g., tensile strength of materials, engine thrust per lb. of fuel) are plotted against time on linear or logarithmic scales. Using "eyeball" extrapolation, or statistical "best fit" procedures, a growth-of-technology line is drawn through the data points and extended into the future. An assumption of technology saturation effects produces the biological growth pattern with its S-shaped curves; an assumption of no saturation leads merely to longer straight lines. Poor fit of the data to a single line suggests the need for alternative technological projections, and often leads to a forecast of an envelope of possible technological states. When two sets of these progress parameter curves appear to be correlated, with one curve consistently leading the other in time (e.g., the speed of bombers versus commercial transports), similar trend extrapolations are applied. In this case, the process is referred to as forecasting by the analysis of precursive events.

The trend extrapolations, both intuitive and formal, fail to state explicitly their underlying assumptions. As Jantsch points out, ". . . the simple extrapolation of secular trends does contain one analytical element —the intuitive expectation that the combined effect of internal and external factors which produced a trend over a past period will remain the same during a future period, or that it will undergo an estimated gradual change."[5] Yet the changes occurring in numerous areas of technology deny the validity of these stability-oriented assumptions.

THE EXPERIENCES OF ECONOMIC FORECASTING

Rather than continue to berate the undeveloped state of exploratory forecasting it appears wiser to apply the forecasters' own tools. The development of exploratory forecasting techniques seems to be following the path previously taken by economic forecasting (in a precursive event relationship). A review of the parallels involved indicates that exploratory forecasting can advance more rapidly by skipping some of the developments that occurred in economic forecasting.

Economic forecasting is now beginning its fifth stage of development, with an obvious sixth stage just over the horizon. These stages of evolution are:

(1) wisdom, expert or genius forecasting;
(2) "naive" models;
(3) simple correlative forecasting models;
(4) complex multi-variate econometric forecasts;
(5) dynamic causally-oriented models; and
(6) learning models.

Expert Forecasts

The first stage of development of economic forecasting was the intuitive judgmental expert forecast. Perceptive economists, applying their mental models to analyses of economic factors, predicted future economic performance, often with excellent foresight. This nonquantitative "genius" stage has been (and still is being) paralleled in the technological field.

"Naive" Forecasting Models

As economists began applying quantitative techniques to economic forecasting, so-called "naive" models came to the front. The most naive forecasts are the "same level" and the "same trend" predictions. The "same level" model assumes that next year will be the same, economically, as this year. The "same trend" forecast says that the economic trend from this year to next will be the same as from last year to this one. Economists themselves have labelled these approaches as "naive," yet technological forecasters are using them almost exclusively. (The use of S-shaped curves and log scales by technical forecasters merely reflects their higher mathe-mathematical training relative to their earlier economic counterparts.)

Simple Correlative Models

In the third stage of development of economic forecasting two or three variables were interrelated by statistical correlation (or just by charts) to forecast economic behavior. The use of "leading" economic indicators is the simplest representation of this phase of forecasting and is replicated in technological forecasting by precursive event forecasts. Recent work by Mansfield in predicting the rate of diffusion of technological innovations indicates that exploratory technological forecasting is now in this third stage.[6]

Complex Multi-variate Econometric Forecasting

The great growth of quantitative economics accompanied its movement into large-scale multi-variate statistical models for explaining and predicting economic performance. No longer were the models simple or naive, and the computer quickly found an important role in implementing the needed calculations. (Input-output models of the economy can be associated with this fourth stage of evolution.) But the models were not usually causally-oriented; rather the "best fit" criterion, applied to tests on past data, was the primary measure of acceptability. It is not surprising, therefore, that these complex but non-causal forecasting models usually performed no more accurately than did simpler models and naive forecasts. Nor even have they consistently outperformed the "expert" forecasts of the business economists. Although technological forecasting has not yet moved openly into this fourth phase, it is likely to do so soon unless effectively urged in other directions.

Dynamic Causally-oriented Forecasting

Recently a change has begun to show up in the style and structure of economic forecasting models. The model-builders have attempted to include more a priori causal structuring, mixed linear and nonlinear relationships are being represented, feedback phenomena are included in the models, and dynamic computer simulation is being used to project economic forecasts.[7]

Moreover, this new type of economic forecasting model has the unique feature of coupling exploratory and normative purposes in a consistent manner. Not only can the models be initialized with present and historical inputs to project the future economy, but simulated tests can be run using proposed normative changes in policies and parameters. Contemplated resource allocations, for example, are thus fed into the "exploratory" model to project anticipated consequences, and these in turn suggest alternatives to the proposed allocations. This type of iteration between exploratory forecasts and normative recommendations has been proposed as the ultimate for technological forecasting.[8]

As shall be pointed out in the last section of this paper, much work has already been done along similar lines in technology-related areas. But the review of literature recognizes only the contributions of Lenz to the dynamic modelling phase of exploratory forecasting and views his work, unfortunately, as "hardly useful for any practical purpose."[9] Until this work and related dynamic models are indeed recognized for their potential, exploratory forecasting will stall in its third stage of development or waste itself needlessly in the unproductive fourth stage it is about to enter.

Learning Models

The next logical stage of development for economic forecasting is the creation of learning models. These would be structured similar to those used in stage five, but they would be paired with real-time data collection and data interpretation systems. The combination, monitored by computer routines for analyzing model adequacy, would permit parameter and possibly even structural changes in the forecasting model based upon experienced model and economy performance. But no serious activity is yet underway in this stage in either the economic or the technological forecasting area.

This review of exploratory forecasting has concluded that pathetically simple methods are being used to predict what technology will be in the future. The techniques parallel an earlier stage of growth of economic forecasting, and as yet have not recognized the importance of causal dynamic models. Jantsch seems to agree with this condemnation of exploratory forecasting's underdevelopment: ". . . no model has so far succeeded in taking into account more than a limited number of influencing factors by assuming relationships that are generally unproved or not known in detail, and mathematical formulations do not yet include even all of these recognized factors."[10]

The empirical "research on research" of the past decade has now produced an impressive basis of understandings of the influences on scientific and technological progress.[11] Surely it is important to begin embodying these findings into the development of improved exploratory models.

An Appraisal of Normative Technological Forecasting

Normative technological forecasting activities attempt to provide a basis for allocating technology-generating resources so as to maximize attainment of organizational goals. The effectiveness of any normative method depends upon:

(1) the meaningfulness of its treatment of goals;
(2) the correctness of its assumed relationships between allocated resources and generated technology;
(3) the adequacy of its balancing of the resources-to-technology considerations against the worth of goal fulfillment; and
(4) the implementability of the method, including the ability to acquire reasonable inputs at reasonable costs as well as the ability to persuade organizational decision-makers to use the generated outputs.

Most of the effort in the development of normative forecasting techniques has gone into items 1 and 3 above. The expression of goals, the establishment of values for them, the accounting for the conflicting interests of various groups, are primary questions debated by the designers of normative forecasting methods. The techniques for manipulating the resources being allocated against these assumed values are also many and varied, ranging from simple linear and dynamic programming to elaborate embodiments of Bayesian analyses and Monte Carlo techniques. And these techniques are under continuing refinement, with accompanying developments of the computer software needed for the desired calculations. These areas can be left to others to criticize.

Yet items 2 and 4 above have been largely ignored. Little effort has been devoted to making the forecasting techniques practicable or believable by the manager. The most sophisticated, perhaps even the best, normative approach requires thousands of estimate inputs for every use. Moreover, the assumed relationships between allocated resources and generated technological outputs are seldom even explicitly identified in the normative techniques. Usually, the forecasts receive as inputs the estimates of the technical outputs that would be produced by various funding levels. In other words, in most cases no exploratory forecasting techniques is used to generate the basis for normative manipulations! The assumed technical outputs are guesses only.

TECHNICAL OUTPUT GENERATION

Let me treat first the question of how technical outputs are handled in normative forecasting. If resources are to be deployed wisely by a company, a government agency, or a nation, that deployment should be based upon the best understandings available of the likely results of the use of those resources. The area of exploratory forecasting is devoted to a search for and an expression of these understandings. But the exploratory forecasters have made little impact on their normative brethren. An examination of the leading normative forecasting techniques demonstrates this failing.

Profile

PROFILE (Programmed Functional Indices for Laboratory Evaluation), developed by Marvin J. Cetron for the U.S. Navy, is among the better known methods for resource allocation in R&D.[12] PROFILE uses three basic criteria—Military Utility, Technical Feasibility, and Application of Resources—plus a fourth criterion, Intrinsic Value to the Laboratory, which acts as a "fudge factor" to influence the final weighted index that is developed.

In his PROFILE paper Cetron asserts, "Research and development tasks become more technically feasible if they are being executed by personnel who have the necessary expertise, have confidence in the successful completion of the task and recognize the benefits to other applications."[13] This is an interesting albeit empirically unsubstantiated theory of the technology generation process. The theory is interpreted in PROFILE by criteria for Applicability to Long Range Plan and Mission, Probability for Achieving Task Objective, and Technological Transfer. Of the three only the "probability of achievement" estimate is related to a forecast of anticipated technological output, and that is a single-valued "genius" forecast, produced generally by a "non-genius." The fact that the man who must do the work is usually the estimator as well raises further questions as to the meaningfulness of the input. The "applicability" measure assesses *value* of the output's contribution to lab objectives generally, while "technological transfer" identifies output *value* in terms of possible contributions to other technical tasks. These estimates are hardly related to the likelihood of future technology being generated, yet PROFILE misuses them in this fashion.

PROFILE's Application of Resources sector treats availability of manpower, facilities, and funding for the R&D project being contemplated. Yet this treatment mixes considerations of factors that might be included in a model of technology generation with project cost considerations. And, of course, all of these are weighted in PROFILE as if they are measures of value, and added in a linear combination of factors. The failure to appreciate the difference between worth of an outcome, the influences upon the attainment of that outcome, and the cost of the outcome thus characterizes the PROFILE approach. Most critical is that the explicit "exploratory" forecast is limited to a "hunch" probability estimate by the staff member filling out the PROFILE forms.

Quest

What PROFILE is designed to do for an individual laboratory, the QUEST system (Quantitative Utility Estimates for Science and Technology), developed by Cetron, is supposed to do for the entire Navy R&D program.[14] The complexity of QUEST's matrices of Value of Technology to Missions and Relevance of Science to Technology illustrates the heavy emphasis placed upon the valuing procedure. The technology generation procedure, however, is largely ignored by QUEST. In its examination of the contribution of a technical effort to a given mission, "the assumption is that the objective of the technical effort will be accomplished."[15] In its evaluation of the relevance of each science area to each technology area, a subjective single-value estimate is assigned by the forms-filling engineer and researcher to describe the essentiality of the science to the technology. These estimates range from 0, "the technology does not draw on this science at all," to 10, "no progress is possible in this technology without vigorously pursuing this science." This estimate is hardly what would be described as an elaborate exploratory forecasting method.

Pattern

PATTERN (Planning Assistance Through Technical Evaluation of Relevance Numbers), developed by Honeywell's Military and Space Sciences Department, is perhaps the most extensive and expensive normative forecasting technique in use.[16] Yet PATTERN's sophistication is largely concentrated in its allocation methodology, as opposed to its generation of exploratory forecasts. Primarily "genius" forecasting, trend extrapolation and envelope curves are employed to predict the possible technical state of the art, and resource allocations are not fed back to affect technological developments. In particular, the key exploratory forecast embodied in PATTERN is someone's estimate of the number of years that a system in question will remain in each of several sequential stages of advancement. The stages considered are: research, exploratory development, advanced development, product design, and availability This series of timing estimates is a rather modest recognition of exploratory forecasting capabilities.

Probe

Finally, an examination of TRW's Probe II approach further indicates the conflict between simple exploratory forecasting and elaborate normative procedures.[17] Based on a modified Delphi technique, TRW determines Desirability, Feasibility, and Timing of each forecast event. Then to determine appropriate corporate response, SOON (Sequence of Opportunities and Negatives) charts, similar to PERT networks, are prepared to demonstrate the details of specific accomplishments that will be needed to realize the forecast event. Apparently no one is concerned (at least, not in print) that collective wisdom alone produces the exploratory forecasts whereas detailed R&D planning is the basis of the normative reaction.

Investigation of other well-known and highly regarded normative forecasting techniques (e.g., TORQUE) provides further evidences to support the point already established. Very sophisticated methods of valuing technology and allocating resources are being combined with very trivial methods of forecasting technical outputs. The methods appear to be aimed at producing five decimal-place accuracy outputs from one decimal-place accuracy inputs, a task comparable to acquiring silk purses from sow's ears. The inconsistency of this practice, and the obvious notion that a chain is only as strong as its weakest link, have not yet shifted enough attention to the needed improvement of exploratory forecasting methodology.

IMPLEMENTABILITY OF NORMATIVE FORECASTS

If the problem just cited were corrected, if the normative allocations were indeed based on legitimate and respectable efforts at exploratory forecasting, a number of problems would still exist in gaining effective implementation of the normative techniques. Some of the observed problem areas are:

(1) the costliness of the inputs;
(2) the dubious accuracy of the estimates;
(3) the inflexibility of the methods; and
(4) the probable limited impact upon managerial decisions.

Costliness

Each of the primary normative methods described above is a heavy user of resources. Jantsch estimates the original setup cost for a PATTERN scheme at $250,000 to $300,000 with annual "maintenance" costs of roughly $50,000.[18] QUEST requires estimates for a "value of technology to missions" matrix that may be of the order of 30 by 50 and for a "relevance of science to technology" matrix of approximately 50 by 130 size. Each of these QUEST inputs may have to be provided for the three time frames of now, five years from now, and ten years from now, as well as for several sets of assumed funding levels.[19] Probe II required inputs from 140 experts.[20] Many organizations, including those already cited, may find the expenditure of these resources to be an awesome consideration, especially as the techniques require resubmittal of all the inputs on a reasonably regular basis. To be sure, learning must take place which reduces these input acquisition costs, but each estimator is still needed to regenerate on a regular basis his inputs to the forcasting systems.

Dubious Accuracy

A second problem is the questionable believability of the inputs submitted. The scientific-technological expert is a doer who understands the state of knowledge in his fiield and the process employed for advancing that state. Instead of asking the expert to assess that state or to describe that process, the normative methods principally call upon him to become a crystal-ball gazer and to leap inferentially to a conclusion (usually probabilistic) as to what will occur in the future. Little objective evidence exists to defend this kind of expert testimony.

This problem of input accuracy is worsened by the likelihood that the estimator providing the inputs will be affected by the conclusions derived from his inputs. The scientist entering data into a normative forecast has to guard against "signing his own death warrant." This participative role in what are likely to be self-fulfilling or self-defeating forecasts almost assures that the inputs will be biased consciously or unconsciously, and surely not in any systematic manner.

Inflexibility

In many areas of critical decision-making resource allocators evaluate their alternatives using quantitative techniques such as, for example, the cost-effectiveness analyses used by the DOD in selecting weapon systems. These cost-effectiveness evaluations permit wide latitude in the mode of costing adopted, as well as in the method for value assessment. Top level Defense management reviews each analysis for its soundness in order to qualify the adequacy and acceptability of the derived recommendations. Following these formal reviews the over-all resource allocation is still subject to a balancing against other usually nonquantified social, economic and political considerations.

Of the managerial areas being subjected to quantitative resource allocation techniques, research and development consists of more unique programs, with more uncertain outcomes, and less uniformity of types of results than any other area. Yet the normative forecasting techniques proposed and somewhat adopted for selecting and funding R&D programs are supposed to be applied uniformly to all programs, regardless of scope, phase, duration, criticality, technology, or what-have-you. This degree of unjustified standardization is not matched by the flexible view taken for DOD weapon system tradeoffs. Moreover, the complexity and mathematical sophistication of the normative technological forecasting methods again exceeds by far the relatively simple formats and seldom-more-than-arithmetic computation procedures used in DOD cost-effectiveness determinations. Is it possible that the current style of normative technological forecasting is an overreaction to the difficulties of managing research and development?

Limited Impact

The characteristics of normative forecasting just described, as well as the characteristics of the decision-making process, combine to suggest that the present generation of techniques is likely to have only limited impact on specific managerial decisions. The costliness, dubious accuracy, and inflexibility of approach will naturally tend to limit the use of these methods. But more important is that experience in other related areas has shown that comparable techniques are seldom responsible for selection decisions.

In their excellent review of formal project selection methods, Baker and Pound found that few organizations of the 50 studied were employing the formal selection processes that were described in published papers by their employees.[21] Perhaps this is indicative only of the low state of managerial decision-making generally, but other evidences suggest that the problem is more fundamental.

In a study by the author of about 100 R&D contractor selection decisions, informal person-to-person factors were found to influence the awards far more than did formal evaluation procedures.[22] In fact, six to eight months prior to formal award announcements, long before the formal proposal evaluations, all but ten percent of the awards of R&D contracts up to several millions of dollars in magnitude were predictable from the available data.

When major decisions are to be made it appears that management needs to consider factors other than those generally included in formal complex evaluation procedures. Investigation of 51 of the largest contract awards by the National Aeronautics and Space Administration revealed that NASA headquarters did not follow the suggestions of its Source Evaluation Boards in 25 percent of the cases.[23] But these 25 percent accounted for 67 percent of the total funds contracted on the 51 awards. It is possible that formal evaluation methods are followed only when the outcome is not regarded as vital to the organization.

Previously this paper pointed out that the PROFILE technique contains a "fudge factor" criterion, Intrinsic Value to the Laboratory, that permits managerial "overrides" of otherwise elaborate evaluations. More recently Cetron has indicated that consideration of so-called "sacred cows" in another technique under investigation by the Navy also permits the rest of a complex evaluation procedure to be scrapped in favor of explicit management preferences.[24] Is it not reasonable that in the important cases such "sacred cow" factors would limit the impact of formal evaluations oriented against a top manager's desires?

Evidence gathered in a series of other studies also argues that real decisions are not made in the manner suggested by the formal, complex decision-aiding systems in R&D.[25] These data do not suggest that the formal evaluation systems are without value. Indeed these methods seem to stimulate a more thoughtful and more orderly planning process that enhances management effectiveness. But the data do indicate that the present type of normative forecasting techniques is likely to have only limited impact on managerial resource allocation for R&D.

Integrating Exploratory and Normative Forecasting With Dynamic System Models

Throughout this paper the inconsistencies between the developments of exploratory and normative forecasting techniques have been highlighted. In mathematical sophistication and level of detail the simple schemes used by those trying to predict technology of the future look pallid when matched against the techniques employed by those who are allocating the resources that will create the future. The examination of exploratory forecast methods indicates that what is known about the process that generates future technology is not presently included in the forecasting models. This lack shows up further as a critical weakness of the normative techniques, which are attempting to select and budget R&D projects based on meager schemes for forecasting future technological possibilities.

An earlier section of the paper pointed out the potential of dynamic models which are oriented toward the inclusion of those cause-and-effect relationships that are likely to alter future technological developments. These models are being utilized in economic analysis, forecasting and policy design, i.e., in both exploratory and normative modes. Jantsch has realized how much these dynamic system models might contribute to technological forecasting. However, he has seriously underestimated the degree of their present development.

Rigid computer models are on the threshold of becoming useful for technological forecasting. In particular, "dynamic forecasting" is serving as a guideline in a number of serious attempts; this term, introduced by Lenz to denote the modelling of all significant cause-effect relationships which influence the growth of technology in general or a functional capability, may be extended here so as to include technology transfer in general. The hope, of course, is to achieve adequate results with a limited dynamic model. The "Industrial Dynamics" concept of Forrester for complex business decision-making provides the background to many attempts in this area.[26]

The "Industrial Dynamics" concept that Jantsch references emphasized the importance of feedback relationships in influencing the dynamic evolution of a situation.[27] For example, the connections between exploratory and normative forecasting form the kind of feedback loops that significantly affect future behavior. An exploratory forecast generates a prediction that a desired outcome is highly feasible within a reasonable time period; this leads to a high value index established for the related R&D project in the normalized forecast, which in turn influences increased funding for the project. The resultant strengthened research support enhances the likelihood of timely completion of the project, and this status improvement is reflected in the exploratory forecast. This type of feedback relationship is critical to the technological growth process and it demands the integration of the exploratory and normative phases Dynamic feedback system models are the most likely candidates for accomplishing this integration.

DYNAMIC SYSTEM MODELS IN TECHNOLOGY-RELATED AREAS

Though generally unrecognized by Jantsch and other reviewers of the technological forecasting field, dynamic models of technology-related feedback systems have been under development for ten years. A brief review of these models will demonstrate their present availability for broader exploitation in technological forecasting and their traditional integration of exploratory and normative considerations.

R&D Projects

As the primary present use of technological forecasting is in the area of R&D project selection and budget allocation, it seems appropriate to mention the dynamic systems models oriented toward examining these projects. The major effort here is the author's books on the factors affecting R&D project life cycles.[28] The mathematical model of the project process follows the scheme illustrated in Figure 1.

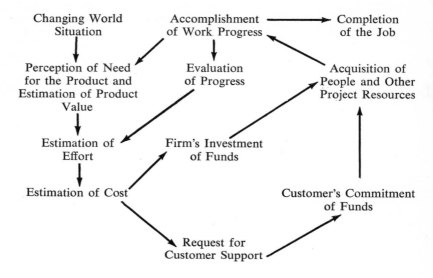

Figure 1. Dynamic system underlying project life cycles.

Indeed the model treats both the exploratory and normative sides of the project process and contains a detailed sector that represents the technology-generating process. Initially this model was intended as a conceptual tool only, but it has already been applied to specific technological forecasting in the United States and Japan, resulting in publications in both countries.[29]

Multi-project and Multi-phase Allocations

Beyond looking at projects singly, technological forecasters are concerned with the problems of beneficial and conflicting "cross-support" between multiple projects. This problem has been treated in dynamic feedback system models aimed at two subtopics—the cross-support between projects and the cross-support between various phases of R&D activity in a technical organization. The former area has been the subject of one excellent graduate thesis, while the latter has been covered by a variety of high quality thesis efforts.[30]

Technical Organization Forecasting

Several dynamic system models have been developed as attempted to analyzing and causally predicting the growth (or decline) of a technical organization (exploratory style) and the effect of various policies on that growth (normative style). Two papers and an array of good quality graduate theses document this area of activity.[31] The paper listed by Robert

Spencer describes ventures undertaken at the Dow Chemical Company to better plan and allocate resources for one of its major divisions.

Technological Growth Forecasts

A number of dynamic system models emphasizing feedback effects have tackled the question of the growth of a new technology. Lenz and Reisman have concerned themselves with the training and employment of the professional people who cause a new technological area to develop.[32] Nord has focused on the growth process for a new product, while Forrester has written on the growth of a new technology-based firm.[33]

Many other papers, theses, and unpublished studies have also dealt with exploratory and normative aspects of scientific and technological developments. The wide variety of models identified here does indicate that "rigid computer models," as Jantsch refers to them, or, preferably, "dynamic feedback system models" are part of the presently available state-of-the-art of technological forecasting.

TOWARD EFFECTIVE USE OF DYNAMIC SYSTEM MODELS

It is clear that the large-scale dynamic simulation models described above have the capacity to include realistically the cause-and-effect relationships believed to generate technological advances. What is not clear is how to use these models most effectively.

A focus on the previously asserted need for consistency between exploratory and normative forecasting seems to provide a clue toward effective use. Although many of the general factors influencing growth of a technological area are understood, this understanding does not extend down to rather minute details or up to any high degree of accuracy. The uncertainties of research and development, the uniqueness of the program, the intangibility of the progress, and the long time delays in the feedback of results constrain the possible accuracy of understanding to a marked extent. Thus, exploratory forecasting models are similarly limited in the accuracy and detail that can be demanded of them. And, consistently, attempted normative forecasts must be confined to the same range of uses. To attempt to use normative technological forecasting to select and allocate funds to hundreds or thousands of individual projects is obviously beyond the effective capacity of the models that can be built. Much more knowledge is needed, not about allocation techniques but rather about the technological development process, before such a high degree of disaggregation becomes meaningful.

It seems reasonable that dynamic feedback system models can be developed to help answer a number of fundamental resource allocation questions. Should more money in total be expended on research and development activities? How should the R&D budget be split between its research and its developmental components? How should the budget treat new potentially important areas of science and technology as opposed to the older on-going activities? How should funds be allocated in support of various broad missions or goals? These and other key questions are now largely being ignored in the mistaken rush to decide quantitatively but unjustifiedly the selection and funding of each and every R&D project. But it is in the realm of these policy issues that integrated exploratory and normative technological forecasting, enriched by the use of dynamic feedback systems models, will make its most potent contribution.

REFERENCES

1. Cetron, M. J., et al., *A Proposal for a Navy Technological Forecast* (Washington, D.C.: Naval Material Command, May 1966, AD 659–199 and 659–200).
2. Gabor, D., *Inventing the Future* (London: Seckery Warburg, 1963).
3. Jantsch, E., *Technological Forecasting in Perspective* (Paris: Organisation for Economic Co-operation and Development, 1967), pp. 15, 17.
4. Gordon, T. J. and Helmar, O., "Report on a Long-Range Forecasting Study' (Santa Monica, California: The RAND Corporation, September 1964, Paper P–2882).
5. Jantsch, *ibid.*, p. 156.
6. Mansfield, E., "Technical Change and the Rate of Imitation," *Econometrica,* October 1961.
7. Examples of this "new" type of economic forecasting model are: Duesenberry, J. S., et al. (editors), *The Brookings Quarterly Econometric Model of the United States* (New York: Rand McNally, 1965); Fromm, G. and Taubman, P., *Policy Simulations with an Econometric Model* (Washington, D.C.: The Brookings Institute, 1968); Hamilton, H. R., et al., *Systems Simulation for Regional Analysis* (Cambridge: The M.I.T. Press, 1968); Weymar, F. H., *The Dynamics of the World Cocoa Market* (Cambridge: The M.I.T. Press, 1968).
8. Jantsch, *ibid.*, p. 17.
9. Lenz, R. C., Jr., *Technological Forecasting*, Second Edition (Wright-Patterson Air Force Base: U.S. Air Force Aeronautical Systems Division, June 1962, Report ASD–TDR–62–414), as cited Jantsch, *ibid.*, p. 241.
10. Jantsch, *ibid.*, p. 155.
11. Among the recent summaries of aspects of this research are: D. G. Marquis (editor), *Second Report of the M.I.T. Research Program on the Management of Science and Technology* (Cambridge: M.I.T. Sloan School of Management, October 1967); and Isenson, R. D., "Factors Affecting the Growth of Technology—As Seen through Hindsight," unpublished paper presented at the NATO Defense Research Group Seminar, Teddington, England, November 1968.
12. Cetron, M. J., "Programmed Functional Indices for Laboratory Evaluation (PROFILE)," presented at the 16th Military Operations Research Symposium; Seattle, Washington; October 1966.
13. *Ibid.*, p. 5.
14. Cetron, M. J., "QUEST Status Report," *IEEE Transactons on Engineering Management*, vol. EM–14, no. 1, March 1967.
15. *Ibid.*, p. 62.
16. Jestice, A. L., *Project PATTERN—Planning Assistance Through Technical Evaluation of Relevance Numbers* (Washington, D.C.: Honeywell, Inc., 1964).
17. North, H. A., "Technological Forecasting in Industry," presented to NATO Defense Research Group Seminar; Teddington, England; November 12, 1968.

18. Jantsch, *ibid.*, p. 226.
19. Cetron, *ibid.*
20. North, *ibid.*, p. 9.
21. Baker, M. R. and Pound, W. H., "R and D Project Selection: Where We Stand," *IEEE Transactions on Engineering Management,* vol. EM–11, no. 4, December 1964.
22. Roberts, E. B., "Questioning the Cost/Effectiveness of the R&D Procurement Process," in Yovits, M. C., et al. (editors), *Research Program Effectiveness* (New York: Gordon and Breach, Publishers, 1966).
23. Bergsteinsson, P., *The Evaluation and Selection of Sources for Major NASA Contracts* (unpublished Master of Science thesis, M.I.T. Sloan School of Management, 1967).
24. Cetron, M. J., "Prescription for the Military R&D Manager," presented at the NATO Defense Research Group Seminar; Teddington, England; November 12, 1967, pp. 19, 21–22.
25. Roberts, E. B., "Facts and Folklore in Research and Development Management," *Industrial Management Review,* vol. 8, no. 2, Spring 1967.
26. Jantsch, *ibid.*, p. 202.
27. Forrester, J. W., *Industrial Dynamics* (Cambridge: The M.I.T. Press, 1961). Figure. 1. Dynamic system underlying project life cycles.
28. Roberts, E. B., *The Dynamics of Research and Development* (New York: Harper & Row, Publishers, 1964).
29. Schlager, K. J., "How Managers Use Industrial Dynamics," *Industrial Management Review,* vol. 6, no. 1, 1964. Reference to the Japanese application is contained in a private communication to the author from S. Sakakura.
30. Nay, J. N., *Choic and Allocation in Multiple Markets: A Research and Development Systems Analysis* (unpublished Master of Science thesis, M.I.T. Department of Electrical Engineering, 1966); D. C. Beaumariage (1961), P. W. Lett (1961), G. R. Wachold (1963), and G. Welles III (1963) produced thesis studies at the M.I.T. Sloan School of Management on the allocation of funds and effort among several series-related phases of work.
31. Roberts, E. B., "Problems of Aging Organizations," *Business Horizons,* vol. 10, no. 4, Winter 1967; Spencer, R. W., "Modelling Strategies for Corporate Growth," presented at the Society for General Systems Research Conference, Washington, D.C., 1966; and M.I.T. Management theses by L. Salba (1967), C. H. Perrine (1968), and J. Troutner (1968).
32. Lenz, *ibid.*; Reisman, A., "Higher Education: A Population Flow Feedback Model," *Science,* vol. 153, July 1, 1966.
33. Nord, O. C., *Growth of a New Product* (Cambridge: The M.I.T. Press, (1963); Forrester, J. W., "Modelling the Dynamic Processes of Corporate Growth," presented at the IBM Scientific Computing Symposium; Yorktown Heights, New York; December 1964.

"I wish to have no connection with any ship that does not sail fast for I intend to go in harm's way." — JOHN PAUL JONES 1778

APPENDIX C

FORECAST: MATERIAL SUPPORT TECHNOLOGY
(SEA FLOOR ENGINEERING)

WHAT FOLLOWS is an example of how a specific decision can be analyzed, based on some technological forecasts generated by the Naval Civil Engineering Laboratory. Forecasts for metallic materials and seals are given in terms of toughness, yield strength, and corrosion resistance. The next consideration might take us into the area of concrete and ultimate concrete strengths for, say, structural concrete versus polymer concrete, or possibly plastic composites. We also might want to consider Forecasts of weight handling devices, heating for sea floor sites and underwater observations. Each of these functional considerations key into the total sea floor site construction problem, in the same manner that each of the pacing parameters key into each functional area. In this fashion we can work our way through the Chart (Figure A), eventually going into any degree of detail or considering as many functional areas as we wish.

This information is used for very practical decisions. For instance the pacing parameters of toughness, yield strength and corrosion resistance are forecast for the functional metallic materials and seals are shown in the attached graphs (Figure B). The complete technological forecast on metallic materials and seals and five other functional areas covered in Figure A follows in the remainder of this appendix. All the materials covered in the Navy Technological Forecast are shown in the matrix appearing on page 291.

530 MATERIAL SUPPORT TECHNOLOGY (SEA FLOOR ENGINEERING)

535–6 Metallic Materials and Seals
Prepared by:
NAVAL CIVIL ENGINEERING LABORATORY
J. F. Jenkins, L–52

A. BACKGROUND

In order to successfully construct and maintain structures on the ocean bottom at great depths for extended periods of time behavior at depth of materials of construction and the limitations of construction designs and methods must be well defined.

263

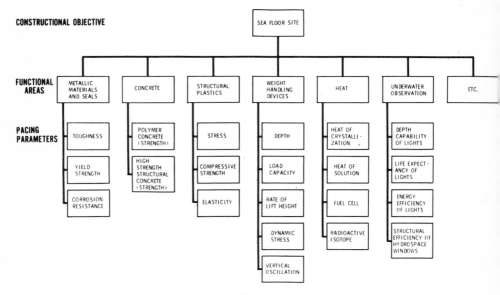

Figure A

Many of the parameters affecting the corrosion of metallic materials such as O_2 conc., pH, pressure, salinity, temperature, etc., were found to vary extensively in the deep ocean. These parameters change with location, depth, and season. In order to better define the behavior of construction materials in the deep ocean, test exposures of 10,995 specimens of 500 materials have been made at 2,500 and 6,000 ft. in the Pacific Ocean off the coast of Southern California for varying periods of time up to 1,064 days. Evaluation of these specimens has shown that the corrosion behavior of materials at these two depths is different in both degree and nature and is different from their behavior in sea water at the surface.

One particular area of inadequate information pertinent to the installation and maintenance of structures in the deep ocean is that of the behavior of seals and gaskets during long term loading while exposed to sea water.

Investigation of the long term seal loading and deterioration effects in the deep ocean is underway at NCEL. In July 1968, 40 specimens of 15 static seal configurations constructed from five flange materials will be exposed to the deep ocean at a depth of 6,000 feet. This initial exposure is scheduled to be six months in length.

Metal components of sea floor structures and equipment will be subjected to very severe and environmental and service conditions and are likely to be covered with plastic or paint coatings, where practical, to protect them from corrosion. Such coverings will be subject to abrasion and impact damage and the bare metal thus exposed will be subject

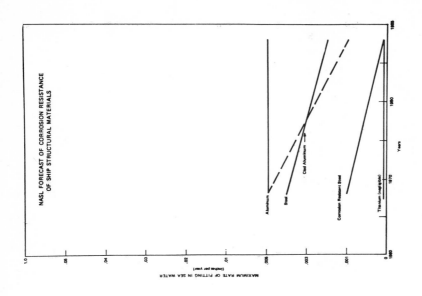

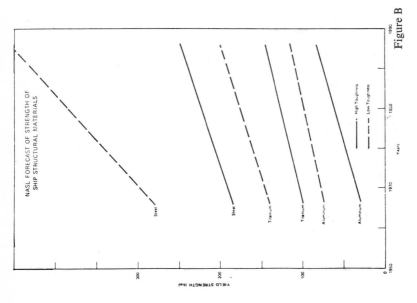

Figure B

to rapid corrosion unless protected by some system such as cathodic protection.

B. PRESENT STATUS

Materials—Of the 500 materials exposed to date in the deep ocean test program, many have shown promise for application in the deep ocean. However, as in all applications of materials in a corrosive environment, a material selection must be made by evaluation of pertinent performance data, material requirements, and actual exposure conditions (environment, stress, crevices, and galvanic corrosion possibilities).

Corrosion data from the six deep ocean exposure tests has added significantly to the body of corrosion knowledge used in material selection for deep ocean structures.

Also, note the available strengths of steel, titanium and aluminum in the forecast table.

Seals—Evaluation of the present seal technology has revealed a dearth of published information about the use of seals for external pressure applications and for long term loading and deterioration effects in sea water. A compilation of the limited available service data for seals in the deep ocean, taken primarily from deep submersible vessel applications, indicates that the major difficulty in the design of seal which will be effective without maintenance for long periods is the corrosion of the flange faces and not the deterioration of the actual sea material. Seals of the O-Ring type are considered to be of primary importance for deep ocean applications. The deep ocean performance of this type of static seal in various configurations is presently being investigated by this laboratory. Preliminary tests have confirmed the usefulness of static O-Ring seals for deep ocean use, as there were no seal failures in the laboratory short term hydrostatic loading tests simulating depths up to 10,000 feet.

Cathodic protection has been quite an effective method of corrosion control for steel ships, piling, buoys, etc., in shallow sea water applications but in deep ocean exposures only small test specimens have been cathodically protected to date, and relatively little knowledge is known about cathodic protection in such environments.

C. FORECAST

Materials—The deep ocean corrosion data obtained in the previous exposure tests has made it possible to predict long term behavior in the deep ocean for many materials in environments similar to those in which the corrosion tests were made. However, many materials were found to corrode in such a way that long term generalized predictions of corrosion are impossible, e.g., increasing pitting rate or increasing corrosion rate. Also, due to the wide variation of corrosion related parameters, long term, and in many cases short term corrosion behavior can only at best be approximated from present corrosion data and theory. Corrosion exposures for extended periods and in numerous locations will better define the corrosion behavior of metallic materials throughout the deep ocean. Laboratory tests which to date have been stifled by inability to maintain corrosion related parameters at desired values may prove to be of great future value in this definition of corrosion behavior if proper testing equipment can be designed.

One particular aspect of the corrosion behavior of materials in the deep ocean and indeed in any marine environment which will require future investigation in order to clearly define actual corrosion behavior is that of galvanic, or metal couple corrosion. Since nearly any structure of apparatus must be constructed of more than one material the possibility of accelerated corrosion of one or more of the materials exposed to the sea water must be considered in any realistic materials selection. The dearth of present information on this subject may in the future be studied in two ways. Either actual metal combinations must be exposed to the environment or the electrochemical behavior of each of the metals to be investigated must be determined by measurements taken on the metals at intervals during their exposure.

The development of new alloys which by virtue of their high strength, low density or supposed corrosion resistance will require testing by either deep ocean exposure or by exposure in a well regulated simulation facility in laboratory if the latter proves to be a reliable means of predicting corrosion behavior in the deep ocean.

Seals—The development of a static seal system which is reliable from a deterioration standpoint over extended periods in the deep ocean should be the result of the present investigation at NCEL. Seal flanges constructed of corrosion resistant materials and compatible with most proposed construction materials are now being tested and are hoped to prove successful. Other proposed methods of improving flange life are: cathodic protection, painting, and development of a seal system which eliminates corrosion-accelerating crevices. Development of a dynamic shaft type seal which is reliable for long periods in the deep ocean should be undertaken in the near future. The main problem envisioned is the development of an elastomeric material to affect the seal. Problems of flange corrosion should be well delineated by test on static seal systems.

Present and Future Capabilities of Structural Materials: the following table and projections are extracted from the Technical Development Plan (46–36X), Deep Ocean Technology Project of 1 May 1968.

Material	Density ($\#$/in.^{3})	Strength (psi)	
		Available Now	Available 1970–80
Steel	0.283	130,000 to 180,000	300,000
Titanium	0.160	110,000	160,000
Aluminum	0.100	70,000	90,000
Fiber Reinforced Plastic (FRP)	0.080	100,000	150,000
Glass	0.090	100,000	250,000

In general, these values are based on forecasts from the SEABED study. For present state-of-the-art materials, particularly glass, strengths less than accepted laboratory values are indicated. In the case of glass, the scatter of data is so great (i.e., 60,000 to 350,000 psi for simple compression joint tests of chemically strengthened glass) that a nominal fracture stress of 100,000 psi was used.

Analyses of known materials and configurations of pressure-resistant structures, coupled with predicted R&D support for their use in operational vehicles, indicate the following projected capabilities:

- In the present time frame, fiber-reinforced plastic and massive glass are the best candidate materials for 20,000-foot operations.
- Development of high yield-strength aluminum (150,000 psi) will permit its use for cylindrical hulls with $W/D = 0.5$ to operating depths of 20,000 feet.
- The development of a higher strength titanium will permit its use of cylindrical hulls with $W/D = 0.4$ to operating depths of 20,000 feet.
- A metallic or FRP cylindical or spherical hull capable of 10,000-foot submergence can be envisioned within five years.
- A metallic of FRP cylindrical or spherical hull with 15,000-foot depth capability can be available within ten years.
- A 20,000-foot depth capability, with various hull configurations and material options is possible within 15 years.
- The development paths which can minimize the time/depth demonstration sequence are as given below:

    6,000 feet—4 years—Steel cylinder or sphere
    10,000 feet—5 years—Steel cylinder or sphere
    15,000 feet—5 years—FRP cylinder
    20,000 feet—8 years—FRP or glass sphere

The Naval Applied Science Laboratory (NASL) has submitted Figures 1 and 2 to show yield strength and corrosion resistance predictions for structural aluminum, steel and titanium allows. The difference between the high and low toughness materials referred to in the yield strength curve is that the former are estimated capable of sustaining a minimum of approximately 7% plastic deformation before fracture. For later refinement of data, see the NASL technological forecast on materials.

Cathodic protection systems will be used in conjunction with other corrosion control measures (coatings, sheaths, inhibitors, etc.), to reduce costs and obtain the most dependable level of protection.

D. OPERATIONAL IMPLICATIONS

The definition of the corrosion behavior of metallic materials in many deep ocean environments will enable the construction of a deep ocean structure with a long projected life span.

The definition of the behavior of many seal systems in many deep environments will provide seal and flange materials for construction of a deep ocean structure with a long projected life span.

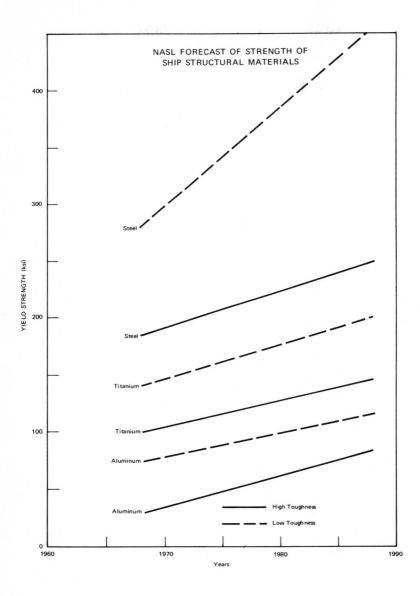

Figure 1

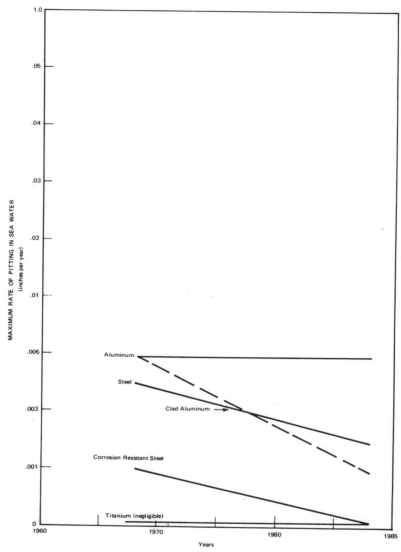

NASL FORECAST OF CORROSION RESISTANCE
OF SHIP STRUCTURAL MATERIALS

Figure 2

E. REFERENCES

1. NCEL Technical Report 345, "Deep Ocean Civil Engineering," Back-up Report Undersea Technology Panel, Project SEABED, September 1964.

2. NCEL Technical Note N–380, "Properties of materials in the Deep Ocean Environment, A Progress Report," March 1960.

3. NCEL Technical Note, "Properties of Materials in the Deep Ocean Environment, A Progress Report," July 1962.

4. NCEL Technical Note N–605, "Preliminary Examination of Materials Exposed on STU I–3 in the Deep Ocean (5,640 feet of depth for 123 days)."

5. NCEL Technical Note N–781, "Effect of the Deep Ocean on the Corrosion of Selected Alloys," October 1965.

6. NCEL Technical Note 793, "Visual Observations of Corrosion of Materials on STU I–1 after 1,064 Days of Exposure at a Depth of 5,300 Feet in the Pacific Ocean."

7. NCEL Technical Note N–900, "Corrosion of Materials in Hydrospace—I, Irons, Steels, Cast Irons and Steel Products," July 1967.

8. NCEL Technical Note N–915, "Corrosion of Materials in Hydrospace—II, Nickel and Alloys," August 1967.

9. NCEL Technical Note N–921, "Corrosion of Materials in Hydrospace—III, Titanium and Titanium Alloys," September 1967.

F. ASSOCIATED R&D ORGANIZATIONS

NASL, Brooklyn, New York
NRL, Washington, D.C.
NSRDC, Washington, D.C.
NAMIC, Pensacola, Florida
NAEC, Philadelphia, Pennsylvania
Lockheed Aerospace & Missiles Co., Sunnyvale, California

530   MATERIAL SUPPORT TECHNOLOGY (SEA FLOOR ENGINEERING)

535–7 Concrete

Prepared by:
NAVAL CIVIL ENGINEERING LABORATORY
H. H. Haynes, L–52

A. BACKGROUND

For the past 40 years concrete has been used as an ocean construction material for coastal and harbor installations. The performance of underwater foundations, piers, and piles which were poured in-place at depths to 200 feet using the methods of tremie, bucketing, and pumping have shown good structural integrity except for a number of incidents where concrete members exhibited major deterioration. In all these cases the cause for deterioration could be directed to low-quality concrete. High quality concrete (high cement-factor, low water-cement ratio, high density, etc.) not only resisted deterioration but also resisted attack by marine organisms.

Experience has also been gained using concrete as a pressure hull material for subaqueous transportation tunnels. Tunnels have been constructed from large precast sections at depths to 120 feet, although high factors of safety were always present with static working stresses below 500 psi.

B. PRESENT STATUS

The feasibility of deep ocean concrete installations was shown in research studies on model spherical hulls subjected to hydrostatic loadings. Concrete hulls developed stresses on the order of 14,000 psi, while the strength of the concrete from uniaxial cylinder tests was only 10,000 psi. Present developments in concrete technology, such as polymer concrete or plastic impregnation of concrete, may eliminate the problem of sea water premeating through the material and also increase the ultimate strength of the material to 24,000 psi. Further developments in fiber reinforcement techniques and sandwich construction methods offer the potential capability of concrete installations to undergo dynamic and cyclic loading conditions.

C. FORECAST

Within 20 years technological advances for concrete will allow working stresses on the order of 12,000 psi will eliminate the problem of concrete permeability to sea water. Major developments in construction techniques such as assembling concrete pressure hulls from prefabricated elements or mixing and pouring concrete on-site using sea floor aggregate and sea water as materials will have significant impetus in broadening the applications for concrete as a construction material in the oceans. Underwater semi-permanent and permanent installations will range in size from small instrumentation capsules to large "gymnasium-size" manned habitats. Very large pressure hulls are feasible in so far as the wall of a concrete hull can be constructed to any thickness. It is foreseen that concrete structures will be employed to maximum operational depths of 3000 feet, even though the material is capable of withstanding hydrostatic pressures at operational depths of 10,000 feet and greater.

Design data obtained from extensive research on the physical properties and structural behavior of concrete under hydrostatic loading will be available for predicting the behavior of any concrete structure in the ocean. Future trends in development work on polymer concrete, glass

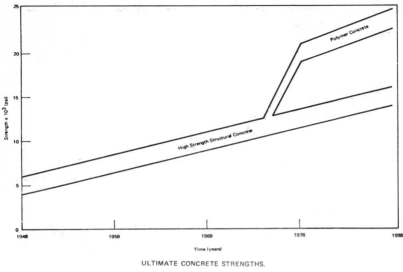

ULTIMATE CONCRETE STRENGTHS.
Figure 1

fiber reinforced concrete, and other unknown methods will not only continue to increase the strength of the material (Figure 1) but also the
economic advantages and the reliability of the material for sea floor
installations.

D. OPERATIONAL IMPLICATIONS

Permanent installations on the ocean floor are technically feasible if
constructed from high-quality concrete. Advantages of fixed ocean floor
habitats are that personnel can be transferred to/from the surface easier
than an entire habitat can be transported, the structure does not have to
undergo cyclic loading, and certain structures such as nuclear reactor
containment vessels will be negatively buoyant, and therefore designed
on the criterion of a permanent underwater pressure hull.

Very large underwater concrete structures can be fabricated by cast
in-place techniques or precast methods of assembling sections in-situ.
Large hulls constructed from other materials have maximum size limitations because of a lack of welding technology for thick walls or elastic
instability problems which require many hull stiffeners. The need for
tall, wide installations could be for oil drilling operations which house
man and equipment.

Buoyant concrete pressure hulls can have application within the continental shelf regions as long term subsurface buoys and instrumentation
capsules.

E. REFERENCES

1. Gerwick, B. C., "Techniques for Concrete Construction on the Ocean Floor," Proceedings of the conference of Civil Engineering in the Oceans, ASCE, September, 1967.

2. Stachiw, J. D., "Behavior of Spherical Concrete Hulls Under Hydrostatic Loadings," U.S. Naval Civil Engineering Laboratory, TR–547, October 1967.

530   MATERIAL SUPPORT TECHNOLOGY (SEA FLOOR ENGINEERING)

535–9 Structural Plastics

Prepared by:
NAVAL CIVIL ENGINEERING LABORATORY
H. McPherson, L03B

A. BACKGROUND

Plastics have been utilized in structures for undersea use for several decades. Where high strength-to-weight ratio and dimensional stability was required glass fiber epoxy laminates were employed whose mechanical properties showed tensile strengths of up to 150,000 psi and compressive strengths of up to 100,000 psi. The premium strengths were reached only by directional winding of glass fibers, while for lower strengths of 20,000 to 40,000 psi hand-laid up glass cloth and matting sufficed. The structures fabricated from glass fiber epoxy and polyester laminates ranged from fairings for submersibles to large underwater buoys and capsules with depth capability of up to 5,000 feet and 0.3 weight to displacement ratio.

For applications where high strength-to-weight ratio is not the over-riding requirement, but resistance to corrosion and economy are, plastics like polyvinyl chloride, acrylic, and polycarbonate have displaced in a large measure the much heavier and expensive corrosion resistant metals. Polyvinyl chloride plastic battery containers, motor housings, oil filled instrumentation capsules, cable reels and pressure compensated piping are typical examples of applications to which the nonreinforced plastics have been put. The strength of these nonreinforced plastics is in the 3000 to 15,000 psi range; but, because of their specific gravity (which is just slightly above one) a strength to weight ratio approaching that of mild steel is realized.

B. PRESENT STATUS

Glass fiber reinforced epoxy has frequently been used for nonmetallic construction material for undersea structural applications where no corrosion can be tolerated and compressive or tensile stresses of less than

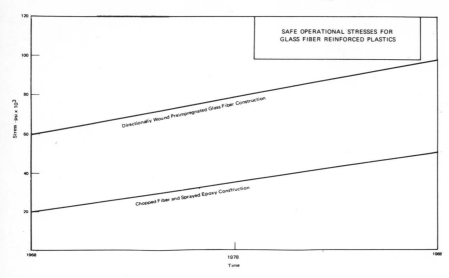

Figure 1

40,000 psi are encountered. For applications where no permeability by water can be tolerated polyethylene and neoprene coatings are widely utilized. This group of materials, however, has yet to see application as the main pressure hull of a manned submersible or habitat.

Nonreinforced plastic materials are usually considered for undersea structural applications where the primary requirement is resistance to corrosion while stresses to be withstood are triaxial—either of hydrostatic nature, or of hydrostatic nature with tensile or compressive loads of less than 5,000 psi magnitude superimposed on them. The most widely used plastic of this kind is polyvinyl chloride. Because of the ease with which it can be sawed, drilled, machined, bonded, and welded, polyvinyl chloride displaced stainless steel #316 and Monel as a construction material of low stresses structural members.

C. FORECAST

1978—Sufficient experimental data will have been accumulated to permit design and construction of man-rated glass fiber reinforced plastic pressure hulls for depths to 2,000 feet, while hulls for instrumented capsules are routinely used to depths of 20,000 feet. The same material would have completely displaced steel in the construction of ambient pressure habitats on the continental shelf.

1988—Man-rated glass fiber reinforced plastic pressure hulls routinely perform dives to depths of 10,000 feet. New, currently unknown glass and other fiber plastic laminates in addition to epoxy laminates will make their appearance in the ocean engineering field. The new laminates will

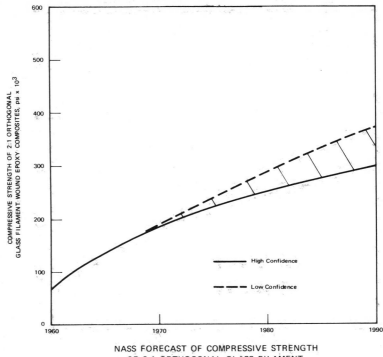

NASS FORECAST OF COMPRESSIVE STRENGTH
OF 2:1 ORTHOGONAL GLASS FILAMENT
WOUND PLASTIC COMPOSITES

Figure 2

be less permeable to sea water than the epoxy laminates and will be subject also to less creep under long term submersion. Improved fabrication
methods will make it possible to achieve construction of pressure hulls
and buoys resulting in a monolithic structure with tensile and compressive stress carrying capabilities of 40,000 to 50,000 psi.

*Tensile and Compressive Strengths and Modulus. Although elastic
moduli exceeding 5×10^5 psi are rare, some polyimid laminates approach
$2-3 \times 10^6$ psi. Modified carbons, many of which are considered organic
copolymers, are expected to supersede these values, particularly if they
are crystalline (Whiskerized) and properly crosslinked. Products with
elastic moduli of $5-10 \times 10^6$ psi should become available during the next
10–20 years. Due to their polynuclear aromatic nature, their temperature
stability will be in the order of 1000°C or even higher, providing that
their hydrogen content is low.

*Whiskerized Graphite Fiber. Graphite fiber composites offer to the
aerospace designers a structural material unsurpassed in modulus and

* Extracted from NSRDC, Annapolis, Maryland Technological Forecast on
Organic Materials.

strength-to-weight ratio. Graphite fibers, with modulus of 50 to 50 mil-
to usefulness, however, because of the low composite interlaminar shear
lion psi and tensile strength exceeding 300,000 psi, have been limited as
strength they exhibit. The interlaminar shear problem has been overcome
through a process called "Whiskerizing," which entails the growth of
silicon-carbide whiskers not only on the external fibers of the graphite
strand bundles, but also completely within the interstices of the fiber
bundle and around each fibril in the graphite bundle. These whiskers have
provided an improvement in composite shear strength from approximately
3000 psi to well over 11,000 psi. Figures 1, 2, and 3 show the forecasts
of operational stress for glass fiber reinforced plastics compressive
strengths of glass filament wound plastics and modulus of elasticity of
filament wound plastic composites, respectively.

D. OPERATIONAL IMPLICATIONS

The availability of glass fiber reinforced plastic laminates with well
understood and proven reproducible properties will also completely elim-

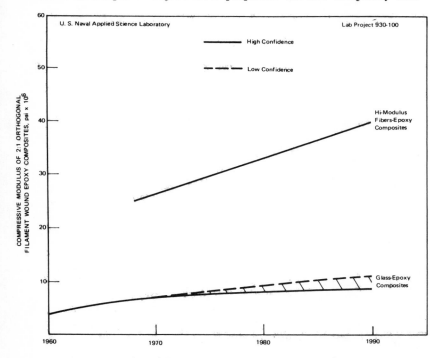

NASL FORECAST OF MODULUS OF ELASTICITY
IN COMPRESSION OF 2:1 ORTHOGONAL FILAMENT
WOUND PLASTIC COMPOSITES

Figure 3

inate corrosion resistant metals from underwater habitats and vehicles where the tensile and compressive stress levels are less than 50,000 psi. This will result in structures that are easier and more economical to build, transport, and emplace in its ocean bottom location. Repairs to damages will be effected on ship deck or in the nearest convenient harbor by semi-skilled labor with automated plastic and chopped fiber dispensers insuring high quality end product.

E. REFERENCES

"Investigation of Advanced Design Concepts for Deep Submersibles," Prepared to NAVSHIPS under Contract NObs–90180, Project R–007–03–04 Task 1008, by H. I. Thompson Fiber Glass Company, 1965.

F. ASSOCIATED R&D ORGANIZATIONS

NSRDC, Carderock and Annapolis, Maryland

530   MATERIAL SUPPORT TECHNOLOGY (SEA FLOOR ENGINEERING)

535–15 Weight Handling Devices
Prepared by:
NAVAL CIVIL ENGINEERING LABORATORY
H. McPherson, L03B

A. BACKGROUND

The conventional way to place and remove objects of all kind into and out of the ocean is from ships. As these objects have become heavier, however, and the desired depths greater, there has developed a need for considerably improved handling devices and techniques. Existing devices do not have sufficient capacity, and ship motions introduce dynamic stresses in the cables and undesirable motions in the object being handled. Also, as construction operations are performed within the ocean, rather than from the surface, there will be a need for new weight handling devices that operate in the hydrospace without any support from the surface.

B. PRESENT STATUS

The present state-of-the-art concerned with weight handling devices may be evaluated in terms of three potential realms of operation: the ocean surface, the ocean bottom, and the water column from surface to bottom.

Surface-supported suspension systems utilize long lines (cables, etc.)

to transmit the lifting force to the bottom. Theoretical prediction of the stresses in these lines has been formulated, but testing and evaluation have been carried out only to the 1,200-foot depth. Techniques for manufacturing, spooling, and storing high-capacity (large diameter) long-length cables are inadequately developed.

C. FORECAST

See table below.

Characteristics	1973	1978	1988
Surface-Independent Subsystem			
Depth	6,000 ft	12,000 ft	18,000 ft
Load capacity	20–100 tons	400–600 tons	600–900 tons
Rate of lifting	1–3 fps	2–4 fps	3–5 fps
Maximum dynamic stress in cable (% of static stress)	10–50%	5–10%	4–6%
Maximum vertical oscillation of object	1–2 ft	0.1–1.0 ft	0.1–0.5 ft
Surface-Supported Subsystem			
Depth	600 ft	6,000 ft	12,000 ft
Load Capacity	10–30 tons	50–100 tons	200–400 tons
Height of lift	30–50 ft	50–100 ft	1,000 ft

D. OPERATIONAL IMPLICATIONS

Increased weight handling capacity and control will allow the Navy to place in the ocean larger and more sophisticated equipment and facilities with greater capability. It will also allow the Navy to recover heavier objects from greater depths.

E. REFERENCES

Technical Development Plan 46–36X, Deep Ocean Technology Project, April 1968.

Holmes, P., Ph.D., "Mechanics of Raising and Lowering Heavy Loads in the Deep Ocean: Cable and Payload Dynamics," NCEL Technical Report R–433, Port Hueneme, California, April 1966.

Muga, B. J., Ph.D., "Mechanics of Raising and Lowering Heavy Loads in the Ocean: Experimental Results," NCEL Technical Report R–543, Port Hueneme, California, September 1967.

F. ASSOCIATED R&D ORGANIZATIONS

NUWC, San Diego, California

530   MATERIAL SUPPORT TECHNOLOGY (SEA FLOOR ENGINEERING)

535–26 Heat

Prepared by:
NAVAL CIVIL ENGINEERING LABORATORY
H. McPherson, L–03B

A. BACKGROUND

The heat supply system is one of the most important requirements of sea floor engineering. Heat is required for underwater operations in a variety of ways; e.g., to provide a warm comfortable environment in the cold hostile surroundings, and hot water for various uses of the personnel living and working at the ocean depths. In other instances, efficient means of heat rejection are needed for equipments which generate heat during their operation. All types of rotating machines fall in this category. In yet other instances, efficient means of heat transfer are required in power generating equipments which use fluids to convert the heat obtained from burning various fuels into electric power. With the exception of batteries and fuel cells, the memory of all power sources depends largely upon the efficiency of the predominant mode of heat transfer in the equipment. Often the heat transfer rates are limited by either the critical heat flux or the mechanism of condensation in heat ransfer phenomenon involving phase changes, and by the resistance of the thermal boundary layer in the case of convective heat transfer.

All possible sources of heat or thermal energy may be divided into three broad categories:

a. shore-based heat sources
b. surface-tendered heat sources, and
c. in situ (emplacement of the ocean floor) heat sources.

Each type of heat source has its advantages and limitations which make them suitable for use under a limited range of conditions. For example, shore-based heat sources are suitable for underwater work at only short distances from the shore, the maximum practicable distance being dependent upon the cost of connecting supply lines and their effect upon the efficiency of the system. Shore-based sources, therefore, lack the flexibility required for salvage operations at large distances from the shore.

The surface-tendered heat sources are useful for limited depths only. If used to supply hot water to the diver or habitat at depths of, say, over 1000 feet, the power and heat losses in the umbilical will make the system inefficient and uneconomical. In "situ" heat sources, however, offer the most efficient means of generating and distributing heat where required. If the requirements from the heat source are not too high, the source could be compact enough to be easily transportable to various locations.

Small power sources, in general, offer the flexibility which make them useful even under the most demanding conditions. They can be carried by divers with them on short notice. However, they are usually limited as to the duration in their use before replenishment becomes necessary.

B. PRESENT STATUS

The divers are kept warm by circulating hot water through their suits. The hot water for this purpose is produced on board a barge or ship and sent to the diver through a rubber umbilical. The technology is not advanced enough to produce efficient, compact, and reliable heat sources which could be placed at the ocean depths near the habitat or the diver's working area. Similarly, because of the absence of dependable underwater heat sources, the habitat heating requirements are met by electrical heaters powered from surface-located energy sources.

C. FORECAST

Heat sources based upon the heat of crystallization or heat of solution may become a practical reality in the next 10 years for application where small amounts of heat are required over relatively short periods of time. For example, a diver's suit may be made by sandwiching lithium nitrate between two sheets of flexible insulating materials and then using the heat of crystallization to keep the divers warm for 2 hours. Heating systems using heat of solution may also be developed for keeping divers warm using a closed cycle loop. These systems, however, are required to be regenerated after a few hours of use making their uninterrupted long term use difficult.

Radioactive isotopic heating is at the demonstration stage at this moment and may become feasible during the next 10 years. However, the cost of radio-isotopes will forbid the applications of this system of heating for undersea operations since other less expensive methods are

TABLE 1

| Power Source | FORECAST | |
	1978	1988
Heat of crystallization	May keep divers warm for 2–3 hours.	May be successfully used for 4–5 hours.
Heat of Solution	May keep a diver warm for 3 hours.	May be successfully used for 4–5 hours.
Radioactive Isotope	Too expensive to be of practical value.	Too expensive to be of practical value.
Fuel Cell	20% improvement in specific weight and volume.	50% improvement in specific weight and volume.

available. The use of radioactive isotopic heating, therefore, cannot be foreseen during the next 20 years.

The fuel cell principle may also be used to generate heat for undersea work. At the 30 KW power level, an estimated specific weight of 55 pounds per KW will be required. This figure does not include the weights associated with the fuel storage and waste products. For the larger energy requirements, these will constitute a major portion of the equipment weights and volumes. During the next 10 and 20 years, however, extensive development work may increase the efficiency of the system sufficiently to reduce the system weight and volume requirements by 20 and 50 percent, respectively. The improvements in various sources for small power requirements during the next 10 and 20 years are compared in Table 1.

The nuclear reactor plant has been proven to be very important and successful source of heat and power for undersea applications. Energy storage with the nuclear reactor requires very small weight and volume. It is the only practical self-contained power source for power and energy levels required at ocean depths. It is almost certain that nuclear energy will be the most widely used, and the least expensive, source of electrical power in the next decade or so. With wide use of nuclear energy, and the accompanying development work in better heat transfer surfaces, the cost of producing heat may be reduced significantly during the next 20 years.

The actual cost of power per KW from a nuclear reactor will depend largely upon the type and size of the reactor and the conditions under which it will be used. It is estimated that cost improvements of 10 and 20 percent may be safely expected during the next 10 and 20 years, respectively. These improvements are significant in view of the fact that dramatic developments are not expected in the foreseeable future. These improvements in cost, weight and volume are expected to be caused by a series of small developments in the fairly advanced art of reactor heat transfer. These improvements are shown along with the present costs in Table 2.

TABLE 2

COST OF NUCLEAR POWER PLANT ($ MILLIONS)

Power (KW)	Operation of depth (ft)	Present (Ref(1))	1978 (Projected)	1988 (Projected)
30	2,000	5.8	5.2	4.6
30	20,000	8.1	7.3	6.5
100	2,000	6.2	5.6	5.0
100	20,000	10.1	9.1	8.1
300	2,000	6.6	6.0	4.9
300	20,000	15.8	14.2	12.6

D. OPERATIONAL IMPLICATIONS

Dives of up to 600 feet are expected to be achieved by the year 1968. Developments during the next 10 and 20 years may make it possible to operate at depths to 5000 and 20,000 feet, respectively using mechanical equipments. These developments will have to come in areas other than heat transfer since the heat generating equipment is not the restricting criterion.

The present day pressurized type water reactors could be reduced in weight and volume by an improved understanding of the boiling mechanism and its dependence upon the boundary layer behavior. Similarly, advances in the art of achieving dropwise condensation for indefinite periods will reduce the condenser sizes by a factor of between 2–10 depending upon the level of research efforts and the application of the equipment. These are the high payoff areas where adequate financial support may lead to greater potential gain and an earlier improved operational capability.

In summary the maximum payoff will result from improved reactor design through steady advances in heat transfer technology.

E. REFERENCES

"Conceptual Study of Electrical Power Transmission Systems to Deep Ocean Installations (U)," General Dynamics Corporation, Electric Boat Division, Report No. CR 68.004, Contract N62399–67–C–0015, Aug. 1967.

530   MATERIAL SUPPORT TECHNOLOGY (SEA FLOOR ENGINEERING)

535–30 Underwater Observation

Prepared by:
NAVAL CIVIL ENGINEERING LABORATORY
H. McPherson

A. BACKGROUND

Operations in sea can be observed directly by men looking through viewports at scenes illuminated by lamps; or indirectly, with TV (assisted by buoys, and by acoustic sensors, and by photography). In some instances the equipment is exposed to ambient, in others it must be protected from pressure or fouling. These equipments have evolved from other industrial uses, e.g., TV systems, or from military surveillance systems, e.g., high resolution sonar. Remote systems require hard wire telemetry links between the coast site and the viewer (observer).

B. PRESENT STATUS

Todays lamps are common tungsten filament incandescent lights, mercury vapor, quartz iodine, tungsten halogen, and thallium iodide. The efficiency of these illumination sources vary from 10 lumens per watt for the incandescent to 80 lumens per watt for the thallium iodide. The length of useful life of these illumination sources varies greatly from 10 hours for arc lights to 1000's of hours for the incandescent lights.

Viewing distances of 10 to 20 feet are considered normal for the unaided eye while distances of 25 and 35 feet are approximate distances, respectively, for the vidicon and image orthicon.

The underwater viewing (visual display) capability of sonar devices has not been applied to ocean floor engineering.

An ultrasonic telemetry system has recently been developed and is in prototype stage for use in depths greater than 6000 feet. The system has 3 channels and provides 10% of full scale accuracy.

Ultrasonic holography is in the R&D stage.

Acrylic windows of conical frustrum shape seating in steel flanges with conical cavities are considered standard for submersibles. Design factors in the range of 8 to 18, based on short term implosion pressure at room temperature are considered to be acceptable design criteria for such windows. Although a factor of 12 is looked upon as standard, it is known to be over-conservative.

Other acrylic window shapes, like flat disc and spherical shell sector have been investigated under short term loading. As a result flat disc acrylic windows are also being utilized in few shallow depth submersibles, diving bells, and hyperbaric chambers. The spherical shell sector acrylic windows have found no application yet in operational systems although they are being considered for some.

Glass windows find only very limited application. Their use is limited almost exclusively to diving bells and hyperbaric chambers of less than 1000 psi pressure capability. But even there they are being displaced by acrylic material whose behavior under the combination of stresses found in a hydrospace window is more repeatable than that of currently available glass.

Fouling of the window's surface exposed to sea water limits the optical usefulness of windows to about 24 hours. A recently introduced Tributyl Tin Oxide transparent coating extends the optical usefulness of windows to somewhat in excess of 100 hours. No difference in resistance to fouling has been found between glass, acrylic or polycarbonate materials.

C. FORECAST

1978—The light source will increase 50% in efficiency and 100% in length of life. The main area of improvement will be to match the wave length of the generated light with the band in which the receiving sensor has its greatest efficiency. (See Figures 1 and 2.)

The pressure case will become 20% lighter. The electrical connection will become 95% reliable. (See Figure 3.)

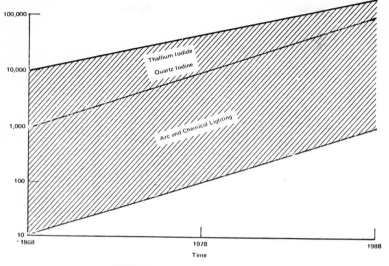

LIFETIME OF UNDERWATER LIGHTS

Figure 1

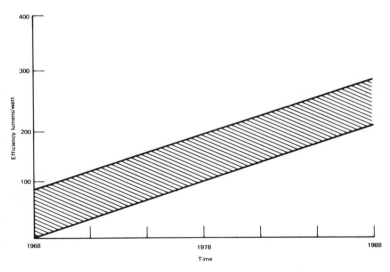

ENERGY EFFICIENCY OF UNDERWATER LIGHTS

Figure 2

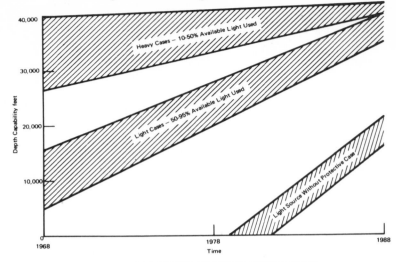

DEPTH CAPABILITY OF UNDERWATER LIGHTS

Figure 3

Acrylic windows, regardless of their shape, will be completely understood and detailed design standards and specifications will be available for their design and fabrication. Factors of safety of 6 to 8 (compared with present design factor of 12) will encourage the incorporation of larger windows in submersibles. (See Figure 4.)

Spherical shell sector shape acrylic windows will further increase in size permitting the occupants of submersibles to have a panoramic view of hydrospace. Window diameters of up to 8 ft for continental shelf depths, and 1 foot for abyssal depths will become state of the art of a acrylic windows. Very little improvement in acrylic windows beyond the state of the art forecast for 1968 will be feasible unless the limitation imposed by the mechanical properties of the currently available acrylic are lifted.

Research conducted on the basic mechanical properties of glass, and the effect of triaxial stress fields with local stress concentrations on its failure will result in flat disc glass windows of 4 to 8 inches diameter and up to 5000 feet depth capability. Nevertheless, for the same diameter and thickness the acrylic windows will still be capable of withstanding greater depths than glass windows.

Other transparent plastic materials will produce several promising candidates with 20 to 50 percent higher mechanical strength properties of 20 to 50 percent less time dependent strain than currently available acrylics.

Fouling of windows will be eliminated for periods of at least 1000 hours by the development of slow leaching transparent overlays applied to the high pressure face of the windows.

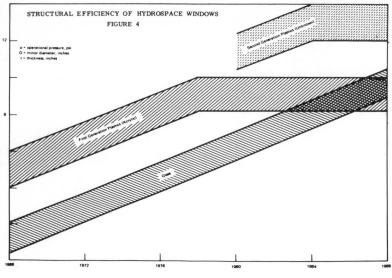

STRUCTURAL EFFICIENCY OF HYDROSPACE WINDOWS
FIGURE 4

p = operational pressure, psi
D = minor diameter, inches
t = thickness, inches

Figure 4

1988—Nuclear and gas power sources will become standard equipment in the 1980's. The length of life will be expanded from weeks to years for small energy supplies. The light source efficiency will be increased to 250 lumens per watt. The length of useful life will be expanded five fold by introduction of better cooling methods, cold light sources and better materials.

For underwater television cameras techniques such as time and range rating, to eliminate some "close" back scattering, may improve range to a limited degree.

For underwater ultrasonic telemetry 1.0% of full scale accuracy appears entirely feasible. Many channels of information will be multiplexed on one ultrasonic carrier using FM-FM techniques. Since most phenomena being monitored are dynamically slow, time sharing will be utilized to increase the amount of information. Surface radio buoys or other radio link facilities, including satellite repeaters, will make the monitored data available anywhere in the world in real time. Data reduction to engineering units will be "computerized."

Control of activities on the ocean floor will be accomplished by using ultrasonic techniques on a "two way street" basis.

With underwater acoustics, objects can be located and dimensioned, readout of tools can be used and guidelines can be provided for the mating of prefabricated structures. Improved resolution, together with greater range will be achieved as the dimension of the transducers are increased. The techniques used in mine detection and anti-submarine warfare ultrasonic devices will be adapted to sea floor engineering requirements. The use of digitally formatted information, at frequencies within the hearing spectrum of the diver will be exploited. Use of these techniques will free packages, which he presently must carry and significantly improve the work efficiency of divers.

Introduction of new transparent plastic as window material will permit the increase of the window diameters further from what they were in 1968 when made from acrylic. The increase in size will be the order of 20 to 50 percent for all depth capabilities. Detailed design and fabrication standards will be available for fabrication of hydrospace windows from the new materials.

The continued investigation of mechanical properties of glass and its behavior under complex stress fields will result in the acceptance of glass on par with plastic windows. The available glass windows will be probably of the same size and thickness as the plastic ones for any given depth range. They will be preferred for applications where water temperatures above 75°F or sustained loading durations or more than 1000 hours are encountered in service.

D. OPERATIONAL IMPLICATIONS

Improvement of underwater lights will make surveillance of surrounding hydrospace more complete and accurate and result in increased safety and ease of operations. Enhanced operating areas would be vessel control, data acquisition, navigation, and search and salvage.

Panoramic visibility approaching that of airplane cockpits and car windshields will permit safer operation of submersibles in close proximity to fixed objects on the ocean floor. Ocean bottom habitats will make the surveillance of surrounding hydrospace more complete and accurate.

E. REFERENCES

NCEL Technical Report R–209, "Analysis of a Pulsed Light Deep Ocean Search System," R. Hitchcock.

NCEL Technical Report R–432, "Submarine Illumination and Television in Harbor Water," R. Hitchcock.

NCEL Technical Report R–532, "Light Housing for Deep-Submergence Applications," by J. D. Stachiw and K. O. Gray.

T. R. Kretschmer, DOTIPOS Sea Performance and Plate Bearing Test, Internal Memo, 5 June 1960.

Snoey, M. R. and Stachiw, J. D., "Windows and Transparent Hulls for Man in Hydrospace," 4th Annual Marine Technology Conference, 1968.

E.E. General References on Sea Floor Engineering

The following references, while not exhaustive, are in the NCEL library and are considered good references on Sea Floor Engineering.

The Encyclopedia of Oceanography, Volume I of Earth Sciences Series, edited by R. W. Fairbridge, Rewhold Publishing Corporation, New York, 1966.

The Oceans, H. V. Sverdrup, M. W. Johnson and Richard H. Fleming, Prentice Hall, 1942.

Ocean Engineering, Volumes I to IV National Security Industrial Association, 1965.

The Sea, Volumes I to III, General Editor M. N. Hill, John Wiley and Sons, 1962.

The Living Sea, Jacques-Yves Cousteau, Harper and Row, 1963.

Abyss, the Deep Sea and The Creatures that Live In It, C. P. Idyll, Crowell, 1964.

Under the Deep Ocean; Twentieth Century Voyages of Discovery, T. F. Gaskell, Norton, 1960.

The Floors of the Ocean, B. C. Heezen, Geological Society of America, 1959.

The Sea Bed, V. Zenkovick, Lawrence and Wishart, 1959.

Ocean Engineering, Volumes I to VIII, North American Aviation, 1964.

Sea Bottom Instrumentation Investigation, C. L. Hayen and C. L. Cohen, Challenger Research, Inc., 1967.

The Ocean Engineering Program of the U.S. Navy; Accomplishment and Prospects, Oceanographic Office, 1967.

Ocean Sciences, E. J. Long, U.S. Naval Institute, 1964.

A Hole In the Bottom of the Sea; The Story of the MOHOLE Project, Williard Bascom, Doubleday, 1961.

IGY World Data Center A: Oceanography Catalogue of Data, Volumes 1 to 5, 1967.

Oceanographical Engineering, R. L. Wiegel, Prentice-Hall, 1964.

Apparatus and Methods of Oceanography, Harold Barnes, N.Y. Interscience Publishers, Inc., 1959.

Oceanography and Marine Biology; A Book of Techniques, Macmillan, 1959.

Oceanography, Proceedings of the International Oceanographic Congress in New York in 1959, American Association for the Advancement of Science, 1961.

New Portrait of Our Planet (map of ocean floors), LIFE, 1960.

Oceanography, 1966, Achievements and Opportunities, 1967, National Research Council, Committee on Oceanography, 1966.

Effective Use of the Sea, U.S. Presidents Science Advisory Committee, U.S. Government Printing Office, 1966.

Oceanography: An Introduction to Marine Sciences, Boston, Little Brown, 1962.

Glossary of Ocean Sciences and Undersea Technology Terms, Edited by Lee M. Hurst and Donald G. Groves, Compass Publications, Arlington, Virginia, 1965.

Glossary of Oceanographic Terms, edited by B. B. Baker, W. R. Deebel, E. D. Geisenderfer, Washington, D.C., 1966.

Oceanography to Geographers, C. A. King, London, E. Arnold, 1962.

Down to the Sea; A Century of Oceanography, J. R. Dean, Glasgow, Grown, Son and Ferguson, 1966.

Marine Sciences Instrumentation, Instrument Society of America, Pittsburg, Pennsylvania, 1962–1965.

F. ASSOCIATED R&D ORGANIZATIONS

Naval Underwater Warfare Center, Pasadena, California
Mine Detection Laboratory, Orlando, Florida
Naval Ship Systems Command, Washington, D.C.
Underwater Sound Laboratory, New London, Connecticut
Naval Electronics Laboratory, San Diego, California
Naval Ship Research and Development Center, Annapolis, Maryland

MATERIAL	STRUCTURAL			MACHINERY		ENVIRONMENTAL						MISCELLANEOUS		
	HOMOGENEOUS	COMPOSITE	ARMOR	PROPULSION & POWER	PIPING & AUXILIARY	CORROSIVE SERVICE	LOW TEMP SERVICE	HIGH TEMP SERVICE	PROTECTION	WIRE ROPE, WIRE, ETC.	ELECTRICAL	UNIQUE PROPERTIES	CAMOUFLAGE & IDENTIFICATION	ENERGY ABSORPTION & INSULATION
ALUMINUM	X	X		X	X	X	X			X	X			
ANTIMONY												X		
BERYLLIUM	X	X		X	X	X	X	X	X			X		
BISMUTH												X		
CADMIUM							X				X	X		
CESIUM														
CHROMIUM		X		X	X			X						
COBALT		X		X	X	X		X	X			X		
COLUMBIUM				X	X	X		X				X		
COPPER		X		X	X	X	X				X			
GALLIUM											X	X		
GERMANIUM												X		
GOLD		X				X						X		
HAFNIUM								X			X	X		
INDIUM											X	X		
IRIDIUM											X	X		
IRON	X	X		X	X	X	X	X	X					
LANTHANUM												X		
LEAD						X						X		
LITHIUM												X		
MAGNESIUM	X	X		X	X	X		X				X		
MERCURY											X	X		
MOLYBDENUM	X			X	X			X				X		
NICKEL	X	X		X	X	X	X	X	X					
NIOBIUM											X			
OSMIUM											X	X		
PALLADIUM		X		X	X			X				X		
PLATINUM		X		X	X			X				X		
POTASSIUM												X		
RHENIUM						X					X	X		
RHODIUM												X		
RUTHENIUM											X	X		
SELENIUM												X		
SILICON											X			
SILVER		X				X					X	X		
SODIUM												X		
STEEL – SEE IRON														
TANTALUM				X	X	X	X				X	X		
TECHNETIUM												X		
TELLURIUM												X		
THALLIUM											X	X		
TIN						X					X	X		
TITANIUM	X	X		X	X	X	X	X		X		X		
TUNGSTEN				X	X			X			X	X		
URANIUM											X	X		
VANADIUM				X				X			X	X		
ZINC						X						X		
ZIRCONIUM											X	X	X	
ADHESIVES		X							X			X		
COATINGS									X					
COMPOSITES		X	X	X					X			X	X	
FIBERS & TEXTILES									X					
HYDRAULIC FLUIDS				X					X					
LUBRICANTS				X					X					
PLASTICS	X	X	X	X					X			X	X	X
WOOD	X	X												

NOTE: "X" – MATERIAL / FUNCTION COVERED

"Science is as yet in its infancy, and we can foretell little of the future save that the thing that has not been is the thing that shall be; that no beliefs, no values, no institutions are safe." — J. B. S. HALDANE 1924

APPENDIX D

*ORGANIZATIONS ADDRESSING EFFORT TOWARD A DELINEATION OF THE FUTURE ENVIRONMENT**

Profit, Non-Profit Professional Organizations:

Abt Associates, Boston, Massachusetts (Clark Abt and Robert Rae), has developed an automated scenario generator, allocation of resource models, and consults to private industry in these areas.

Battelle Memorial Institute, Columbus, Ohio (Edgar Cheany and William Swager), has a large data bank of technological forecasts and consults to private industry on the integration of this information on their corporate objectives and long-range R&D programs.

Commission on the Year 2000, American Academy of Arts and Sciences, Boston, Massachusetts (Daniel Bell), has been developing hypothetical alterative futures and related problems likely to emerge, to seek measures by which to judge social performance and pose alternative policy approaches to the solution of such problems.

Conference on the Next Fifty Years (1967–2011), American Institute of Planners, Washington, D.C. (William Ewald), conducts conferences on various types of technological, political, economic, and social problems that may emerge by 2011 and recommends some probable courses of action.

Division of Public Affairs Research, National Industrial Conference Board, New York City, New York (Charles M. Darling), is attempting to identify emerging scientific or technological opportunities derived from forecasting in an attempt to restate them to potential problems in business policy and strategies.

Educational Policy Research Center, Syracuse Research Corporation, Syracuse, New York (Thomas Green), has been focusing its attention on alternative scenarios for society and for education 20 years into the future.

G. E. Tempo, Santa Barbara, California (Theodore Rubin), has designed an information system for environmental forecasting. They do consulting in the area of "future environments."

Harvard University Program on Technology and Science, Cambridge,

---

* An environmental forecast of social/political changes in the 1970's is included as an example at the end of this Appendix.

293

Massachusetts (Emmanuel G. Mesthene), has been looking in depth at the interaction of technological innovation of society, public policy, and the economy, and vice versa.

Hudson Institute, Croton-on-Hudson, New York (Herman Kahn), has developed a number of future scenarios and an analytic summary which has a complete classification system for evaluating social consequences of planned R&D. Hudson has a large consultant business (largely military).

Institute for the Future, Middletown, Connecticut (Olaf Helmer and Theodore Gordon), has been developing data banks, methodologies, and technological and environmental forecasts in order to influence constructively the formulation of long-range public policy to bring about the most desirable possible future through appropriate, purposeful action. This group consults to government agencies as well as private corporations.

Lockheed Corporation, Burbank, California (Harold Linstone), has developed the Military Analysis of the Future Environments of 1975 (Mirage 75) and 1980 (Mirage 80) which compares the United States with other nations, technologically, economically, socially, and politically.

National Planning Association, Washington, D.C. (Leonard Lecht), undertakes policy studies on possible national goals and the probable allocation of scarce resources to meet these goals.

Project on Social Trends, Russell Sage Foundation, New York City, New York (Wilbert Moore), has developed social indicators dealing with Productivity, The Family Unit, Religion, Consumption, Leisure, and The Labor Force.

Stanford Research Institute (SRI), Menlo Park, California (James E. Hacke), has both a Long-Range Planning and Forecasting Service (subscriptions) and individual consultant service on specific technologies as they apply to corporate long-range planning. They also have an Educational Policy Research Center developing methods of portraying alternative qualitative social states with emphasis on education for the next 20 years.

Synergistic Cybernetics Incorporated (SCI), Alexandria, Virginia (Jacob Johnson), aids corporations in setting up a technological forecasting capability and trains their employees on how to "set corporate goals, prepare technological forecasts, and integrate these into a planning system, including an "allocation of resources model."

System Development Corporation, Santa Monica, California (Hasan Ozbekham and Marvin Adelson), has accumulated a large number of software programs which are required in utilizing automated or computerized operations research techniques necessary in developing a large, integrated forecasting program. These programs and the services of the System Development Corporation staff are available for a fee.

The Diebold Institute for Public Policy Studies, New York City, New York (Herbert Blitz), is analyzing public problems created by technological change, hoping to persuade the private sector as well as government to aid in correcting these problems.

TRW, Incorporated, Redondo Beach, California (Harper Q. North), has in operation a modified Delphic approach to "Probing" TRW's future in many technological areas. This probe is used in developing TRW's long-range plans.

World Resources Inventory, Carbondale, Illinois (John McHale), has developed a program to look at the world as a totality in terms of prospective resources, probable demand for these resources for mankind, and strategies for optimum utilization of these resources.

In the Academic Community:

Columbia University (Aaron Warner), Seminar on Technological and Social Change.

University of California at Berkeley (Mel Weber), The School for Environmental Design.

University of California at Los Angeles (Werner Hirsch), The Institute for Government and Public Affairs.

University of Michigan (Floyd Mann), The Center for Research on the Utilization of Scientific Knowledge.

The George Washington University, Washington, D.C. (Louis Mayo), Program of Policy Studies in Science and Technology dealing with alternative policy strategy to improve the future environment.

State University of New York at Albany, Albany, New York (Eugene McLaren), Center for Study of Science and the Future of Human Affairs (both factulty and student participation).

Case Western Reserve University, Cleveland, Ohio (Dennis Livingston), Course on Alternative Futures of the International Political System.

Congressional Activities:

Technology Assessment Seminar (Congressman Emellio Daddario), proposed that Congress be concerned with how forecasted technology could affect the United States' social, economic, and political goals and then set priorities on broad national goals to bring about the most desirable future environment.

Proposal for a Select Senate Committee on Technology and the Human Environment (Senator Edmund Muskie), dealt with why it is imperative to begin long-range conceptualization of technological innovation and its social consequences.

The future environment is also being worked on abroad by:

Futuribles (Bertrand de Jouvenel)—This work deals with institutionalizing the research for possible futures and the democratic processes of choosing among them. (France)

Imperial College (Dennis Gabor)—Inventing the future deals with the need for "social engineering" to avert potential social disaster. (England)

Committee on the Next 33 Years, British Social Sciences Research Council (Michael Young) —Deals with trying to create a better future. (England)

Office of Economic Co-Operation and Development (OECD) (Erik

Jantsch)—Technological and economic forecasts to aid in the development of 21 different nations. (France)

Europe (Claude Bourdet, Robert Jungk and Maurice Rickards), is working on an exhibition to be called "Mankind 2000."

ENVIRONMENTAL FORECASTS

The following are forecasts of social/political changes in the 1970's which will affect the construction industry:

(1) the notion that hard or unpleasant work must be tolerated because it is unavoidable is on the way out. Many companies may find they cannot pay the premium that workers demand for unpleasant jobs.

(2) By 1975 professional and technical people will outnumber skilled craftsmen. Companies must be prepared to hire and train personnel at the lower end of the educational scale.

(3) The public is developing a lower frustration tolerance for anything that impairs ability to work, live in decency as judged by current economic standards, and to express oneself. There will be no tolerance of circumstances created by poverty, unemployment, sickness, reduced income at retirement, and strikes.

(4) The cost of laying off a worker will be as high as keeping him on the job because of higher unemployment compensation and other benefits; hence, there will be a strong incentive to keep industry on an even keel.

(5) The public will expect more attention be paid to safety in design. Industry will be expected to pay more of the social costs of problems it helped create; such as, air pollution, water pollution and traffic congestion.

(6) The Government will have increasing say in where new plants are to be located, will compel location in rural development areas, will control land usage and pollution, and will have much more to say on building codes.

(7) Farming in the oceans.

(8) Mining on the moon.

(9) Less leadership from business, more from government, research centers and universities.

(10) The end of democratic government as people lose interest and leave decisions to an intellectual, technological elite.

(11) Emergence of new more dangerous weapons, permitting even poor countries to destroy any other country.

BIBLIOGRAPHIES

TECHNOLOGICAL FORECASTING BIBLIOGRAPHY
(Partially Annotated)

Abt Associates, Inc., "Survey of the State of the Art: Social, Political, and Economic Models and Simulations," report prepared for the National Commission on Technology, Automation, and Economic Progress; published in *Applying Technology to Unmet Needs,* Appendix, Vol. V, *Technology and the American Economy,* Washington, D.C.: Government Printing Office, February, 1966.

Abt, Clark, "The Impact of Technological Change on World Politics," *The Futurist,* pp. 21–25 (4/68).

Aerospace Industries Association, *Aerospace Technical Forecast—1962–1972.* Washington, D.C., 1962.

AIR FORCE (U.S.) PUBLICATIONS:

Technology for Tomorrow, 5th ed., 1962–63, Aeronautical Systems Division, AFSC, Wright-Patterson AFB, Ohio; 62ASOP–300, December, 1962. (SECRET)

> "Technology for Tomorrow" is a preparation of motivational concepts, outlining the approach to an optimum plan. It is a guide to the organization and selective application of resources and capabilities for an aggressive support of the long-range Air Force technical mission. Thus it represents a step in the planning process. The contents and organization of the document reflect, in themselves, the fact that a cohesive detailed plan exists collectively in the minds of the engineers, scientists, and management personnel who have contributed to its formulation.

Operation FORECAST, 14 vols., SCGF–46–7 Forecast Special Project Office, HQ, AFSC, Andrews AFB, Maryland, January, 1964. (SECRET)

Project FORECAST, Organization and Mission Planning Group Report dated April 13, 1963.

> Discusses organization and planned operation of the 1963 study, *Project FORECAST,* conducted by the Air Force. Explains duties of the individuals and panels and how it was expected the panels would interact. Project Forecast Panel Reports:
> a. Navigation and Guidance (AD 354–060)
> b. Electronic Countermeasures and Counter-Countermeasures (AD 354–062)
> c. Intelligence and Reconnaissance (AD 354–063)
> d. Communications, Volumes I and II (AD 354–058, AD 354–059)
> e. Weapons (AD 354–057)
> f. Power Generation (AD 354–053)
> g. Flight Dynamics (AD 354–051)

A Systems Development Planning Structure, an interim report by Abt Associates, Inc., 14 Concord Lane, Cambridge, Mass., to HQ, Air Force Systems Command (SCLS), Andrews Air Force Base, Washington, D.C., November 18, 1965.

In the development of systems, this computerized technique is intended to provide the decision maker with an estimate of the implications of placing special emphasis on particular policies. It describes possible situations related to each policy. The technique is designed to assist with the assignment of a consistent set of relative values to any number of objectives by eliciting "Yes" or "No" responses from the decision maker to questions about preferences for various combinations of objectives.

An Approach to Research and Development Effectiveness, a paper presented by A. B. Nutt, Air Force Flight Dynamics Laboratory, Wright-Patterson Air Force Base, Dayton, Ohio, to 17th NAECON Conference Proceedings, May 12, 1965.

This paper describes the rationale and use of RDE (Research and Development Effectiveness)—a computerized planning program developed in-house and designed to utilize analytical techniques in the management of R&D resources in the Air Force Flight Dynamics Laboratory, RTD, AFSC.

AFSC Technological War Plan, prepared by Deputy Chief of Staff, Plans, AFSC, Washington, D.C., Basic Plan No. TWP Basic SCL–65–3, dated March, 1965. (SECRET)

This report is the AFSC Command Plan for the conduct of R&D activity in support of their assigned responsibility. The TWP consists of a basic plan and five supporting annexes. The purpose of each is briefly stated as follows:

The "Basic Plan" integrates the content of the annexes and provides the transition of planning effort into programs and budgets.

Annex A, "Environment," discusses the broad setting within which the technological threat and military policy goals are evolved.

Annex B, "Threat," describes the expected evolution of aggressor systems and technology.

Annex C, "Systems," projects and describes concepts and capabilities which may evolve into the systems of the future AF force structure.

Annex D, "Technology," describes technology for deriving system capabilities, and projects efforts to strengthen the Command's technological base.

Annex E, "Resources," projects mission man-years, technical facilities and RDT&E funds necessary to develop, test and evaluate both technology and systems.

Technical Objectives Documents, Research and Technology Division, AFSC, 36 Technical Area Reports, November, 1965. (UNCLASSIFIED)

These documents are prepared to provide means of communicating with science and industry and to describe the Air Force's objectives in each of 36 different technical areas. As in any selective grouping in science and technology, it is difficult to draw sharp boundaries between areas, and thus overlapping does occur.

RTD Technological War Plan/Long Range Plan, Research and Technology Division, AFSC, Washington, D.C., Report No. RTL 64, April 25, 1964 and changes. (SECRET)

This plan describes the future course of action that the Research and Technology Division will take in managing the Air Force Exploratory and Advanced Development Programs. It is prepared by the people most familiar with these programs—the working scientists and engineers in the Air Force Laboratories. It is an attainable Plan. It describes how RTD will allocate those resources which it may realistically expect to have available over the next decade.

The Plan is oriented toward achieving the level of technology required to attain the future Air Force capabilities identified by *Project FORECAST*. It also recognizes that a major objective of this Division is the building and maintaining, in our laboratories, of a strong in-house technical capability.

Changes will undoubtedly alter various parts of this Plan. Breakthroughs will occur and unsuccessful efforts will be terminated. On the whole, however, the Plan represents a coordinated picture of where RTD is going over the next decade, as we now see it.

ARMY (U.S.) PUBLICATIONS:

Long Rang Technological Forecast, 3d ed. Prepared by the Office of the Chief of Research and Development, Department of the Army, 3 vols., April, 1965. (SECRET)

The Army *Long Range Technological Forecast* (LRTF) is designed to be of value in both technical and operational planning. It covers a period of twenty years.

The Forecast describes knowledge, capabilities, and examples of material which science and technology can be expected to produce if supported by orderly programs of research and development. It represents one element of a current and comprehensive plan for long-range technical planning. The document is published in 3 volumes, entitled: "Scientic Opportunities, "Technological Capabilities," and "Advanced Systems Concepts."

Forecast in Depth—Information Processing Systems for the Field Army, H. T. Darracott, Technical Forecasting and Objectives Branch, Research and Development Directorate, U.S. Army Materiel Command, Washington, D.C. (UNCLASSIFIED)

Comprehensive study of the peripheral equipments in an automatic information processing system. Part of its purpose was to provide a tool to aid in the design of such equipment for tactical data processing systems.

The Army Research Plan, Industry Edition, Office of the Chief of Research and Development, Department of the Army, No. ARP–65, dated March 1, 1965. (CONFIDENTIAL)

The Army Research Plan (ARP) is an extension of the Army Research and Development Long Range Plan. Its purpose is to afford guidance to those commanders and agencies responsible for the detailed formulation of the Army's research programs by assigning relative levels of recognition to scientific and technological areas of interest to the Army.

Combat Development Objectives Guide, Combat Development Command, Department of the Army, dated August 15, 1964. (SECRET)

The purpose of the *Combat Development Objectives Guide* is to provide guidance for the development of future operational concepts, organizations, and materiel. It states general combat development objectives and consolidates the studies, and lists field experiments and approved qualitative materiel requirements which are pointed toward the attainment of those objectives.

The Army Study System, Director Special Studies, Department of the Army, Office of the Chief of Staff, Washington, D.C., 3 vols. dated May 18, 1964. (Official use only)

Examines current (1964) Army major study activities and evaluates effectiveness of the studies as inputs to planning, programming, budgeting, and other needs. The three volumes are: Basic Study (Vol. I), Study Documentation and Information Retrieval (Vol. II), and Bibliography of Current Major Army Studies, 1962 to date (1964) (Vol. III).

The Army Master Study Program 1967, Army Study Advisory Committee, Chief of Staff, Department of the Army, dated December 27, 1966. (CONFIDENTIAL)

1. A formal, approved list of those major studies being pursued under the sponsorship of the Army Staff Agencies, HQ., Department of the Army, which are considered to be of prime importance to over-all Army planning, force development and programming.

2. A mechanism for the use of the Army Staff to determine gaps or unbalanced emphasis within the over-all study effort and thus enable studies to provide more effective support to the orderly development of the well-balanced, multipurpose Army of the future.

3. An orientation of the Army's study processes toward the unifying concepts, missions and guidance for the Army of the future which are enunciated in the document "Assessment of the Army, 1964."

4. A useful compendium of major Army study efforts for the information of the Office of the Secretary of Defense and other interested government agencies.

Allen, *Technology and Social Change*, Appleton, 1957.

Ayres, Robert U., *On Technological Forecasting*, report HI–484–DP. Hudson Institute, Harmon-on-Hudson, N.Y., January 17, 1966. (Restricted)

———, *Technology and the Prospects for World Food Production*, report HI–640–DP (Rev. 2), Hudson Institute, Harmon-on-Hudson, N.Y., April 19, 1966. 71 pp.

Baade, Fritz, *The Race to the Year 2000. New York*: Doubleday & Company, Inc., 1962. 246 pp.

Bagby, F. L., et al., *A Feasibility Study of Techniques for Measuring and Predicting the State-of-the-Art*. Battelle Memorial Institute, Columbus, Ohio, July, 1959. DDC Report (AD 233–350)

Discusses the results of a feasibility study on techniques for measuring and predicting the state of the art. The method used relied heavily on case histories in systems development. The study was conducted for the Air Force.

Bell, Arthur S., *Toward the Year 2000*. Daedalus, Summer 1967.

Bell, Daniel, "Twelve Modes of Prediction," in *Penguin Survey of the Social Science*, ed. J. Gould, Baltimore, Md.; Penguin Books, 1965.

Bergsteinsson, P., *The Evaluation and Selection of Sources for Major NASA Contracts* (unpublished Master of Science thesis, M.I.T. Sloan School of Management, 1967).

Bernstein, George B., *A Fifteen-Year Forecast of Information-Processing Technology, Naval Supply Systems Command*, Washington, D.C. 1969.

——— and Cetron, Marvin J., "SEER: A Delphic Approach Applied to Information Processing," *Technological Forecasting*; American Elsevier, N.Y.C.; Spring 1969.

Bicker, Robert E., *The Changing Relationship Between the Air Force and the Aerospace Industry*, Memorandum RM–4101–PR. The RAND Corporation, Santa Monica, Calif., July, 1964. 79 pp.

Bisplinghoff, R. L., *New Technology, Its Selection and Development*. Office of Advanced Research and Technology, National Aeronautics and Space Administration, Washington, D.C., February 1965.

Blackett, P. M. S., "Tizard and the Science of War," *Nature*, March, 1960.

Bliven, Bruce, *Preview for Tomorrow: The Unfinished Business of Science*. New York: Alfred A. Knopf, 1953. 345 pp.

Bright, James R., "Opportunity and Threat in Technological Change," *Harvard Business Review*, November–December, 1963.

———, ed., *Research, Development, and Technological Innovation*. Homewood, Ill.: Richard D. Frwin, Inc., 1964. 783 pp.

———, *Technological Planning on the Corporate Level*, Division of Research, Harvard Business School, Boston, Mass., 1961.

———, ed., *Technological Forecasting for Industry and Government, Methods and Applications*, Prentice-Hall, Inc., Englewood Cliffs, N.J., 1968.
Comprised of the following articles: "A Sociologist Looks at Technical Prediction," S. C. Gilfillan; "Technological Forecasting Lessons from Project Hindsight," R. S. Isenson; "Forecasts of Exploding Technologies by Trend Extrapolation," R. C. Lenz, Jr.; "Envelope Curve Forecasting," R. U. Ayres; "A Methodology for Trend-Forecasting of Figures of Merit," A. L. Floyd; "Techniques for Measuring Uncertainty in Technological Forecasting," F. J. Husic; "Analysis of the Future: The Delphi Method," O. Helmer; "New Approaches to Delphi," T. J. Gordon; "An Evaluation and Appraisal of Various Approaches to Technological Forecasting," M. J. Cetron, et al.; "An Integrated Model of Technological Change," F. H. Buttner, et al.; "The Multiple Contingency Concept of Long-Range Technological Planning," R. H. Rea, et al.; "On Mirages," H. A. Linstone; "Technology, Policy, and Forecasting," T. J. Rubin; "The Use of Technological Forecasts for Planning Research," J. P. Martino; "Generation and Application of Technological Forecasts for R&D Programming," A. W. Schmidt, et al.; "Technological Forecasting in Product Planning with Emphasis on Systems Development," H. A. Wells; "Technological Projection and Advanced Product Planning," F. S. Pardee; "The Manager and Technological Forecasting," J. R. Bright; "Technological Forecasting for the Canadian Pulp and Paper Industry," L. R. Thiesmeyer; "The Application of Strategic Forecasting to the Coal Industry," C. M. Mottley; "Developing and Using the U.S. Army Long Range Technological Forecast," J. R. Bird, et al.; "Technology, the Chicken—Corporate Goals, the Egg," H. Q. North; "Integrating Forecasting and Planning Through a Function-oriented Approach," E. Jantsch.

Brown, Bernice, and Olaf Helmer, *Improving the Reliability of Estimates, Obtained from a Consensus of Experts*, report P–2986. The RAND Corporation, Santa Monica, Calif., 1964.

Brown, Harrison, *The Challenge of Man's Future: An Inquiry Concerning the Condition of Man during the Years that Lie Ahead*. New York: The Viking Press, 1954, 290 pp.

Brown, J. H., and E. S. Cheaney, *Report on a Study of Future Research Activity and Pertinent Forecasting Technique for Battelle's Trends in Research Study.* Battelle Memorial Institute, Columbus, Ohio, 1965. 51 pp.

Brozen, Yale, "Determination of the Direction of Technological Change," *American Economic Review*, Vol. 43 (May, 1953), 288–302.

Bruce, Robert D., *The Dimensions of Change.* Paper presented at the First National Joint Meeting, Operations Research Society of America and The Institute of Management Sciences, San Francisco, Calif., November 9, 1961.

Calder, Richie, *After the Seventh Day: The World Man Created.* New York: Simon and Schuster, Inc., 1961. 448 pp.

————, ed., *The World in 1984*, 2 vols., Penguin, 1965.

Cetron, Marvin J., "Using Technological Forecasts," *Science and Technology*, July 1968, No. 79, pp. 57–63.

————, "Forecasting Technology," *International Science & Technology*, September, 1967. 83–92.

————, "Prescription for the Military R&D Manager," presented at the NATO Defense Research Group Seminar; Teddington, England; November 12, 1968, pp. 19, 21–22.

————, "Quantitative Utility Estimates for Science and Technology (QUEST)," *IEEE Transactions on Engineering Management*, Vol. EM–14, No. 1 (March, 1967), 51–62.

———— and Dick, Donald, "Practical Technological Forecasting Problems and Pitfalls," *European Business*, Fontainebleau, France; Winter 1969.

———— and Mahinske, E. B., "The Value of Technological Forecasting for the Research and Development Manager," *Futures*; Iliffe Science and Technology Publication Ltd., London, England, September 1968, Vol. 1, No. 1.

———— and Monahan, T. I., "An Evaluation and Appraisal of Various Approaches to Technological Forecasting." *Technological Forecasting for Industry and Government*, ed. J. F. Bright; Prentice Hall, Englewood Cliffs, N. J., 1968.

———— and Weiser, A. L., "Technological Change, Technological Forecasting and Planning R&D—A View from the R&D Manager's Desk," *The George Washington Law Review—Technology Assessment and the Law*, Vol. 36, No. 5, Washington, D.C., p. 1091.

————, P. H. Caulfield and R. D. Freshman, "Facts and Folklore in R&D Management Revisited," submitted to *Management Science* (TIMS) for publication in the Winter of 1969.

————, et al., *A Proposal for a Navy Technological Forecast*, Parts I and II 2 vols. Headquarters Naval Material Command, Washington, D.C., May 1, 1966. (AD 659–199) and AD 659–200)

> *Part I, Summary Report*, presents in concise form the results of a six month study carried out by the Navy Technological Forecasting Study Group. The document recommends a Navy technological forecast and describes the nature and utility of such an effort in addition to the procedure for accomplishing it.
>
> *Part II, Back-up Report*, presents much detail supporting material, sample forecasts, methodologies and a classification scheme. The backup report will aid those responsible for actually generating technological forecasts.

————, Joseph Martino and Lewis Roepcke, "The Selection of R&D Program Content—Survey of Quantitative Methods," *IEEE Transactions on Engineering Management*, Vol. EM–14, No. 1 (March, 1967), 4–12.

Changes Facing Business in '70's, U.S. News and World Report, 3 June 1968.

Cheany, E. S., *Technical Forecasting as a Basis for Planning,* ASME paper 66–MD–67, presented at the Design Engineering Conference, Chicago, Ill., May 9–12, 1966.

Clarke, Arthur S., *Profiles of the Future,* Harper.

Conant, James B., *Science and Common Sense,* New Haven: Yale University Press, 1952; Yale Paperbound (tenth printing) July, 1964, 344 pp.

Conference of Senior Officials of National Bodies Concerned with Urban and Regional Research, Economic Commission of Europe Committee on Housing, Building and Planning, Stockholm, 24 April–1 May 1968.

Conklin, ed., *17X Infinity,* Dell, 1963.

Dalkey, N., and Olaf Helmer, "An Experimental Application of the Delphi Method to the Use of Experts," *Management Science,* 9 (April, 1963), 458–67.

Darwin, Charles Galton, *The Next Million Years.* London: Rupert Hart-Davis, 1952. 210 pp.

De Solla Price, D. J., "The Acceleration of Science—Crisis in Our Technological Civilization," *Product Engineering,* 32 (March 6, 1961), 56–59.

———, "A Calculus of Science," *International Science and Technology,* No. 15, March, 1963.

———, *Little Science, Big Science,* New York: Columbia University Press, 1963; Columbia Paperback Edition, 1965. 118 pp.

Duesenberry, *et al.* (editors), *The Brookings Quarterly Econometric Model of the United States,* Rand McNally, 1965.

Dockx, S., and P. Bernays, eds., *Information and Prediction in Science,* New York: Academic Press, 1965. 272 pp.

Domar, E. D., "On the Measurement of Technological Change," *Economic Journal,* 71 (December, 1961), 709–29.

Doyle, L. B., *How to Plot a Breakthrough.* System Development Corporation, Santa Monica, Calif., December, 1963. (AD 427–161)

Ellingsworth, K., "Technology Assessment," an unpublished masters paper in R&D Management, American University, Washington, D.C., June, 1968.

Ellison, ed., *Dangerous Visions,* Doubleday, 1968.

Ellul, Jacques, *The Technological Society.* New York: Alfred A. Knopf, Inc., 1964. 449 pp.

Emme, Eugene M., *A History of Space Flight.* New York: Holt, Rinehart & Winston, Inc., 1965.

Ewell, L. N., "Uncle Sam Gazes into His Crystal Ball," *Armed Forces Chemical Journal,* Vol. VI (January, 1953), 9–15.

Falk & Mendlovitz, eds., *The Strategy of World Order,* World Law Fund, 1968.

Fedor, Walter S., Senior Editor, "Commodity Forecasting by Computer Time Sharing," *C&EN Feature,* September 12, 1966.

Foreign Policy Assoc., *Toward the Year 2018,* Cowles, 1968.

Forrester, Jay, *Industrial Dynamics.* Cambridge, Mass.: The M.I.T. Press, 1961.

———, "Modeling the Dynamic Processes of Corporate Growth," presented at the IBM Scientific Computing Symposium; Yorktown Heights, New York, December 1964.

Fromm, G., and Taubman, P., *Policy Simulations With an Econometric Model,* The Brookings Institute, 1968.

Furnas, C. C., *The Next Hundred Years—The Unfinished Business of Science.* Baltimore, Md.: Williams & Wilkins, 1936.

"The Future," *New York Times Magazine* Section 6, Part 2, April 19, 1964, pp. 86–118.

"The Future as Suggested by the Development of the Past 75 Years," *Scientific American*, October, 1920.

Gabor, Dennis, *Inventing the Future*. London: Secker & Warburg, 1963; Pelican Book A 663, Penguin Books, Harmondsworth, Middlesex, 1964. 199 pp.

Garrison, W. L., and D. F. Marble, *A Prolegomenon to the Forecasting of Transportation Development*. Northwestern University, Evanston, Ill., August, 1965. (AD 621–514).

Gilfillan, S. Colum, "The Prediction of Inventions," in U.S. National Resources Committee, *Technological Trends and National Policy*, Part One, Section II, pp. 15–23. Government Printing Office, June, 1937.

———, *The Sociology of Invention*. Chicago, Ill.: Follett Publishing Company, 1935.

———, "The Prediction of Technical Change," *The Review of Economics and Statistics*, Vol. XXXIV (November, 1952), 368–385.

Gilman, William, *Science: USA*. New York: The Viking Press, 1965.

Gordon, T. J., and O. Helmer, *Report on a Long-Range Forecasting Study*, report P-2982. The RAND Corporation, Santa Monica, Calif., September, 1964. (UNCLASSIFIED)

> Describes an experimental trend-predicting exercise covering a period extending as far as fifty years into the future. The experiment used a sequence of questionnaires to elicit prediction from individual experts in six broad areas: scientific breakthroughs; population growth; automation; space progress; probability and prevention of war; and future weapons systems.

———, *The Future*. New York: St. Martin's Press, 1965. 185 pp.

Granger, Charles H., "The Hierarchy of Objectives," *Harvard Business Review*, May–June, 1964, pp. 63–74.

Greenberger, Martin, ed., *Computers and the World of the Future*. Cambridge, Mass.: The M.I.T. Press, 1962.

Griliches, Zvi, "Hybrid Corn: An Exploration in the Economics of Technological Change," *Econometrica* (Journal of the Econometric Society), Vol. 25, No. 4 (October, 1957), 501–22.

Guth, W. D. and R. Tagiuri, "Personal Values and Corporate Strategy," *Harvard Business Review*—Cambridge, Mass., Sept.–Oct. 1965.

Haase, R. H., and W. H. T. Holden, *Performances of Land Transportation Vehicles*, Memorandum RM–3966–RC. The RAND Corporation, Santa Monica, Calif., January, 1964, p. 138.

Hamilton, H. R., *et al.*, *System Stimulation for Regional Analysis*, Cambridge, M.I.T. Press, 1968.

Heinlein, L. J., *The Past Through Tomorrow*, Doubleday, 1968.

Helmer, Olaf, *Social Technology*, report P-3063. The RAND Corporation, Santa Monica, Calif., February, 1965. ((AD 460–520)

———, and N. Rescher, *On the Epistemology of the Inexact Sciences*, report R–353. The RAND Corporation, Santa Monica, Calif., February, 1960. (AD 236–439)

Hertz, D. B., "The Management of Innovation," *Management Review*, April, 1965, pp. 49–52.

Herz, *International Politics in the Atomic Age*, Columbia, 1962.

Hetrick, J. C., and G. E. Kimball, "A Model for the Discovery and Application of Knowledge," in *Basic Research in the Navy*, Vol. II. U.S. Department of Commerce, Washington, D.C., 1959, pp. 5–29.

Hitch, Charles J., *Decision-Making for Defense*. Berkeley and Los Angeles: University of California Press, 1965.

Holton, Gerard, ed., "Science and Culture—A Study of Cohesive and Disjunctive Forces," *The Daedalus Library*, Vol. 4. Boston, Mass.: Houghton Mifflin Company, 1965.

Isenson, Raymond S., "Technological Forecasting in Perspective," *Management Science*, October, 1966.

———, and C. W. Sherwin, *Project Hindsight* (Interim Report), Office of the Director of Defense Research and Engineering, CSTI (AD 642 400) Springfield, Va., June 30, 1966 (Revised, Oct. 13, 1966).

———, "Factors Affecting the Growth of Technology—As Seen through Hindsight," presented at the NATO Defense Research Group Seminar, Teddington, England, November 1968.

Industrial Research, "Exploring the Sea, etc.," series of articles in *Industrial Research*, March, 1966, pp. 7–114.

Institute of Radio Engineers, "Communications and Electronics—2012 A.D." *Proceedings of the IRE*, Vol. 50, No. 5. The Institute of Radio Engineers, Inc. (IEEE—The Institute of Electrical and Electronics Engineers), New York.

Jantsch, Erich, *Technological Forecasting in Perspective*, Organization for Economic Cooperation and Development, Paris, France, April, 1967.
    Undoubtedly the most comprehensive international survey of the field of Technological Forecasting.

Jestice, A. L., "Project PATTERN—Planning Assistance Through Technical Evaluation of Relevance Numbers." Paper presented to Operations Research Society of America, October 7–8–9, 1964. Pamphlet Minn.-Honeywell, Inc.
    Discusses a method of evaluating and determining how to structure a research and development program, utilizing Honeywell's relevance tree approach.

Jewkes, John, David Sawers and Richard Stillerman, *The Sources of Invention*. London Macmillan & Co., Ltd., 1958.

deJouvenel, B., *Futuribles*, report P–3045. The RAND Corporation, Santa Monica, Calif., January 1965. (AD 610–217)

———, *The Art of Conjecture*, trans. Nikita Lang, New York: Basic Books, Inc., Publishers, 1967.

Kahn & Wiener, *The Year 2000*. Macmillan, 1967.

———, The Year 2000: *A Framework for Speculation on the Next Thirty-Three Years*, Macmillan, 1968.

Kaplan, *New Approaches to International Relations*. St. Martin, 1968.

Kiplinger-Hammond Forecast Atlas of the World, An Encyclopedic Atlas of the World Today, 1964.

Lenz, R. C., Jr., *Technological Forecasting*, 2d ed., Aeronautical Systems Division, AFSC, ASD–TDR–62–414, Wright-Patterson AFB, Ohio, June 1962. (AD 408–085)
    Presents several methods of forecasting rates of technological advance. The methods include forecasting by extrapolation of existing rates; by analogies to biological growth processes; by precursive events; by derivation from primary trends; by interpretation of trend characteristics; and by dynamic simulation of the process of technological improvement. The investigation included a search of the literature for references to principles of technological progress and for methods which have been used for predictive purposes.

————, and Reisman, A., "Higher Education: A Population Flow Feedback Model," *Science*, vol. 153, July 1, 1966.

Lessing, Lawrence, "Where the Industries of the Seventies Will Come From," *Fortune*, January, 1967, p. 96.

Arthur D. Little, Inc., *Patterns and Problems of Technical Innovation in American Industry*, report to National Science Foundation, Boston, Mass., September, 1963 (available OTS, Washington, D.C., PB–181573).

Litton Systems, Inc., *U.S. Defense Posture—Overview 1964–1974*, Guidance Control Systems Division, Publication No. 3373, OPR 64–1. June, 1964.
Provides an overview of the economic, political and military context of the defense market over the next ten years. The major environmental conditions that will shape the domestic and international economic and political climate which will prevail during this time period are evaluated in light of their impact on the defense market.

Linstone, H. A., *Mirage 75—Military Requirements Analysis Generation 1970–75*, Report No. LAC/592371. Lockheed Aircraft Corporation, Burbank, Calif., January, 1965. (SECRET)
This report is the Lockheed corporate planning study on military requirements. It projects the environment to 1970–75 and forecasts systems and technology to meet the projected environment. A similar study, "Mirage 80," has just been published.

Livingston, "Science Fiction as Source Material for Futurists," *Futures*, March, 1969.

Lovewell, P. J., and R. D. Bruce, Stanford Research Institute, "How We Predict Technological Change," *New Scientist*, No. 274, February 15, 1962.

Martino, Joseph P., et al., *Long Range Forecasting Methodology*, A Symposium held at Holloman AFB, Alamogordo, New Mexico, 11–12 October 1967. Comprised of the following articles: "Delphi," N. C. Dalkey; "Unsolved Problems in Selecting Experts in Planning and Long-Range Forecasting," C. W. Taylor; "Demographic Projection Techniques," D. S. Akers, et al.; "Technological Forecasting and Its Role in Planning," H. Q. North; "The Mirage Studies and Some Implications," H. A. Linstone; "Long-Range Projections of Labor Force," D. F. Johnston; "Anticipating Socioeconomic Consequences of a Major Technological Innovation," J. E. Hacke, Jr.; "Numerical Weather Forecasting Techniques," G. D. Hamilton; "Technological Forecasting in Military Planning," M. J. Cetron, et al.

————, *Longe-Range Forecasting and Planning*—A symposium held at the U.S. Air Force Academy, Colorado (16–17 August 1966), comprising the following articles: Marvin J. Cetron, "Background and Utility of Technological Forecasting;" Thomas I. Monahan, "Current Approach to Forecasting Methodology;" James E. Hacke, Jr., "A Methodological Preface to Technological Forecasting;" Howard A. Wells, "Weapon System Planner's Guide;" Robert H. Rea, "A Comprehensive System of Long-Range Planning;" H. T. Darracott, "The U.S. Army Long-Range Technological Forecast—Its Past, Present and Future;" E. S. Cheaney, "Technological Forecasing by Simulation of Design;" Donald Yeager, "Planning and Organizing a Technological Forecast;" Ralph C. Lenz, Jr., "Technological Forecasting;" J. E. McGrolrick, "Planning Launch Vehicles for Space Science and Application;" T. J. Rubin, 'Environmental Information Systems: New Aids for Decision Making;" Clearing house, U.S. Dept. of Commerce, Springfield, Va.

McGraw-Hill, *Research and Development in American Industry*, Department of Economics, New York: McGraw-Hill Publications, May 6, 1966.

McLuhan, Marshall, *Understanding Media: The Extensions of Man*. New York: McGraw-Hill Paperbacks, McGraw-Hill (third printing), 1966. 364 pp.

Magee, John F., "Decision Trees for Decision-Making," *Harvard Business Review*, Vol. 42 (July-August, 1964), 126–38.

Mansfield, E., "Technical Change and the Rate of Imitation," *Econometrics*, October 1961.

———, and Carlton Hensley, "The Logistic Process: Tables of the Stochastic Epidemic Curve and Applications," *The Journal of the Royal Statistical Society*, 1960, pp. 332–37; Reprint No. 60, Graduate School of Industrial Administration, Carnegie Institute of Technology, Pittsburgh, Pa., 1960.

Marquis, D. G., editor, "Second Report of the M.I.T. Research Program on the Management of Science and Technology," M.I.T. Sloan School of Management, October 1967.

Mestene, Emmanuel G., "On Understanding Change: The Harvard University Program on Technology and Society," *Technology and Culture*, Spring, 1965, pp. 222–35.

Mumford, L. S., "Loneliness of the Long Range Forecaster," *Chemical Industry*, 1788–96 (November 9, 1963).

Myers, Sumner, *Industrial Innovations—Their Characteristics and Their Scientific and Technical Information Bases*, a special report to the National Science Foundation, National Planning Association, Washington, D.C., April, 1966. 24 pp.

NAVY (U.S.) PUBLICATIONS:

Navy Long Range and Strategic Study (NLRSS)–73, prepared by Strategic Plans Division (Op–60), Chief of Naval Operations, May 9, 1965. (SECRET)

Navy Mid-Range Objectives Through 1975 Under Limited Funding Assumptions (MRO–75), prepared by Long Range Objectives Group (Op–93), Chief of Naval Operations, June 1, 1964. (SECRET)

Bureau of Naval Weapons Research and Development Planning Guide, Plans Division, RDT&E, BuWeps, July 1, 1963. (SECRET)

Bureau of Ships Long Range Plan for Research and Development (LRP–62), Volume IA (CONFIDENTIAL), Volume IB (SECRET), Volume IC (CONFIDENTIAL), Department of the Navy, Washington, D.C., August, 1962.

Index of Navy Development Requirements, DCNO(D), Encl (1) to CNO 0201P70, January, 1965. (CONFIDENTIAL)
    Contains: (A) A list of Planning Objectives, General Operational Requirements, Specific Operational Requirements and Advanced Development Objectives (Part I) for use in verifying that requirements files are current; (b) An index of Operational Requirements and Development Characteristics (Part II), which will be phased out as they are replaced by undated GOR's and SOR's.

Department of the Navy RDT&E Management Guide, vols. I and II, NAVEXOS P–2457, July, 1964.
    Published in two volumes: "Vol I—Organization and Procedures" and "Vol II—Appendixes." Prepared to aid both newcomers and practicing "journeymen."

Rationales for Goals in Part I—The Undersea Target of Goals for Technology in Exploratory Development. Draft report, Chief of Naval Development (MAT 311), August 31, 1965. (SECRET)

Gives rationales used in deriving the Goals for Technology in Exploratory Development.

Goals for Technology in Exploratory Development—The Undersea Target. Preliminary report published by the Chief of Naval Development (MAT 311), August 31, 1965. (SECRET)

Purpose is to assist in formulating the Exploratory Development Program of the Navy. The goals included herein are based on various formal long-term statements of need expressed by the Chief of Naval Operations and the Commandant of the Marine Corps. This document is intended for in-house use by personnel concerned with planning and programming the Exploratory Development Program at all levels of the technical community.

Goals for Technology in Exploratory Development—The Air Target. Preliminary report published by the Chief of Naval Development (MAT 311), November 17, 1965. (SECRET)

Purpose is to assist in formulating the Exploratory Development Program of the Navy. The goals included herein are based on various formal long-term statements of need expressed by the Chief of Naval Operations and the Commandant of the Marine Corps. This document is intended for in-house use by personnel concerned with planning and programming the Exploratory Development Program at all levels of the technical community.

Goals for Technology in Exploratory Development—The Air Target. Preliminary report published by the Chief of Naval Development (MAT 311), November 17, 1965. (SECRET)

Purpose is to assist in formulating the Exploratory Development Program of the Navy. The goals included herein are based on various formal long-term statements of need expressed by the Chief of Naval Operations and the Commandant of the Marine Corps. This document is intended for in-house use by personnel concerned with planning and programming the Exploratory Development Program at all levels of the technical community.

"Advanced Developments and Advanced Development Candidates for Tactical Missiles and Weapons," *PROJECT SMEADO '67* Missile Development Office (RM), Bureau of Naval Weapons, RM–67–1A, June, 1965. (SECRET)

Main body, Sections 1 through 9, consists of brief summaries of FY 67 plans for Advanced Developments and Advanced Development Candidates in the Tactical Missiles and Weapons Area. These summaries are abstracts of forty individual current planning documents, prepared under PROJECT SMEADO. Taken together, the forty summaries constitute a SMEADO '67 Catalog for Missile Development Office (RM) operations. Plans for the Missile Flight Evaluation Systems Area are not included.

Navy Program Factors, Office of Chief of Naval Operations (OPNAV 90P–02, revised May, 1965. (CONFIDENTIAL)

"Navy Program Factors" supplements the Navy Programming Manual (OPNAV 90P–1). It is comprised of Program Factor Description Sheets and Program Factor Data Sheets grouped by the major resource areas of ships and aircraft. The program factors will be used in the Navy planning and programming analytical procedure

(Cost Model) for estimating the resource implications (materiel, personnel, dollars) of various force levels and varying levels of support of these forces.

"Project SEABED," *Advanced Sea-Based Deterrence Summer Study 1964,* Naval Ordnance Laboratory, Silver Spring, Md., July, 1964. (SECRET) Four-volume report giving the results of the summer study held in Monterey, California, by the Special Projects Office. The four volumes are as follows:
Volume I—Summary
Volume II—Contemporary Analysis of Sea-Based Deterrence
Volume III—Weapons Systems for Sea-Based Deterrence
Volume IV—Advanced Underseas Technology.

Pellini, W. S., *Status and Projections of Developments in Hull Structural Materials for Deep Ocean Vehicles and Fixed Bottom Installations,* Naval Research Laboratory, NRL Report 6167, Washington, D.C., November 4, 1964.
Projects state of the art in materials for deep ocean operation. Used at PROJECT SEABED in defining the potentials for deep-ocean vehicles and installations in the 1980's and the R&D necessary to make these potentials a reality.

Nay, J. N., *Choice and Allocation in Multiple Markets: A Research and Development Systems Analysis* (unpublished Master of Science thesis, M.I.T. Department of Electrical Engineering, 1966).

Nelson, Richard A., *The Link Between Sciences and Invention: The Case of the Transistor.* The RAND Corporation, P–1854–RC, December 15, 1957. (AD 222,163)

Neumann, John von, "Can We Survive Technology," *Fortune,* June, 1955.

Nord, O. C., *Growth of a New Product,* Cambridge: The M.I.T. Press, 1963.

Ozbekhan, Hasan, *The Idea of a "Look-Out" Institution,* System Development Corporation, Santa Monica, Calif., March, 1965. 20 pp.

———, *Technology and Man's Future,* report SP–2494. System Development Corporation, Santa Monica, Calif., May 27, 1966. 41 pp.

Page, Robert Morris, "The Origin of Radar," *Science Study Series.* Garden City, N.Y.: Anchor Books, Doubleday & Co., 1962. 198 pp.

Pardee, F. S., *State of the Art Project and Long Range Planning of Applied Research.* The RAND Corporation, Santa Monica, Calif., 1965. (AD 618–516)

Peterson, M. S., "The Trouble with Technological Forecasting," *Science,* 144, May 15, 1964, pp. 795–96.

Prehoda, Robert W., *Designing the Future,* Chilton, 1967.

Quade, E. S., ed., *Analysis for Military Decisions.* The RAND Corporation, R–387–PR, November, 1964.

Quinn, James Brian, "Technological Forecasting," *Harvard Business Review,* March–April, 1967.
Report on Technological Forecasting, interservice ad hoc study group sponsored by the Army Materiel Command, the Naval Material Command, and the Air Force Systems Command, 30 June 1967. Available from the Department of Defense Documentation Center, Cameron Station, Alexandria, Va. This Report assesses the state of the art and synthesizes available information.

Ridenour, Louis N., "Physical Science and the Future," in Lyman Bryson, ed.,

Facing the Future's Risks—Studies Toward Predicting the Unforeseen, New York: Harper & Brothers, 1953, pp. 60–89.

Roberts, E. B., "Facts and Folklore in R&D Management," *Industrial Management Review,* Sloan School of Management, Cambridge, Mass., Spring 1967.

———, "Facts and Folklore in Research and Development Management," *Industrial Management Review,* vol. 8, no. 2, Spring 1967.

———, "Problems of Aging Organizations," *Business Horizons,* vol. 10, no. 4, Winter 1967.

———, "Questioning the Cost/Effectiveness of the R&D Procurement Process," in M. C. Yovits, *et al.,* (editors), *Research Program Effectiveness,* New York: Gordon and Breach, Publishers, 1966.

Rogers, Everett M., *Diffusion of Innovations,* New York: The Free Press, 1962. 367 pp.

———, "Interpersonal Relationships: U.S.A. 2000," *Journal of Applied Behavioral Science,* pp. 265–280 (July 9, 1968).

Rosecrance, "Bipolarity, Multipolarity, and the Future," *Journal of Conflict Resolution,* pp. 314–327 (August 1966).

Russett, "The Ecology of Future International Politics," *International Studies Quarterly* (March 1967).

Samson Science Corporation, *Microelectronics—Revolutionary Impact of New Technology,* Samson Report No. 2, available from Samson Science Corporation, 270 Park Avenue, New York, N.Y. 34 pp.

———, *Satellite Communications—Comsat and the Industry,* Samson Report No. 1, Samson Science Corporation, 270 Park Avenue, New York, N.Y., December, 1964. 84 pp.

Sarnoff, David, "By the End of the Twentieth Century," *Fortune Magazine,* May, 1964, pp. 116–19.

Schaeffer, K. H., J. B. Fink, M. Rappaport, L. Wainstein, and C. J. Erickson, *The Knowledgeable Analyst: An Approach to Structuring Man-Machine Systems.* Project IMU 3546, Stanford Research Institute, Menlo Park, Calif., 1963. (AD 297–432)

Schlager, K. J., "How Managers Use Industrial Dynamics," *Industrial Management Review,* vol. 6, no. 1, 1964.

Schon, D., et al., *The Role of the Federal Government in Technological Forecasting,* Interagency Task Groups on Technological Forecasting in Federal Government, January, 1966.

> A report to the President's Committee on Manpower and to the National Commission on Technology, Automation and Economic Progress. Specifically, the investigation focused on:
> 1. Action points in government at which technological forecasting might be useful, if available;
> 2. Criteria for information at these points;
> 3. Current technological forecasting activities and methodologies and their adequacy to federal requirements.

Scientific American, a symposium comprising the following articles: J. Bronowski, "The Creative Process;" Paul R. Halmos, "Innovation in Mathematics;" Freeman J. Dyson, "Innovation in Physics;" George Wald, "Innovation in Biology;" John R. Pierce, "Innovation in Technology;" John C. Eccles, "The Physiology of Imagination;" Frank Barron, "The Psychology of Imagination;" Warren Weaver, "The Encouragement of Science;" Scientific American, September, 1958.

Science Journal, a special issue of forecasting the future: Robert Jungk, "The Future of Future Research;" Erich Jantsch, "Forecasting the Future;" Olaf Helmer, "Science;" Ali Bulent Cambel, "Energy;" Hasan Ozbekhan, "Automation;" John R. Pierce, "Communication;" Robert C. Seamans, Jr., "Space;" Gabriel Bouladon, "Transportation;" Robert V. Ayres, "Food;" William L. Swager, "Materials;" Roger Revells, "Population;" Herman Kahn, "World Futures" (October, 1967) Vol. 3, No. 10 (London, England).

Semkov, B. F., "Soviet Scientists Discuss Methodology and Planning of Scientific Research" translation from Voprosy (Problems of Philosophy) (Vopr. Filosofii), No. 7, TT–65,30027, Joint Publ. Research Service, OTS U.S. Department of Commerce, Washington, D.C., 1964.

Siegel, Irving H., "Technological Change and Long-Run Forecasting," *The Journal of Business of the University of Chicago*, Vol. XXVI, No. 3 (July, 1953), 141–56.

Sigford, J. V., and R. H. Parvin, "Project PATTERN: A Methodology for Determining Relevance in Complex Decision-Making," *IEEE Transactions on Engineering Management*, Vol. EM–12, No. 1 (March, 1965), pp. 9–13.

Silberman, C. E., "Is Technology Taking Over?" Philosophies of J. Ellul and M. McLuhan, *Fortune*, 73 (February, 1966), pp. 112–15.

Smith, Bruce L., *The Concept of Scientific Choice: A Brief Review of Literature*, report P–3156. The RAND Corporation, June, 1965. 54 pp. (AD 616,977)

Spanier, *World Politics in an Age of Revolution*, Praeger, 1968.

Spencer, R. W., "Modelling Strategies for Corporate Growth," presented at the Society for General Systems Research conference, Washington, D.C., 1966.

Squibb, Andrew, Jr., *What Will Life Bring in 2,000*. 1967 World Book Encyclopedia, Science Service, Inc.

Stanford Research Institute, *The World of 1975* (composite of following SRI Reports: 232, 233, 234, 235, 236). (n.d.)
> Composite of reports on forecasts by SRI Long Range Planning service in predicting the world of 1975. It includes the following subjects:
> 1. The International Prospect
> 2. Economic Trends
> 3. Governmental and Political Trends
> 4. Science and Technology
> 5. Social and Cultural Framework.

Stockfish, J. A., ed., *Planning and Forecasting in the Defense Industries*, (papers presented at a UCLA seminar on 4–5 May 1960). Belmont, Calif.: Wadsworth Publishing Company, 1962.

Stromer, P. R., *Long-Range Planning and Technological Forecasting: An Annotated Bibliography*, SRB–63–12. Lockheed Missiles and Space Co., Sunnyvale, Calif., November, 1963. (AD 441–618)

————, *Longe-Range Planning and Technological Forecasting: An Annotated Bibliography, Supplement I*, SRB–65–1. Lockheed Missiles and Space Co., Sunnyvale, Calif., February, 1965. (AD 457–949)

Swager, William L., *Industrial Implications of Technological Forecasting*. Paper presented to the Fourth Symposium of the Engineer-Economy Division of the American Society for Engineering Education in Chicago, Ill., June 19, 1965. Battelle Memorial Institute.

Sweezy, Eldon E., *Technological Forecasting—Principles and Techniques*. Paper presented at the 4th Symposium of the Engineering Economy

Division, The American Society for Engineering Education, Chicago, Ill., June 19, 1965.

Syracuse University Research Corporation, *Science and Technology in the 1985 Era* (Project 1985), DDC Report AD 613–525 (Appendix AD 613–526), May 1964.

    Prepared in response to a request by the Marine Corps to predict what certain aspects of the world will be like in 1985. In the language of the Marine Corps, "This study will examine projected national objectives and policies, and international and domestic miltiary, economic, and technological factors affecting the United States in the 1985 era."

Syracuse University Research Corporation, *Science and Technology in the 1985 Era* (Project 1985), DDC Report AD 613–525 (Appendix AD 613–526), May 1964.

    Covers the technological aspects of the projection. Forecasts technology as related to the Marine Corps in the next two decades.

Teilhard de Chardin, Pierre, *The Future of Man*. London: Collins, 1964.

Thirring, Hans, *Energy for Man: From Windmills to Nuclear Power*. New York: Harper and Row, Publishers, 1958. 409 pp.

Thompson, Sir George, *The Foreseeable Future*. London: Cambridge University Press, 1955. 166 pp.

Ubbelohde, A. R., *Man and Energy*. New York: George Braziller, Inc., 1955. 247 pp.

U.S. Department of Labor, *Measurement of Technological Change*, by Solomon Fabricant, Seminar on Manpower Policy and Program, No. 4, October, 1964. 32 pp.

U.S. National Academy of Sciences, National Research Council, *Chemistry: Opportunities and Needs*, publication 1292. Academy of Sciences, National Research Council, Washington, D.C., 1965.

————, *Physics: Survey and Outlook: Reports on the Subfields of Physics*. National Research Council, Washington, D.C., 1966.

————, *Theoretical Chamistry—A Current Review*, Publication 1292–D. National Research Council, Washington, D.C., 1966. 44 pp.

U.S. National Bureau of Economic Research, *The Rate and Direction of Inventive Activity—Economic and Social Factors*. A Conference of Universities, Princeton, N.J.: Princeton University Press, 1962.

U.S. National Commission on Technology, Automation, and Economic Progress, report, Vol. I, *Technology and American Economy*. Washington, D.C., February, 1966. 115 pp.

U.S. National Resources Committee, *Technological Trends and National Policy—Including the Social Implications of New Inventions*, a report of the subcommittee on Technology. U.S. Government Printing Office, Washington, D.C., June, 1937.

United Nations, *A Select Bibliography on Industrial Research, from 1944 to June 1964*, reference paper 1, prepared for the Interregional Seminar on Industrial Research and Development Institutes in Developing Countries, November 30–December 12, 1964, Beirut, Lebanon: Centre for Industrial Development, Department of Economic and Social Affairs, United Nations, New York, 1964. 37 pp.

Vassilev, M., and S. Gouschev, eds., *Life in the Twenty-First Century*, translated from Russian, first published in Russia 1959, Penguin Special, Penguin Books, Harmondsworth, Middlesex, 1961. 222 pp.

Wagle, B., "Some Statistical Aids in Forecasting," internal report Esso Petroleum Co., Ltd., London; introduction published under the title "A Review of Two Statistical Aids in Forecasting," *The Statistician*, Vol. 15, No. 2 (1965).

Wainerdi, R. E., Dr. et al., *Engineering in the 70's*, Convocation Proceedings, Texas A&M University College of Engineering, 1967.

Warner, Aron W., and Dean Morse, eds., *Technological Innovation and Society*. New York: Columbia University Press, 1966.

————, and Alfred S. Eichner, eds., *The Impact of Science on Technology*. New York: Columbia University Press, 1965.

Ways, Max, "The Road to 1977," *Fortune,* January, 1967. p. 93.

Weymar, F. H., *The Dynamics of the World Cocoa Market*, Cambridge, The M.I.T. Press, 1968.

Wolstenholme, Gordon, ed., *Man and His Future*. A Ciba Foundation Volume. Boston, Mass.: Little Brown and Company, 1963, 410 pp.

Zwicky, Fritz, *Morphology of Propulsive Power*, Monographs on Morphological Research No. 1, Society for Morphological Research, Pasadena, Calif.; available from the Bookstore of the California Institute of Technology, Pasedena, Calif., 1962. 382 pp.

BIBLIOGRAPHY FOR APPRAISAL TECHNIQUES

Ackoff, Russell L. *Scientific Method: Optimizing Applied Research Decisions.* New York: John Wiley and Sons, 1962.

———, (ed.). *Progress in Operations Research*, Vol. I. New York: John Wiley and Sons, Inc., 1961.

———, "Specialized Versus Generalized Models in Research Budgeting." Paper presented at the Second Conference on Resarch Program Effectiveness, Washington, D.C., July 27–29, 1965.

———, Arnoff, E. Leonard, and Churchman, C. West. *Introduction to Operations Research.* New York: John Wiley and Sons, Inc., 1957.

Adams, J. G., Nellums, Howard, R. E. "Engineering Evaluation—Tool for Research Management," *Industrial and Engineering Chemistry*, XLIX, (May, 1957), 4OA.

Albertini, J., *The QMDO Planning Process as it Relates to the U.S. Army Material Command.* Cornell Aeronautical Lab. Report No. VQ–2044–H–1 on USAMC Contract DA–49–185 AMC–237(X), Aug. 31, 1965.

———, *The LRTP Planning Process* as it *Relates* to the *U.S. Army Material Command*, Cornell Aeronautical Lab. Report No. VQ–2044–H–2 on USAMC Contract DA–49–186 AMC–237(X). Oct. 30, 1965.

———, *LRTP Mathematical Model Brochure.* Cornell Aeronautical Lab. Report No. VQ–2044–H–3 on USAMC Contract DA–49–186 AMC–237(X). Oct. 30, 1965.

Amey, L. R. "The Allocation and Utilization of Resources," *Operations Research Quarterly*, (June, 1964).

Andersen, Sigud L. "Venture Analysis, A Flexible Planning Tool," *Chemical Engineering Progress* (March, 1961), 80–83.

———, "A 2x2 Risk Decision Problem," *Chemical Engineering Progress* (May, 1961), 70–72.

Anderson, Carl A. "Notes on the Evaluation of Research Planning." Paper presented at the Research Program Effectiveness Conference, Washington, D.C., July 21–23, 1964.

Ansoff, H. I., Evaluation of applied research in a business firm, Technological Planning on the Corporate Level, J. R. Bright, Ed., Proc. Conf. at Harvard Business School, Harvard University, Cambridge, Mass., 1962, pp. 209–224.

Andrew, G. H. L., Assessing priorities for technical effort, *Operational Research Quart.*, Vol. 5, September 1954, pp. 67–80.

Anthony, Robert N., and Day, John S. *Management Controls in Industrial Research Organizations.* Cambridge: Harvard University Press, 1952.

Asher, D. T. "A Linear Programming Model for the Allocation of R&D Efforts," *IRE Transactions on Engineering Management*, EM–9, No. 4 (December, 1962), 154–157.

———, and S. Disman, Operations Research in R&D, *Chemical Engineering Progress*, Vol. 59:1, January 1963, pp. 41–45.

Aumann, R. J., and Kruskal, J. B. "Assigning Quantitative Values to Qualitative Factors in the Naval Electronics Program," *Naval Research Logistics Quarterly* (March 1959), 15.

Bakanas, V., *An Analytical Method to Aid in the Choice of Long Range Study Tasks*. Cornell Aeronautical Lab. Report No. VQ–1887–H–1. AMC contract DA–49–186 AMC–97(X). May 19, 1964.

Baker, N. R., and Pound, W. H., "Rand D Project Selection: Where we stand," *IEEE Transactions on Engineering Management,* Vol. EM–11, No. 4, December 1964.

Battersby, A., *Network Analysis for Planning and Scheduling*, St. Martins Press, New York, 1964.

Barmby, John G., "The Applicability of PERT as a Management Tool," *IRE Transactions on Engineering Management,* Vol. EM–9, No. 3 (September 1962).

Baumgartner, John Stanley, *Project Management*. Homewood, Illinois: Richard Irwin Press, 1963.

Beckwith, R. E., "A Cost Control Extension of the PERT System," *IRE Transactions on Engineering Management,* Vol. EM–9, No. 4 (December 1962).

Belt, John Robert, "Military Applied R&D Project Evaluation," U.S. Navy Marine Engineering Laboratory, Annapolis, Md.; June 1966 (Unpublished Thesis).

Berman, E. R., "Research Allocation in a PERT Network Under Continuous Activity Time-Cost Functions," *Management Science*, Vol. 10, No. 4, 1964.
———, Draft: *Theoretical Structure of a Methodology for R&D Resource Allocation*. Research Analysis Corp., May 26, 1965.

Bensley, Dean E., "Planning and Controlling a Research and Development Program: A Case Study." Master's Thesis, Massachusetts Institute of Technology, Cambridge, 1955.

Berstein, Alex, and Ithiel de Sola Pool, "Development and Testing of an Evaluation Model for Research Organization Substructures." Paper presented at the Research Program Effectiveness Conference, Washington, D.C., July 21–23, 1964.

Blinoff, V., and C. Pacifico, *Chemical Processing*, Vol. 20, November 1957, pp. 34–35.

Blood, Jerome W., (ed). *The Management of Scientific Talent*. New York: The American Management Association, Inc., 1963.

Blum, Steven, *Time, Cost, and Risk Analysis in Project Planning*. U.S. Army Frankford Arsenal Report, Aug. 22, 1963.

Bock, R. H., and Holstein, W. K., *Production Planning and Control*. Columbus: Charles E. Merrill Books, Inc., 1963.

Bonini, Charles P., Jaedicke, Robert K., and Wagner, Harvey M., *Management Controls: New Directions in Basic Research*. New York: McGraw-Hill Book Company, Inc., 1964.

Boothe, Norton, and others. *From Concept to Commercialization, A Study of the R&D Budget Allocation Process*. Stanford University Sloan Program, The Graduate School of Business. Stanford, California: Stanford University, 1962.

Brandenburg, R. G., *A Descriptive Analysis of Project Selection*. A Summary Report. Pennsylvania: Carnegie Institute of Technology, July 1964.
———, *Toward a Multi-Space Information Conversion Model of the Research and Development Process*, Carnegie Inst. of Tech. Management Sciences Research Report No. 48, Aug. 1965.

Bright, James R., (ed). *Technological Planning on the Corporate Level.* Proceedings of the Conference at Harvard Business School, Harvard University, Boston, 1962.

Busacker, Robert G. and Saaty, Thomas L., *Finite Graphs and Networks: An Introduction With Applications.* New York: McGraw-Hill Book Company, Inc., 1965.

Bush, George P., *Bibliography on Research Administration, Annotated.* Washington, D.C.: The University Press, 1964.

Carroll, Phil, *Profit Control—How to Plug Profit Leaks.* New York: McGraw-Hill Book Company, Inc., 1962.

Caulfield, Patrick and Freshman, Robert, "Technology Evaluation Workbook," HQ Research and Technology Division, AFSC, Bolling AFB, D.C., January 1967.

Cetron, Marvin J., "Programmed Functional Indicies for Laboratory Evaluation, 'PROFILE'," Paper presented at the 16th Military Operations Research Symposium (MORS), Seattle, Washington, October 10–14, 1965.

———, and Freshman, Robert. Some Results of "PROFILE" paper presented at the 17th MORS, Monterey, California, May 21–25, 1966.

———, "Quantitative Utility Estimates for Science & Technology 'QUEST' " Paper presented at the 18th MORS, Fort Bragg, North Carolina, 19–21 October 1966.

———, & Harold F. Davidson, "Methodology for Allocating Corporate Resources to Objectives for Research and Development (MACRO R&D)" *Industrial Management Review,* Massachusetts Institute of Technology, Cambridge, Mass. Winter 1969.

———, R. Isenson, J. Johnson, A. B. Nutt & H. Wells, *Quantitative Methods for Technological Resources Management,* MIT Press, Cambridge, Mass. 1969.

———, J. Martino and L. Roepke, "The Selection of R&D Program Content—Survey of Quantitative Methods," *IEEE Transaction on Engineering Management,* Vol. EM–14, No. 1, March 1967, pp. 4–12.

———, "Using Technological Forecasts," *Science and Technology,* July 1968, No. 79, pp. 57–63.

——— and Monahan, T. I., "An Evaluation and Appraisal of Various Approaches to Technological Forecasting," *Technological Forecasting for Industry and Government,* ed. J. F. Bright; Prentice Hall, Englewood Cliffs, N.J, 1968.

——— and Weiser, A. L., "Technological Change, Technological Forecasting and Planning R&D—A View from the R&D Manager's Desk," *The George Washington Law Review—Technology Assessment and the Law,* Vol. 36, No. 5, Washington, D.C., p. 1091.

Charnes, A., "Conditional Chance-Constrained Approaches to Organizational Control." Paper presented at the Research Program Effectiveness Conference, Washington, D.C., July 21–23, 1964.

———, and Stedry, A. C. "Optimal Real-Time Control of Research Funding." Paper presented at the Second Conference on Research Program Effectiveness, Washington, D.C., July 27–29, 1965.

Churchman, C. West, *Prediction and Optimal Control.* Englewood Cliffs, New Jersey: Prentice-Hall, Inc., 1960.

———, Kruytbosch, C., and Ratoosh, Philburn. "The Role of the Research Administrator." Paper presented at the Second Conference on Research Program Effectiveness, Washington, D.C., July 27–29, 1965.

Clark, Wallace, *The Gantt Chart.* London: Sir Isaac Pitman and Sons, Ltd., 1938.

Clarke, Roderick W., "Activity Costing—Key to Progress in Critical Path Analysis," *IRE Transactions on Engineering Management,* Vol. EM–9, No. 3 (September, 1962), 132.

Combs, Cecil E., "Decision Theory and Engineering Management," *IRE Transactions on Engineering Management,* Vol. EM–9, No. 4 (December, 1962).

Cook, Earle F., "A Better Yardstick for Project Evaluation," *Armed Forces Management* (April, 1958), 20–23.

Cramer Robert H., and Smith, Barnard E., "Decision Models for the Selection of Research Projects," *The Engineering Economist,* IX, No. 2 (January–February 1964), 1–20.

Crisp, R. D., Product Planning for Future Projects, *Duns's Review and Modern Industry,* March 1958.

Dantzig, George B., *Linear Programming and Extensions.* Princeton: Princeton University Press 1963.

Daubin, Scott C., "The Allocation of Development Funds: An Analytic Approach," *Naval Research Logistics Quarterly,* III (September 1958), 263–276.

Davidson, Harold F., "Surveys as Tools for Acquisition of Research Management Information." Paper presented at the Research Program Effectiveness Conference, Washington, D.C., July 21–23, 1964.

Davis, Keith, "The Role of Project Management in Scientific Manufacturing," *IRE Transactions on Engineering Management,* Vol. EM–9, No. 3 (September, 1962), 109.

Dean, Burton V., (ed.). *Operations Research in Research and Development;* Proceedings of a conference at Case Institute of Technology. Editor Burton V. Dean, New York: John Wiley and Sons, Inc., 1963.

————, *Scoring and Profitability Models for Evaluating and Selecting Engineering Projects, Case Institute of Technology,* Operations Research Group, 1964.

————, "Allocation of Technical Resources in a Firm." Paper presented at the Research Program Effectiveness Conference, Washington, D.C., July 21–23, 1964.

————, "Stochastic Networks in Research Planning." Paper presented at the Second Conference on Research Program Effectiveness, Washington, D.C., July 27–29, 1965.

————, and Sengupta, S., "On a Method for Determining Corporate Research Development Budgets," *Management Sciences, Models, and Techniques,* Vol. II, C. West Churchman, and Michel Verhulst, editors, New York: Pergamon Press, 1960.

————, and Glogowski, *On the Planning of Research.* ONR–AMC Project NONR1141(19), July 1965.

————, and Hauser, L. E., *Advanced Material Systems Planning.* Case Institute of Technology, Operations Research Group Technical Memorandum, No. 65. ONR–AMC Project NONR–1141(19), September 15, 1966.

Dean, Joel, *Managerial Economics.* Englewood Cliffs: Prentice-Hall, Inc., 1951, pp. 249–610.

————, "Measuring the Productivity of Capital." *Harvard Business Review* (January–February, 1954).

De L'Estoile, "Resource Allocation Model," French Ministere Des Armees, Paris, France.

DeVries, Marvin G., *A Dynamic Model for Product Strategy Selection.* Industrial Development Research Program Institute of Science and Technology. Ann Arbor: The University of Michigan, 1963.

————, "The Dynamic Effects of Planning Horizons on the Selection of Optimal Product Strategies," *Management Science*, X, No. 3 (April, 1964), 524–544.

Disman, S., Selecting R&D projects for profit, *Chemical Engineering*, Vol. 69, December 1962, pp. 87–90.

Dooley Arch R., "Interpretations of PERT," *Harvard Business Review*, XLII (March–April, 1964), pp. 160–171.

Drucker, Peter F., "Twelve Fables of Research Management," *Harvard Business Review* (January–February, 1963).

————, *Managing for Results*. New York: Harper & Row Publishers, Inc., 1964, pp. 25–50.

Easton, David, *A Systems Analysis of Political Life*. New York: John Wiley and Sons, Inc., 1965.

Eisner, Hoard, "Generalized Network Approach to the Planning and Scheduling of a Research Program" *Operations Research*, 1962, 115–125.

————, "The Application of Information Theory to the Planning of Research." Paper presented at the TIMS American International Meeting, September 12–13, 1963.

Elmaghraby, Salah E., "An Algebra for the Analysis of Generalized Activity Networks," *Management Sciences*, X, No. 3 (April 1964) 494–514.

Emlet H. E., *Methodological Approach to Planning and Programming Air Force Operational Requirements, Research and Development (MAPORD)*. Analytic Services Report 65–4, October 1965.

Esch, Maurice E., "Planning Assistances Through Technical Evaluation Pattern." Paper presented at the 17th National Aerospace Electronics Conference, Dayton, Ohio, May 10–12, 1965.

Ewing, David W. (ed.). *Long-Range Planning of Management*. New York: Harper & Brothers, 1958.

Flood, Merrill W., "Research Project Evaluation," *Coordination, Control, and Financing of Industrial Research*, Albert R. Rubenstein, editor. New York: (Columbia University); King's Crown Press, 1955.

Fong, L. B. C., "A Visual Method of Program Balance and Evaluation," *IRE Transactions on Engineering Management*, Vol. EM–8, September 1961, pp. 160–163.

Ford, L. R., Jr., and Fulkerson, D. R., *Flows in Networks*. Princeton: Princeton University Press, 1962.

Freeman, Raoul J., "An Operational Analysis of Industrial Research." Ph.D. dissertation, Department of Economics, Massachusetts Institute of Technology, Cambridge, Massachusetts, 1957.

————, "A Stochastic Model for Determining the Size and Allocation of the Research Budget," *IRE Transactions on Engineering Management*, Vol. EM–7, No. 1 (March 1960), 2–7.

————, "Quantitative Methods in R&D Management," *California Management Review*, XI, No. 4 (Summer 1960), 36–44.

————, "A Generalized Network Approach to Project Activity Sequencing," *IRE Transactions on Engineering Management*, Vol. EM–7, No. 3 (September 1960), 103–107.

————, "A Survey of the Current Status of Accounting in the Control of R&D," *IRE Transactions on Engineering Management*, Vol. EM–9, No. 4, (December 1962), 179–181.

Fry, B. L., "SCANS—System Description and Comparison with PERT," *IRE Transactions on Engineering Management*, Vol. EM–9, No. 3 (September 1962), 122.

Galbraith, John Kenneth, *The Affluent Society*. New York: Mentor Books, 1958.

Gargiulo, G. R., and others, "Developing Systematic Procedures for Directing Research Programs," *IRE Transactions on Engineering Management*, Vol. EM–8, No. 1 (March 1961), 24–29.

———, "Research on a Research Department: An Analysis of Economic Decisions on Projects," *IRE Transactions on Engineering Management*, Vol. EM–7, No. 4 (December 1960), 166–172.

Gloskey, C. R., M.A. thesis, Massachusetts Institute of Technology, Cambridge, 1959.

Goldberg, L. C., "Dimensions in the Evaluation of Technical Ideas in an Industrial Research Laboratory, M.S. thesis," Northwestern University, Evanston, Illinois, 1963.

Guy, K., *Laboratory Organization and Administration*. London: Macmillan & Company, Ltd. Also New York: St. Martin's Press, 1962.

Hackney, J. W. "How to Appraise Capital Investments," *Chemical Engineering* (May 15, 1961), 146–167.

Hahn, W. A., and Pickering, H. D., "Program Planning in a Science-Based Service Organization." Paper presented at the Second Conference on Research Program Effectiveness, Washington, D.C., July 27–29, 1965.

Hansen, B. J., *Practical PERT Including Critical Path Method*. Washington: America House, 1964.

Harrel, C. G., Selecting projects for research, in *Research in Industry: Its Organization and Management*, C. C. Furnas, editor. New York: Van Nostrand, 1948, ch 7, pp. 104–144.

Henke, Russ, *Effective Research & Development for the Smaller Company*. Houston Gulf Publishing Company, 1963.

Heckert, J. E., and Willson, J. B., *Business Budgeting and Control*. New York: The Ronald Press Company, 1955.

Hertz, David B., *The Theory and Practice of Industrial Research*. New York: McGraw-Hill Book Company, Inc., 1950.

———, and Rubenstein, A. H., *Costs Budgeting and Economics of Industrial Research*: proceedings of the first annual conference of industrial research. New York: Columbia University Press 1951.

———, and A. H. Rubenstein (eds.), *Proceedings of the Third Annual Conference on Industrial Research: Research Operations in Industry*. New York: Columbia University Press, 1953, Esp. Stewart, J. A., p. 55, and Hartstone E., p. 153.

———, and Phillip G. Carlson, Selection, evaluation, and control of research and development projects, in *Operations Research in Research and Development*, B. V. Dean, editor. New York: Wiley, 1963, pp. 170–188.

Hess, Sidney W., "On Research and Development Budgeting and Project Selection." Ph.D. dissertation, Case Institute of Technology, Cleveland, 1960.

———, "A Dynamic Programming Approach to R&D Budgeting and Project Selection," *IRE Transactions on Engineering Management*, Vol. EM–9, No. 4 (December 1962), 170–178.

Heyel, Carl (ed.), *Handbook of Industrial Research Management*. New York: Reinhold Publishing Corporation, 1959.

Hickey, Albert E., Jr., "The Systems Approach: Can Engineers Use the Scientific Method?" *IRE Transactions on Engineering Management*, Vol. EM–7, No. 2 (June 1960), 72.

Hildenbrand, W., "Application of Graph Theory to Stochastic Scheduling." Paper presented at the Second Conference on Research Program Effectiveness, Washington, D.C., July 27–29, 1965.

Hill, F. I. and Roepcke L. A., "An Analytical Method to Aid in the Choice of Long Range Study Tasks." A paper presented at the 1964 U.S. Army Operations Research Symposium at Rock Island Arsenal, May 25–27, 1964.

Hill, Lawrence S., "Toward An Improved Basis of Estimating and Controlling R&D Tasks." Paper presented at the 10th National Meeting of the American Association of Cost Engineers, Philadelphia, Pa., June 1966.

Hitchcock, L. B., Selection and Evaluation of R&D projects, p. 1, *Research Management*, Vol. 6, May 1963, pp. 231–244.

Hodge, M. H., Jr. et al., "Basic Research as a Corporate Function," The Graduate School of Business, Stanford University Sloan Program, Stanford University, California 1961.

Honig, John G., "An Evaluation of Research and Development Problems." Paper presented at the Research Program Effectiveness Conference, Washington, D.C., July 21–23, 1964.

Horowitz, Ira, "The Economics of Industrial Research." Ph.D. dissertation, Massachusetts Institute of Technology, Cambridge, 1959.

Janofsky, L., and Sobleman, S., "Balancing Equations to Project Feasibility Studies." Paper presented to Operations Research Society of America, Detroit, October 10, 1960.

———, and Milton, Helen S., "A Proposed Cost-of-Research Index," *IRE Transactions on Engineering Management*, Vol. EM–8, No. 4 (December 1961), 172–176.

Johnson, E. A. and H. S. Milton, "A Proposed Cost-of-Research Index," *IRE Transactions on Engineering Management,* Vol. EM–8 (December 1961), pp. 172–176.

Johnson, Richard A., Kast, Fremont E., and Rosenzweig, James E., *The Theory and Management of Systems*. New York: McGraw-Hill Book Company, Inc., 1963.

Karger, D. C., and Murkick, R. G., *Managing Engineering and Research*. New York: The Industrial Press, 1963, pp. 193–253.

Kelley, James E., Jr., and Walker, Morgan R., "Critical-Path Planning and Scheduling." Proceedings of the Eastern Joint Computer Conference, 1959.

———, and Walker, Morgan R., "Critical Path Planning and Scheduling. Mathematical Basis." *Operations Research*, IX (1961), pp. 296–320.

Kiefer, D. M., "Winds of Change in Industrial Chemical Research," *Chemical Engineering News*, Vol. 42, March 1964, pp. 88–109.

Klein, B., and W. Meckling, "Applications of Operations Research to Development Decisions," *Operations Research*, May–June 1958, pp. 352–363.

———, The decision-making problem in development, in *The Rate and Direction of Inventive Activity*. Princeton, New Jersey: Princeton University Press, 1962, pp. 477–508.

Kliever, W. R., and R. Z. Bancroft, "Choosing and Evaluating Research Projects," *Product Engineering*, June 1953.

Koontz, Harold, *Toward A Unified Theory of Management*. New York: McGraw-Hill Book Company, Inc., 1963.

Landi, D. M., *A Model of Investment Planning for Research and Development*. Evanston: Northwestern University, 1964.

Leermakers, J. A. The Selection and Screening of Projects, in *Getting the Most From Product Research and Development*. New York: American Management Association, 1955, pp. 81–94.

Levy, F. K., Thompson, G. L., and Wiest, J. E., "Multiship, Multishop Workload-Smoothing Program" *Naval Research Logistics Quarterly*, XI (March 1962).

Lipetz, Ben-Ami, *Measurement of Effectiveness of Science Research*. Intermedia, Inc.: Carlisle, Massachusetts, 1965.

Lytle, A. A., "The Yardsticks for Research success," *Product Engineering*, Vol. 30, October 1959, pp. 34–37.

Magee, John F., "How to Use Decision Trees in Capital Investment," *Harvard Business Review* (September–October 1964), pp. 79–96.

Manning, P. D., "Long Range Planning of Product Research," *R&D Development Series No. 4*. New York: American Management Association, 1957.

Marples, D. L., "The Decisions of Engineering Design," *IRE Transactions on Engineering Management*, Vol. EM–8, June 1961, pp. 55–71.

Marschak, T. A., Strategy and organization in a system development project, in *The Rate and Direction of Inventive Activity*. Princeton, New Jersey: Princeton University Press, 1962, pp. 509–548.

————, Models, rules of thumb, and development decisions, in Operations Research in Research and Development, B. V. Dean, editor. New York: Wiley, 1963, pp. 247–263.

Marquis, Donald G., "Organization and Management of R&D." Paper presented at the Research Program Effectiveness Conference, Washington, D.C., July 21–23, 1964.

Marshall, A. W., and W. H. Meckling, Predictability of the costs, time and success of development, in *The Rate and Direction of Inventive Activity*. Princeton, New Jersey: Princeton University Press, 1962, pp. 461–475.

McMaster, Samuel B., "Study of Project Selection Techniques in an R&D Organization." Unpublished Master's Thesis, Northwestern University, Evanston, 1964.

McMillian, Claude and Ganzalez, Richard F., *Systems Analysis: A Computer Approach to Decision Models*. Homewood: Richard D. Irwin, Inc., 1965.

Mees, C. E. K., and J. A. Leermakers, *The Organization of Industrial Scientific Research*, 2nd ed. New York: McGraw-Hill, 1950, especially ch 11.

Martino, Joseph; Caulfield, Patrick; Cetron, Marvin; Davidson, Harold; Liebowitz, Harold; and Roepcke, Lewis, "A Method for Balanced Allocation of Resources Among R&D Projects." AF Office of Scientific Research Technical Report: February 1967.

Massey, Robert J. "A New Publication: Department of the Navy RDT&E Management Guide." Paper presented at the Research Program Effectiveness Conference, Washington, D.C., July 21–23, 1964.

Mellon, W. Giles, "An Approach to a General Theory of Priorities: An Outline of Problems and Methods," Princeton University Econometric Research Program, Memorandum No. 42. Princeton: Princeton University Press, 1962.

Miller, D. W., and Starr, M. K., *Executive Decisions and Operations Research*. Englewood Cliffs, New Jersey: Prentice-Hall, Inc., 1960.

Miller, Robert W., *Schedule, Cost and Profit Control with PERT*. New York: McGraw-Hill Book Company, Inc., 1963.

Miller, T. T., *Projecting the Profitability of New Products, Special Report No. 20*. New York: American Management Association, 1957, pp. 20–33.

Morgenstern, O., Shephard, R. W., and Grabowski, H. G., "Adaption of Graph Theory and an Input-Output Model to Research Description and Evaluation." Paper presented at the Second Conference on Research Program Effectiveness, Washington, D.C., July 27–29, 1965.

Moshman, Jack, Johnson, Jacob and Larson, Madalyn, "RAMPS—ATechnique for Resource Allocation and Multi-Project Scheduling," *Proceedings of the Spring Joint Computer Conference*, 1963. Baltimore: Spartan Books, Inc., 1963, pp. 17–27.

Mottley, C. M., and R. D. Newton, "The Selection of Projects for Industrial Research," *Operations Research,* Vol. 7, November–December 1959, pp. 740–751.

National Science Foundation, *Science and Engineering in American Industry,* Final Report on 1953–1954 Survey, Washington, D.C., October 1956.

Norden, P. V., "Curve Fitting for a Model of Applied Research and Development Scheduling," *IBM Journal of Research and Development,* Vol. II, No. 3 (July, 1958), 232–248.

——, The study committee for research, development and engineering (SCARDE). A progress report and an invitation to participate, *IRE Transactions on Engineering Management,* Vol. EM–8, March 1961, pp. 3–10.

——, "Some Properties of R&D Project Recovery Limits." Paper presented at the Second Conference on Research Program Effectiveness, Washington, D.C., July 27–29, 1965.

Norton, J. H., The role of subjective probability in evaluating new product ventures, Chemical Engineering *Progr. Symp.,* Series No. 42, Vol. 59, 1963, pp. 49–54.

Nutt, Ambrose B., "An Approach to Research and Development Effectiveness," *IEEE Transactions on Engineering Management,* September 1965, pp. 103–112.

Nyland, H. V., and G. R. Towle, "How We Evaluate Return From Research," *National Association of Cost Accountants Bulletin,* May 1956.

Olsen, F., The control of research funds, in *Coordination, Control and Financing of Industrial Research,* A. H. Rubenstein, editor, New York, King Crown Press, Columbia University, 1955, pp. 99–108.

Pacifico, C., "Is It Worth the Risk," *Chemical Engineering Progr.,* Vol. 60, May 1964, pp. 19–21.

Pappas, G. F., and D. D. MacLaren, "An approach to research planning," *Chemical Engineering Progr.,* Vol. 57, May 1961, pp. 65–69.

Pound, William H., "Research Project Selection: Testing a Model in the Field," *IEEE Transactions on Engineering Management,* Vol. EM–11, No. 1 (March 1964), 16–22.

Quinn, James Bryan, *Yardsticks for Industrial Research: The Evaluation of Research and Development Output.* New York: The Ronald Press Company, 1959.

——, and Mueller, James A., "Transferring Research Results to Operations," *Harvard Business Review,* XLI (January–February, 1963).

Rae, Robert H., and Synnott, "Project RDE, A Framework for the Comprehension and Analysis of Research and Development Effectiveness," TM 63–22 Air Force Flight Dynamics Laboratory, Dayton, Ohio, October 1961.

——, A Systems Development Planning Structure, ABT Associates, Inc., 18 November 1965.

——, An Automated Scenario Generator, ABT Associates, Inc., January 1966.

Raiffa, Howard and Schlaifer, Robert, *Applied Statistical Decision Theory.* Boston: Division of Research, Harvard Business School, 1957.

Roberts, C. S., "Product Selection—Witchcraft or Wisdom," *IRE Transactions on Engineering Management,* Vol. EM–6, September 1959, pp. 68–71.

Roberts, E. B., *The Dynamics of Research and Development.* New York: Harper & Row Publishers, 1964.

Roman, Daniel D., "The PERT System: An Appraisal of Program Evaluation

Review Technique," *Journal of the Academy of Management*, Vol. V, No. 1 (April 1962).

———, "Organization for Control," *Journal of the Academy of Management* (Proceedings of the Annual Meeting, Pittsburgh, December 27–28, 1962).

———, "Project Management Recognizes R&D Performance," *Journal of the Academy of Management*, VII (March 1964), 7–20.

———, and Johnson, Jacob N., "On the Allocation of Common Physical Resources to Multiple Development Tasks." Paper presented at the 18th Military Operations Research Society, Fort Bragg, North Carolina, 19–21 Oct. 1966.

Roseboom, J. H., Clark, C. E., and Fazer, W., "Application of a Technique for Research and Development Program Evaluation," *Operations Research*, VII (September–October 1959) pp. 651–653.

Rosen, E. M. and Saunder, W. E., "A Method for Allocating R&D Expenditures," *IEEE Transactions on Engineering Management*, Vol. EM–12, No. 3, September 1965, pp. 87–92.

Rubenstein, Albert H. (ed.), *Coordination, Control, and Financing of Industrial Research*. New York: King's Crown Press, Columbia University, 1955.

———, Evaluation of the possibilities of research effort in a new field of technology, Sweden, Vol. 6, 1955, pp. 239–251.

———, "Setting criteria for R&D," *Harvard Business Review*, January–February 1957, pp. 95–104.

———, and I. Horowitz, "Project Selection in New Technical Fields," *Proc. National Electronics Conference*, Vol. 15, 1959.

———, Studies of project selection behavior in industry, in *Operations Research in Research and Development*, B. V. Dean, editor. New York: Wiley, 1963, pp. 189–205.

———, and Maberstroh, C. W. (eds.), *Some Theories of Organization*. Homewood, Illinois: Richard D. Irwin, 1960.

———, "Some Common Concepts and Tentative Findings from a Ten-Project Program of Research on R&D Management." Paper presented at the Second Conference on Research Program Effectiveness, Washington, D.C., July 27–29, 1965.

Saaty, Thomas L., *Mathematical Methods of Operations Research*. New York: McGraw-Hill Book Company, Inc., 1959.

Sacco, W. J., *On the Choice of Long Range Study Tasks*. Ballistic Research Laboratories Memo Report No. 1693, Aug. 1965.

Savage, J. J., *The Foundations of Statistics*. New York: John Wiley and Sons, Inc., 1954.

Scherer, F. M., "Time-Cost Tradeoffs in Uncertain Empirical Research Projects." Paper in *Naval Research Logistics Quarterly*, ONR, Vol. 13, No. 1, March 1966.

Schweyer, Herbert E., "Graphs Can Reveal Project Feasibility," *Chemical Engineering* (September 18, 1961), 175–178.

Seiler, Robert E., *Improving the Effectiveness of Research and Development*, McGraw-Hill Book Co., New York, 1963.

Shaller, H. I., An exploratory study in research planning methodology, ONR Tech. Report ACR/NAR–27, Department of the Navy, Washington, D.C., September 1963.

Shank, R. J., "Planning to Meet Goals," *Optimum Use of Engineering Talent*, *AMA Report No. 58* (Cambridge: Riverside Press, 1961).

Sher, I. H., and Garfield, E., "New Tools for Improving and Evaluating the

Effectiveness of Research." Paper presented at the Second Conference on Research Program Effectiveness, Washington, D.C., July 27–29, 1963.

Silk, Leonard S., *The Research Revolution*. New York: McGraw-Hill Book Company, Inc., 1960.

Simon, H. A., *The New Science of Management Decisions*. New York: Harper & Row Publishers, 1960.

――――, "An Optimal Method for Selection of Product Development Projects." Paper presented at the 15th National Meeting, Operations Research Society of America, May, 1959.

Sobelman, S. A. Modern dynamic approach to product development, Picatinny Arsenal, Dover, New Jersey, December 1958.

――――, An optimal method for selection of product development projects, presented at the 15th National Meeting of the Operations Research Society of America, Washington, D.C., May 1959.

Sobin, Bernard and Proschan, Authur, "Search and Evaluation Methods in Research and Exploratory Development." Paper presented at the Second Conference on Research Program Effectiveness, Washington, D.C., July 27–29, 1965.

――――, *Proposal Generation and Evaluation Methods in Research and Exploratory Development*. Research Analysis Corp. Paper RAC–P–11, Nov. 1965.

Special Projects Office, *PERT Summary Report I*. Washington, D. C.: Bureau of Naval Weapons, Department of the Navy, 1959.

Spencer, M. H., and Siegelman, L. *Managerial Economics*. Homewood, Illinois: Richard D. Irwin, Inc., 1964, pp. 461–567.

Stanley, A. O., and White, K. K. *Organizing the R&D Function*. AMA Research Study No. 72. New York: American Management Association, 1965.

Steiner, George A. *Managerial Long-Range Planning,* New York: McGraw-Hill Book Company, Inc., 1963.

Stilian, C. N., and others: *PERT—A New Management Planning and Control Technique*. New York: American Management Association, 1962.

Stoessl, L., "Linear Programming Techniques Applied to Research Planning," Master's Thesis, U. S. Naval Post-graduate School, 1964.

Stoodley, F. H., *A Study of Methods Which Could Improve the Relevance of Naval Applied Research and Exploratory Development*. Office Naval Research Report. June 1, 1966.

Sullivan, C. I., CPI Management Looks at R&D Project Evaluation, *Ind. and Eng. Chem.,* Vol. 53, September 1961, pp. 42A–46A.

Taylor, Frederick W., *Scientific Management*. New York: Harper & Brothers, Publishers, 1947.

Theil, H., "On the Optimal Management of Research; A Mathematical Approach." Paper presented at the conference of the International Federation of Operations Research Societies, Oslo, Norway, July 1963.

Thompson, R. E., "PERT—Tool for R&D Project Decision-Making." *IRE Transactions on Engineering Management* (September 1962), 116–121.

University of California. *A System Engineering Approach to Corporate Long-Range Planning*. Department of Engineering, Report EEP–62–1. Berkeley: University of California, June 1962.

Wachold, G. R., "An Investigation of the Technical Effectiveness of a Government Research and Development Test and Evaluation Organization." Navy Missile Center, Pt. Mugu, California, July 1965. (Unpublished thesis)

Walters, J. E., *Research Management: Principles and Practice*. Washington, D. C.: Spartan Books, 1965.

Wasson, Chester R., *The Economics of Managerial Decision*. New York: Appleton-Century-Crofts, Inc., 1965, pp. 147–218.

Wells, Howard A., "Systems Planners Guide." Paper presented at the 18th Military Operations Research Society, Fort Bragg, North Carolina, 19–21 Oct. 1966.

———, "The Allocation of Research and Development Resources." Wright-Patterson Air Development Center, August 1958. (Unpublished thesis)

BIBLIOGRAPHY FOR TECHNOLOGICAL FORECASTING IN THE INFORMATION-PROCESSING INDUSTRY

Articles

————, "The Next Generation," *Datamation,* January 1967, Vol. 13, No. 1, pp. 31–35.

————, "The SIGMA 7 from SDS," *Datamation,* March 1966, Vol. 12, No. 3, pp. 53–57.

————, "What Total Computer Control Can Mean To You," October 1967, Vol. 22, No. 10, pp. 35–50.

————, "The Course of the Computer," *Stanford Research Institute Journal,* No. 17, November 1967, p. 13.

————, "Software, Key to Promised Machine Miracles," *Engineering Opportunities,* May 1967, Vol. 5, No. 5, pp. 36–48.

Adelson, Marvin, "The Education Innovation Study," *American Behavioral Scientist,* March 1967, Vol. 10, No. 7, pp. 8–12.

Amdahl, G. M. and L. D., "Fourth Generation Hardware," *Datamation,* January 1967, Vol. 13, No. 1, pp. 25–26.

Bartley, John P., "Planning in NAVSUP," *Navy Supply Corps Newsletter,* November 1967, Vol. XXX, No. 11, pp. 14–19.

Baust, R. T., "Computer Characteristics," *Datamation,* October 1966, Vol. 12, No. 10, p. 123.

Bernstein, George B., *A Fifteen-Year Forecast of Information-Processing Technology, Naval Supply Systems Command,* Washington, D.C. 1969.

———— and Cetron, Marvin J., "SEER: A Delphic Approach Applied to Information Processing," *Technological Forecasting;* American Elsevier, N.Y.C.: Spring 1969.

Brady, Rodney H., "Computer in Top-Level Decision Making," *Harvard Business Review,* Vol. 45, No. 4, July–August 1967, pp. 67–76.

Cetron, Marvin J., "Forecasting Technology," *International Science and Technology,* September 1967, No. 69, pp. 85–92.

————, "Using Technological Forecasts," *Science and Technology,* July 1968, No. 79, pp. 57–63.

———— and Weiser, Alan, "Technological Change, Technological Forecasting and Planning R&D—A View from the R&D aMnager's Desk," The George Washington *Law Review—Technology Assessment and the Law,* July 1968, Vol. 36, No. 5, pp. 1079–1104.

———— and Mahinske, Edmund B., 'The Value of Technological Forecasting for the Research and Development Manager," *Futures,* September 1968, Vol. 1, No. 1, pp. 21–23.

Colilla, R. A., "Time-Sharing & Multiprocessing Terminology," *Datamation,* March 1966, Vol. 12, No. 3, pp. 49–51.

Cooke, Milton J., "The Data Base Revolution," *Systems and Procedures Journal,* March–April 1968, Vol. 19, No. 2, pp. 20–22.

Craver, John S., "A Review of Electromechanical Mass Storage," July 1966 (a reprint).

Doyle, L. B., "Perpetual User Studies," *Datamation,* October 1966, Vol. **12,** No. 10, pp. 28–30.

Eckert, J. P., *et al.,* "Improvements in Hardware Performance," *Datamation,* January 1966, Vol. 12, No. 1, p. 34.

Fano, R. M., "The Computer Utility and the Community," *1967 IEEE International Convention Record,* Part 12.

Feidelman, L. A., "A Survey of the Character Recognition Field," *Datamation,* February 1966, Vol. 12, No. 2, pp. 45–52.

Head, Robt. V., "Management Information Systems: A Critical Appraisal," *Datamation,* May 1967 (a reprint).

Hobbs, L. C., "Impact of Hardware in the 1970's," *Datamation,* March 1966, Vol. 12, No. 3, pp. 36–44.

Horton, H. B., "Computer Memories—The Search for More Speed, Larger Capacity, Greater Economy," *Sperryscope,* First Quarter 1967, Vol. 17, No. 8, pp. 1–5.

Isenson, Raymond S., "Technological Forecasting in Perspective," *Management Science,* October 1966, Vol. 13, No. 2, pp. B-70–B-83.

———, "Technological Forecasting—A Management Tool," *Business Horizons,* Vol. 10, No. 1, Summer 1967, pp. 37–46.

Lerman, H. N., "A Machine-Aided Drafting System," *Datamation,* January 1967, Vol. 13, No. 1, pp. 49–54.

Nauer, Richard S., "Reference It; Retrieve It; Reproduce It," *Systems & Procedures Journal,* March–April 1968, Vol. 19, No. 2, pp. 32–36.

Opler, Asher, "Fourth-Generation Software," *Datamation,* January 1967, Vol. 13, No. 1, pp. 22–24.

Podsiadlo, Edwin, "Small Economical Digital Systems Using Multi-Sector Core Memories," *Computer Design,* April 1967, Vol. 6, No. 4, pp. 72–77.

Schriever, Gen. B. A., USAF-Ret., "Should Technological Forecasting Be Tailored to User Needs?," *Armed Forces Management,* November 1967.

Simms, R. L., Jr., "Trends in Computer/Communications Systems," *Computers & Automation,* May 1968, Vol. 17, No. 5, pp. 22–25.

Ozbekhan, Hasan, "Automation," *Science Journal,* October 1967, Vol. 3, No. 10, pp. 67–75.

Quinn, James Brian, "Technological Forecasting," *Harvard Business Review,* March–April 1967, Vol. 45, No. 2, pp. 89–106.

Quirk, W. J., "Productive, Graphic Data Processing," *Datamation,* October 1966, Vol. 12, No. 10, pp. 31–32.

Ricci, J. M., "Precision Magnetic Tape," *Datamation,* October 1966, Vol. 12, No. 10, pp. 51–60.

Rosse, Edward, "From Checkograph to Computer: The History of Microfilm As Applied to Data Processing Systems," *Information and Records Management,* February–March 1967 (a reprint).

———, "Integrated Electronic Data Processing and Microfilm System at Social Security Administration," *SPSE News,* July–August 1962, Vol. 5, No. 4, pp. 25–26.

———, "Not Much Paper in Their Paperwork," *Systems Management,* March–April 1962 (a reprint).

Ruyle, Adrian, Brackett, Jown W., and Kaplow, Roy, "The Status of System for On-Line Mathematical Assistance," *Proceedings of the 22nd National ACM Conference,* Published by Thompson Book Co., Nat. Press Building, 14th and F Street, N. W., Wash., D. C. 20004, pp. 151–167.

Shurtleff, Donald A., "Studies in Television Legibility—A Review of the Literature," January–February 1967, Vol. 4, No. 1, pp. 40–45.

Simonson, W. E., "Data Communications: The Boiling Pot," *Datamation,* April 1967, Vol. 13, No. 4, pp. 22–25.
Turoff, Dr. Murray, "Immediate Access & The User," *Datamation,* August 1966, Vol. 12, No. 8, pp. 57–58.
Weisberg, D. E., "Computer Characteristics Quarterly—Recent Trends," *Datamation,* January 1966, Vol. 12, No. 1, pp. 55–56.
Yang, C. C., and Yan, S. S., "A Cutback Cellular Associate Memory," *IEEE Transactions on Electronic Computers,* August 1966, Vol. EC–15, No. 4, pp. 38–44.
Young, Stanley, "Organization as a Total System," *California Management Review,* Spring 1968, Vol. X, No. 8, pp. 21–32.

Books

Anshen, Melvin and Bach, George Leland, *Management and Corporations 1985,* New York: McGraw-Hill, 1960.
Barach, Arnold B., *1975 and the Changes to Come,* New York: Harper & Brothers, 1962.
Barnett, C. C., Jr. and Associates, *The Future of the Computer Utility,* New York: American Management Association, 1967.
Becker, Joseph and Hayes, R. M., *Information Storage and Retrieval,* New York: John Wiley & Sons, 1965.
Brown, Harrison, Bonner, James, and Weir, John, *The Next Hundred Years,* New York: The Viking Press, 1957.
Bright, James R. (ed.), *Technological Forecasting for Industry and Government: Methods and Applications,* Englewood Cliffs, N. J.: Prentice-Hall, Inc., 1968.
Diebold, John, *Beyond Automation,* New York: McGraw-Hill Book Co., 1964.
Gannon, W. A. (ed.), *et al., Computer Industry Annual 1967–68,* Chicago: Fawcett-Haynes, 1967.
Gabor, Dennis, *Inventing the Future,* New York: Knopf, 1964.
Jantsch, Erich, *Technological Forecasting in Perspective,* Paris: Organization for Economic Co-Operation and Development, 1967.
Kent, Allen, *Library Planning for Automation,* Washington, D. C.: Macmillan, 1964.
Kahn, Herman and Wiener, Anthony J., *The Year 2000: A Framework for Speculation on the Next Thirty-Three Years,* New York: Macmillan, 1967.
Mackay, Neil, *The Hole in the Card,* St. Paul, Minn.: North Central, May 1966.
Meacham, Alan D., (ed.), *Data Processing Equipment Encyclopedia, Volumes I, II,* Detroit: Gille Associates, Inc., 1961.
Patrick, Robt. L., *Workbook of Computer Programming Terms,* Los Angeles: ed. & pub. Planning Research Corp., 1964.
Scherr, Allan Lee, *An Analysis of Time-Shared Computer Systems,* Cambridge, Mass.: The MIT Press, Research Monograph No. 36, 1967.

Government Documents

Air Force, *Air Force Data Automation Plan (AFDAP) 1966–1975,* 25 April 1966.
Army Missile Command, Department of Army, EDS–0002, *Assessment of Mechanized Capabilities for Processing Engineering Data.*
Army Missile Command, Redstone Arsenal, Alabama, EDS–0004, *Assessment of Pictorial Data Processing Capabilities Final Report,* DOD Standardization Program, Engineering Data Systems Area, Air Force Logistics Com-

mand, United States Air Force, Wright-Patterson AFB, Ohio, 10 February 1964.

Department of Defense, *Conference on Technical Data Management,* Aberdeen Proving Ground, Maryland, May 5–7, 1964.

Department of Defense, *Defense Standardization Manual, M–200:* Standardization Policies, Procedures and Instructions, Chapter 1—Section 5.

Department of Defense, MIL–M–38748, *Microfiche for Engineering, Technical Data, Reports, Studies, and Related Data, Requirements For,* 15 August 1966.

Department of Defense, MIL–STD–188B, *Military Standard Military Communication System Technical Standards,* 24 February 1964.

Office of Naval Material, Dept. of the Navy, NAVMATINST 4000.18, *Technical Data and Standardization Management,* 30 July 1965.

Planning Research Corp. D–1069, *A Methodology for Development of Technological and User Requirements Forecast for Engineering Data Systems, EDS–0019,* Robert Tailer, 16 December 1965.

SECNAVINST 4000.28, *Improved Management of Technical Logistics Data and Information,* 4 March 1964.

Presentation Symposia

Avedon, Donald, "Looking Ahead to Mechanized Handling of Engineering Documents," (pamphlet) April 1967.

——— and Frey, Henry C., *Mechanized Storage, Retrieval, and Transmission of Engineering Documents.* Presentation by Bell Telephone Laboratories, Holmdel, N. J., April 1967.

Cetron, Marvin J., "Background and Utility of Technological Forecasting in the Military," *Long-Range Forecasting and Planning,* A Symposium held at the U. S. Air Force Academy, Colorado, 16–17 August 1966.

McDonald, H. S., Ninke, W. H., and Weller, D. R., *Computer-Aided Circuit Design.* A presentation at the 1967 International Solid-State Circuits Conference, University of Pennsylvania, February 16, 1967.

North, Dr. H. Q., "Technological Forecasting in Industry," A presentation during a Seminar to the NATO Defense Research Group, Teddington, Middlesex, England, 12 November 1968.

Univac, *Annual Report No. 2, Precis,* 15 May 1966.

Technical Reports

ABT Associates, Inc., *The Multiple Contingency Concept of Long-Range Technological Planning,* Rea, R. H. and Miller, Peter S., May 1967.

Aerial Measurements Laboratory, Northwestern University, AFAL–TR–66–66, *Compilation, Storage, and Rapid Retrieval of Current Document Information for Research on Telemetry Techniques,* Schaid, R. J. and Aagaard, J. S., May 1966.

Aeronautical Systems Division, Wright-Patterson AFB, Ohio, *Forecasts of Exploding Technologies by Trend Extrapolation,* Lenz, Ralph C., Jr.

Aerospace Corporation, Electronics Division, TR–669(9990)–8, *Software Design for Real-Time Systems,* Ffary, Paul C. T., November 1966.

Air Force Avionics Laboratory, Air Force Systems Command, Wright-Patterson Air Force Base, Ohio, AFAL–TR–66–167, *Evaluation of Simplified Learning Schemes Applied to Communication Links,* Russell, B. W., June 1966.

Air Force Systems Command, RADC–TR–64–193, *A User-Oriented Information Processing System,* Dion, F. A., June 1964.

Air Force Systems Command, ESD–TR–66–671, Vol. I, *Phase II Final Report on Use of Air Force ADP Experience to Assist Air Force ADP Management,* Gradwohl, A. J., *et al.,* December 1966.

Air Force Systems Command, Griffiss Air Force Base, N. Y., RADC–TR–66–359, *Compendium of 70mm x 100mm Unit Record Production Viewing and Storage-Retrieval Equipment,* Santoro, John G., September 1966.

Air Force Systems Command, Griffiss Air Force Base, RADC Compendium 67–1, *Compendium of Visual Displays,* March 1967.

Air Force Systems Command, ESD–TR–66–671, Vol. II, *Phase II Final Report on Use of Air Force ADP Experience to Assist Air Force ADP Management,* Gradwohl, A. J., December 1966.

Air Force Systems Command, ESD–TR–66–671, Vol. III, *Phase II Final Report on Use of the Air Force ADP Experience to Assist Air Force ADP Management,* Gradwohl, A. J. and Wootan, W. O., Jr., December 1966.

Air Force Systems Command, ESD–TR–66–672, *Primer for Air Force ADP Experience Handbook (Pilot Version),* December 1966.

Air Force Systems Command, ESD–TR–66–673, *Air Force ADP Experience Handbook (Pilot Version),* December 1966.

Air Force Systems Command, RADC–TR–66–37, *Mathematical Models of Information Systems,* Arnold, R. F., *et al.,* April 1966.

American Federation of Information Processing Societies (AFIPS). *AFIPS Conference Proceedings,* Vol. 30. Spring Joint Computer Conference, Atlantic City, N. J., 1967.

ARL, Sylvania, RADC–TR–66–599, *Implementation of Document Format Recognition,* Blitz, M., Stoddard, J., and Sanders, R., *et al.,* October 1966.

Army Electronics Command, Fort Monmouth, N. J., Communications Lab, *A Holographic Approach to Read-Only Memory,* Progress Rpt., Oct. 65–Dec. 66, Chapman, Robert E., and Fisher, Matten J., April 1967, 72 p., Proj. DA–1EO–20401–A327, Task 01, ECOM 2824, Fld. 9/2, 14/5.

Army Electronics Labs, Fort Monmouth, N. J., P17–22, *Looking Ahead in Science and Technology,* Zahl, Harold A., November 1964.

Army Research Office, *Technological Forecast 1961, Vol. I, Army-Wide,* Dec. 1961.

Arthur D. Little, Inc., *CADOS: A System for the Computer-Aided Detailing of Ships,* August 1966.

Arthur D. Little, Inc., ESD–TR–66–405, *Study and Test of a Methodology for Laboratory Evaluation of Message Retrieval Systems,* Guiliano, Vincent E., *et al.,* August 1966.

Auerbach Corp., Philadelphia, Pa., RADC–TR–65–397, Vol. 1, *Analysis of Small Associative Memories for Data Storage and Retrieval Systems,* Green, R. S., Minker, J., and Shindle, W. E., July 1966.

Auerbach Corp., Phila., Pa., 1151–TR–3, *DOD User Needs Study: Phase I, Vol. I,* 14 May 1965.

Auerbach Corporation, Pennsylvania, PR–7500–145, *Information Storage and Retrieval: A State-of-the-Art Report,* Berul, Lawrence, 14 September 1964.

Ballistics Systems Division, Norton Air Force Base, Calif., *Proceedings of the Air Force/Industry Data Management Symposium,* September 1965.

Battelle Memorial Institute, Columbus Laboratories, *Models of Technological Change,* Preliminary Draft, Buttner, F. H. and Cheaney, E. S.

The Bendix Corporation, Baltimore, Md., *Digital Subscriber Terminal and DST Modem; Sixth Quarterly Report,* 31 March 1966.

Bird, J. R. and Darracott, H. T., *Developing and Using the U. S. Army Long Range Technological Forecast.*

The Boeing Co., Seattle, Wash., ECOM–01695–1, *Retrieval of Display Data: First Quarterly Report,* Wilcox, R. C., September 1966.

Booz, Allen, Applied Research, Inc., Bethesda, Md., BAARINC 914–1–1, *Study of Mechanization in DOD Libraries and Information Center,* September 1966.

Bureau of the Budget, Executive Office of the President, . . . *Inventory of Automatic Data Processing Equipment in the Federal Government,* July 1966.

Burroughs Corp., *BORAM Project Report No. 2,* Shafer, P. E., September 1965.

Burroughs Corporation, *BORAM Project Report No. 3; 3rd Quarter Report,* Shafer, P. E., 15 December 1965.

Carnegie Institute of Technology, *Toward Economical Remote Computer Access,* Gold, Michael M., *et al.,* July 1967.

Carson Laboratories, Inc., Bristol, Conn., *Feasibility Demonstration of High-Brightness Laser Display,* Kalman, Dr. Gabor V., June 1966.

Computer Command and Control Co., Phila., Pa., 26–104–5, *An Automatic Classification System to Air R&D Management,* 1 November 1965.

Control Data Corporation, G 03242, *Final Development Report for Hybrid Computer Study,* 31 July 1965.

Cooley Electronics Laboratory, RADC–TR–65–532, *A Study of Information Flow in Multiple-Computer and Multiple-Console Data Processing Systems–II,* Irani, K. B., *et al.,* February 1966.

Dept. of the Air Force, SCGF646, *U. S. Air Force Project Forecast, Geophysics Report,* Kaplan, Joseph, March 1964.

Director of Army Technical Information, Office of the Chief of Research and Development, Department of the Army, EDIS–1, *Engineering Data and Information System (EDIS) Concept and Action Plan Report,* Goldberg, S. A., *et al.,* July 1964.

Director of Army Technical Information, Office of the Chief of Research and Development, Department of the Army, EDIS–2, *Recommended Approaches to Design of the U. S. Army Engineering Data and Information System,* Goldberg, S. A., December 1964.

Director of Army Technical Information, Office of Chief of Research and Development, *Information Data Exchange Experimental Activities—A Concept for a Scientific and Technical Information Network,* Hoffman, A., October 1964.

Directorate of Information Sciences, AFOSR64–0101, *Annual Report, Information Sciences 1963,* January 1964.

Electronics Components Laboratory, ECOM 2782, Application of the *Land Color-Vision Effect to Television Systems (A Feasibility Study),* Fenton, Charles A., December 1966.

Foreign Technology Division, Air Force Systems Command, Wright-Patterson Air Force Base, Ohio, FTD–TT–65–1663, *New Storage Elements for Electronic Digital Computers,* Hans-Juergen Schiller, 1964.

Foreign Technology Div., Wright-Patterson AFB, Ohio, Rpt. No. FTD–HT–67–51, *Ferrite-Core Memory with Semiconductor Control Circuits,* Burian, M. and Kristoutek, K., 28 February 1967, 21 p.

The Franklin Institute Research Laboratories, T1–163, *State-of-the-Art Survey of Message-Processing Equipment,* Cadwell, G. M., Jr., Williams, R. M., and Pandolfi, R. R., November 1965.

General Electric Co., RADC–TR–64–582, *Indexing Accts., Procedures, and Devices,* Korotkin, Arthur L., *et al.,* April 1965.

General Electric Co., Washington, D. C., ESD–TR–66–137, *The Application of Large-Scale Computers to U. S. Air Force Information Systems,* Campbell, J. B., *et al.,* March 1966.

General Electric Co., ECOM–01442–1, *Magneto-Optical Display Panel with Memory,* Eide, J. E., *et al.,* January 1966.

General Precision, Inc., RADC–TR–66–209, Vol. 1, *Study of Associative Processing Techniques,* Bird, R. M., Cass, J. L., and Fuller, R. H., *et al.,* September 1966.

General Technical Services, Inc., Yeadon, Pa., *Advanced Technological Planning for Interdisciplinary Physical Research,* Iberall, A. S., *et al.,* June 1965.

The George Washington University, School of Engineering and Applied Science, Master's Thesis, *Forecasting the Utility of Air Force Applied Research Efforts,* Griswold, T. L., September 1964.

The George Washington University, *Forecast of the Economic, Social and Political Climate in which Managers will Operate in 1975–86 Era,* Chapman, Gerald S., May 1967.

Georgia Institute of Technology, *A Method for Investigating the Behavior of Attributes which Belong to Information Storage and Retrieval Systems,* Heckman, Ralph Paul, August 1965.

Goodyear Aerospace Corporation, RADC–TR–66–281, *Associative List Selector,* Gall, Russell G. and Brotherton, Dale E., October 1966.

The Hebrew University, Jerusalem, TR–22, *Data Retrieval by Computer—A Critical Survey,* Kasher, Asa, January 1966.

Howard Research Corporation, Arlington, Virginia, *EDIS Task I Report—Categorization of Available Data and Information: Work Unit 1.2,* 3 January 1966.

Howard Research Corporation, Arlington, Virginia, *EDIS Task I Report—Identification of Disciplines and Fields: Work Unit 1.4,* 3 January 1966.

Howard Research Corporation, Arlington, Virginia, *EDIS Task I Report—Identification of User Needs: Work Unit 1.3,* 3 January 1966.

HRB-Singer, Inc., Pennsylvania, *A General Model for Simulating Information Storage and Retrieval Systems,* Blunt, Charles R., *et al.,* April 1966.

Hudson Institute, HI–895–BN/1/1, *Methodological Comments,* Kahn, Herman.

Hughes Aircraft, RADC–TR–66–176, *Association-Storing Processor Study,* Savitt, D. A., Love, H. H., and Troop, R. E., June 1966.

Hughes Research Laboratories, Malibu, Calif., Interim Engineering Report No. 2, *Detection and Imaging Technology,* Lehrer, N. H., Ketchpel, R. D., and Scholl, R. F., 15 September 1966.

Human Sciences Research Inc., HSR–TN–59/7a–SM, *A Systematic Framework for Comparison of System Research Methods,* McGrath, J. E., Nordlie, P. S., and Vaughan, W. S., Jr.

IBM Corp., TRN 173, *Organization and Presentation of Image Interpreter Reference and Auxiliary Information,* Nelson, Arthur, *et al.,* June 1966.

IBM, Federal Systems Division, *Research on Automatic Classification, Indexing and Extracting,* April 1967.

IIT Research Institute, IITRI–A6093–12, *Continuous Facsimile Scanner Employing Fiber Optics,* Pontarelli, Donald A., 24 November 1965.

IIT Research Institute, Chicago, Illinois, IITRI–A6093–24, *Continuous Facsimile Scanner Employing Fiber Optics,* Pontarelli, D. A., September 1966.

Industrial College of the Armed Forces, *Office Atuomation and the Use of*

Random Filing, by Stewart, William R., Jr., Thesis No. 158, 31 March 1965, M65–158.

Informatics, Inc., California, RADC–TR–65–387, *Image Interpretation Cell Electronic Data Storage Study,* Howard, Marvin, Shoffner, Ralph, November 1965.

Informatics, Inc., Sherman Oaks, Calif., TR–65–58–19, *MTACC Computer Technology Exploration,* 20 September 1965.

Information Dynamics Corp., *Selective Dissemination of Information Review of Selected Systems and a Design for Army Technical Libraries,* Bivona, William A., *et al.,* August 1966.

Interservice Technological Forecasting Methodology Study Group, *Report On Technological Forecasting,* 30 June 1967.

ITT Federal Laboratories, *Data Buffering Techniques Study: 3rd Quarterly Report,* June 1966.

Johns Hopkins University, Bumblebee Instrumentation Development Group, TG–809, *Air Defense Studies (ADS) Digital System,* February 1966.

Joint Publications Research Service, 18156, *Long Range Plans for Development of Science,* March 1963.

Laboratory for Electronics, Electronics Division, ECOM 01828–2, *Investigation For a "First-In First–Out" Data Buffer Memory,* Battarel, C. P., Spain, R. J., August 1966.

Library of Congress, Aerospace Technology Division, *Computer Technology,* by Doncov, Boris, A TD Report 67–43 of 31 August 1967.

Lincoln Laboratory, MIT, ESD–TR–66–377, *Content-Addressed Memory Using Magneto- or Electro-Optical Interrogation,* Smith, Donald O., *et al.,* 29 October 1965.

Lincoln Laboratory, MIT, TR 377, *An Experimental On-Line Data Storage and Retrieval System,* J. F. Nolan, *et al.,* 24 September 1965.

Litton Systems, Incorporated, *Computers and Displays/Controls State-of-the-Art Technology Studies,* Pizzicara, Donald J., February 1966.

Litton Systems, Inc., Woodland Hills, Calif., AQ50003H65, *First Quarterly Report for Block Oriented Random Access Memory,* Vieth, R. F., July 1965.

Lockheed Missile and Space Co., *Long-Range Planning and Technological Forecasting: An Annotated Bibliography,* Stromer, Peter R., November 1963.

Lockheed Aircraft Corp., Sunnyvale, Calif., SRB–65–1, *Long-Range Planning and Technological Forecasting: An Annotated Bibliography, Supplement 1,* Stromer, P. R., February 1965.

Logistics Management Institute, *Analysis of Department of Defense Conference on Technical Data Management,* October 1964.

Logistics Research Project, George Washington Univ., T–170, *A Survey of Information Requirements for Navy Maintenance and Material Management,* 15 April 1964.

Management and Economics Research, Inc., draft, *Impact of Future Technology on Navy Business Management:* Volume 1—The Report; Volume 2 —Technological Forecast; Volume 3—Appendix, May 1967.

Management Counsel, *Technological Forecasting—Principles and Techniques,* Sweezy, Eldon E., June 1965.

Management and Economics Research, Inc., *Impact of Future Technology on Navy Business Management,* Vol. 1, The Report, 1–3 May 1967.

Management and Economics Research, Inc., *Impact of Future Technology on*

Navy Business Management, Vol. 2, Technological Forecast, 1–3 May 1967.

Management and Economics Research, Inc., *Impact of Future Technology on Navy Business Management,* Vol. 3, Appendix, 1–3 May 1967.

The Marquardt Corporation, ECOM 90862–F, *Research Investigations on Photo Facsimile Transmission Techniques,* Hell, W. H. and Asam, A. R., January 1966.

The Mitre Corp., Bedford, Mass., *How to Estimate the Investment Cost of Electronic Data Processing Equipment,* Jones, M. V., May 1966.

The Mitre Corp., Bedford, Mass., ESD–TR–66–113, *A Method for the Evaluation of Software, Vol. 1,* Budd, A. E., August 1966.

Mitre Corp., MTR–197, Vol. 3, *A Method for the Evaluation of Software: Executive, Operating or Monitor Systems,* Budd, A. E., September 1967.

MIT, Project MAC, MAC–TR–43 (THESIS), *Program Analysis by Digital Computer,* Wilde, Daniel V., August 1967.

MIT, Project MAC, MAC–TR–40, *On-Line Analysis for Social Scientists,* Miller, James R., May 1967.

MIT, Project MAC, MAC–TR–48 (THESIS), *Incremental Simulation on a Time-Shared Computer,* Jones, Malcolm M., January 1968.

Motorola, Inc., Semiconductor Products Div., AFAL–TR–66–305, *Compatible Semiconductor Thin Film Techniques,* Seelbach, W. and Metz, D., October 1966.

National Aeronautics and Space Administration (NASA), NHB 2170.2, *Reportable Items under the New Technology Clause,* Washington: U.S. Government Printing Office, October 1966.

National Microfilm Association, *Engineering Data Micro-Reproduction Standards and Specifications: Monograph No. 1,* February 1967.

Naval Missile Center, Point Mugu, Calif., NP–66–11, *A Versatile, User-Oriented Computerized Library System,* Neuron, Eric, 7 November 1966.

Naval Training Device Center, *A Survey of Various Information Display Devices,* Kleiman, E. B., May 1967.

NAVSO, P–2457 (Rev. 7–67) *Department of the Navy RDT&E Management Guide,* 1 July 1967.

Navy Technological Forecasting Study Group, *A Proposal for a Navy Technological Forecast, Part 1—Summary Report,* Cetron, Marvin J., *et al.,* 1 May 1966.

Navy Technological Forecasting Study Group, *A Proposal for a Navy Technological Forecast, Part 2—Backup Report,* Cetron, Marvin J., *et al.,* 1 May 1966.

North American Aviation, Inc., C6–2442/030, *Final Report User-Needs Study, Phase II, Vol. I,* Goodman, A. F., *et al.,* 30 November 1966.

North American Aviation, Inc., C6–2442/030, *Final Report, User-Needs Study, Phase II, Vol. II,* Goodman, A. F. and Hodges, J. D., *et al.,* 30 November 1966.

Nortronics, Palos Verdes Peninsula, Calif., ECOM–01398–F, *Display Data Recording by Laser: Final Report,* Corson, R. C., September 1966.

Office of Aerospace Research, Arlington, Virginia, *Information System Networks . . . Let's Profit from What We Know,* Swanson, Rowena W., June 1966.

Office of Aerospace Research, *Long-Range Forecasting and Planning,* A Symposium held at the U.S. Air Force Academy, Colorado, 16–17 August 1966.

Office of Aerospace Research, *The Office of Aerospace Research Scientific and Technical Information Program*, Downie, Currie S., *et al.*, 15 March 1967.

Office of Assistant Secretary, Installations and Logistics, Department of Defense, TD–2, *Technical Data and Standardization Glossary*, December 1965.

Office, Chief of Research and Development, U. S. Army Research Office, *U. S. Army Scientific and Technical Information Program, FY 1966–1972*, December 1966.

Office of Naval Research, Washington, D. C., ACR–113, *Information Systems Summaries*, July 1965.

Office of Naval Research, Washington, D. C., ACR–123, *Information Systems Summaries—Fourth Edition*, September 1966.

Office of Naval Research, London, 1 June 1967, 55 p., Rpt. No. ONRL–33–67, *The British Computer Scene, Part IV, The Universities*, Cowie, James, Hemann, and Maycock, P. D.

Planning Research Corp., R–884, *Computer Aided Ship Design Program Plan*, Heitlinger, L., *et al.*, 1 January 1966.

Planning Research Corp., PRC R–1029, *Technical Data Handling Survey, Vol. I: Review of Projected Navy User Requirements and Current Vendor Capabilities*, Bernstein, George B., *et al.*, 30 August 1967.

Planning Research Corp., PRC R–1029, *Technical Data Handling Survey, Vol. II: Review of Projected Navy User Requirements and Projected Vendor Capabilities (Circa 1972)*, Bernstein, George B., *et al.*, 30 August 1967.

Rabinow Electronics, Incorporated, Rockville, Md., SCL–4592, *High-Speed Message Entry Equipment*, Breslaver, Alfred, *et al.*, 30 September 1965.

Radiation Incorporated, *TV Data Compaction Study*, February 1966.

Radio Corporation of America, Somerville, N. J., Interim Technical Report No. 1, *Development of Molecular Electronic Display Structures*, Anrons, R. W., Caplan, R. and Klein, R., October 1966.

Rand Corp., P–1955, *On the Choice of Objectives in Systems Studies*, Hitch, Charles, 30 March 1960.

Rand Corp., P–2511, *Scheduling State of the Art, Anathema or Necessity*, Pardee, F. S., November 1961.

Rand Corp., P–2568, *Technological Change and Local ·Economy*, Novick, D., March 1962.

Rand Corp., P–2982, *Report on a Long-Range Forecasting Study*, Gordon, T. J. and Helmer, Olaf, September 1964.

Rand Corp., P–2986, *Improving the Reliability of Estimates Obtained from a Consensus of Experts*, Brown, Bernice and Helmer, Olaf, September 1967.

Rand Corporation, P–3045, *Futuribles*, de Jouvenel, Bertrand, January 1965.

Rand Corporation, P–3086, *Use of Hybrid Computing in Design Automation*, Rowe, A. J., *et al.*, March 1965.

Rand Corp., P–3106, *A Guide for the Preparation Indexes*, Harris, Eleanor T., April 1965.

Rand Corp., P–3181, *State-of-the-Art Projection and Long-Range Planning of Applied Research*, Pardee, F. S., July 1965.

Rand Corp., P–3279, *The Computer in Your Future*, Ware, W. H., November 1967.

Rand Corp., P–3365–2, *Bibliography on Automation and Technological Change and Studies of the Future*, Harrison, Annette, March 1967.

Rand Corporation, P–3409, *The Impact of the New Technology on Command System Design*, Wessel, Andrew E., July 1966.

Rand Corporation, P–3415, *On the Development of Equitable Graphic I/O*, Ellis, T. O., *et al.*, July 1966.

Rand Corporation, P–3476, *The Catalog: A Flexible Structure For Data*, Ziehe, T. W., November 1966.

Rand Corp., P–3477, *Satellites and Future Communications, Including Broadcast*, Hult, J. L., April 1967.

Rand Corp., P–3478, *Computer Aspects of Technological Change, Automation, and Economic Progress*, Armer, Paul, February 1966.

Rand Corporation, P–3484, *Current Trends in Aerospace Computation and Some Implications*, Boehm, Barry, November 1966.

Rand Corporation, P–3497, *Acquisition, Archiving and Interchange*, Hays, David G., December 1966.

Rand Corp., P–3558, *Analysis of the Future: The DELPHI Method*, Helmer, Olaf, March 1967.

Rand Corp., P–3571, *The Year 2000*, Haydon, Brownlee, March 1967.

Rand Corp., P–3599, *Computer Simulation Programming Languages: Perspective and Prognosis*, Kiviat, Philip J., September 1967.

Rand Corp., P–3622, *Technological Projection and Advanced Product Planning*, Pardee, F. S., July 1967.

Rand Corp., P–3643, *Prospects of Technological Progress*, Helmer, Olaf, August 1967.

Rand Corp., P–3704, *DELPHI*, Dalkey, Norman C., October 1967.

Rand Corp., P–3712, *Satellite Separation and the Allocation and Specification of Shared Spectrum Usage for Intense Exploitation*, Hult, J. L., October 1967.

Rand Corporation, *Bibliography on Automation and Technological Change and Studies of the Future*, Harrison, Annette, October 1966.

Rand Corporation, RM 4645–PR, *The Catalog: A Flexible Data Structure for Magnetic Tape*, Kay, Martin and Ziche, Theodore, October 1965.

Rand Corp., Santa Monica, Calif., RM–5085–PR, *A Computer System for Inference Execution and Data Retrieval*, Levien, R. E., *et al.*, September 1966.

Rand Corp., Santa Monica, Calif., *Computers and our Future*, Maron, M. E., December 1966.

Rand Corporation, RM 5129–PR, *Programming by Questionnaire: How To Construct a Program Generator*, Oldfather, Paula, Ginsberg, Allen S., and Markowitz, Harry M., November 1966.

Rand Corporation, RM–4793–PR, Related Data File: *A Tool for Mechanized Inference Execution and Data Retrieval*, Levien, Roger, *et al.*, December 1965.

Rand Corporation, Santa Monica, Calif., *State-of-the-Art Projection and Long Range Planning of Applied Research*, Pardee, F. S., July 1965.

Rand Corp., Santa Monica, Calif., RM–4849–PR, *Integrating Base Maintenance Management by Unifying its Information Systems in Manual and Computer-Assisted Environment*, Cohen, I. K., Denardo, E. V., and Kiviat, P. J., June 1966.

Redstone Scientific Information Center, Redstone Arsenal, Alabama, RSIC–516, *Methods for Satisfying the Needs of the Scientist and the Engineer for Scientific and Technical Information*, Murray, Hubert, Jr., January 1966.

Redstone Scientific Information Center, U. S. Army Missile Command and NASA George C. Marshall Space Center, RSIC–567, *Converting the IDEP Master File Reports Format*, Martin, Claude E., June 1966.

Research Analysis Corp., TP 103, *Operations Research in the Next 20 Years, A Technological Forecast*, Smith, Nicholas M., January 1964.

Research and Development Directorate, U. S. Army Materiel Command, *Forecast in Depth on Information Processing Systems for the Field Army*, Darracott, H. T., June 1965.

Solid State Electronics Laboratory, AFCRL–66–136, *Research in Ferromagnetics*, Spain, Robert J., et al., April 1965.

Stanford Research Institute, Menlo Park, Calif., ECOM–01901–24, *Graphical-Data-Processing Research Study and Experimental Investigation*, Duda, R. O., et al., August 1966.

Stanford Research Institute, ECOM–01261–2, *High-Information-Density Storage Surfaces*, Priest, R. C., et al., March 1966.

Stanford Research Institute, ECOM–01261–3, *High-Information Storage Surfaces: Progress Report 3*, Priest, R. C., et al., June 1966.

Stanford Research Institute, ECOM–01261–5, *High-Information-Density Storage Surfaces: Progress Report 5*, Rogers, K. T. and Cogswell, D. L., October 1966.

Statistical Techniques Research Group, Princeton Univ., Minotor: AhOD 1715 40, *The Future of Data Analysis*, Tukey, John W.

Syracuse University Research Corp., *Science and Technology in the 1985 Era*, March 1964.

Syracuse Univ. Research Corp., *Appendix to Science and Technology in the 1985 Era*, May 1964.

Syracuse University Research Corp., *The United States and the World in the 1985 Era*, March 1964.

Syracuse Univ. Research Corp., *Appendixes One and Two to the United States and the World in the 1985 Era*, May 1964.

System Development Corp., ESD–TR–67–452, *Cost Reporting for Development of Information Processing Systems*, Nelson, Edward A. and Fleishman, Thomas, 11 April 1967.

System Development Corp., Santa Monica, Calif., TM–1391/000/01, *Planning: A Bibliography*, Thornton, S. F., 14 February 1964.

System Development Corp., TM–2550/016/01, *Decision Information Distribution System: Cost-Benefits Analysis*, Wellisch, Jean B. and Maloy, J. K., 27 December 1967.

System Development Corp., Santa Monica, Calif., TM–2913/000/00, *A User's Guide to SURF: Support of User Records and Files*, Wallace, E. M., 24 June 1966.

System Development Corporation, TM–3008/002/00, *A Bibliography on Information Science and Technology for 1966—Part II*, Neeland, Frances, 15 September 1966.

System Development Corp., TM–3008/004/00, *A Bibliography of Information Science and Technology for 1966, Part IV*, Neeland, Frances, 16 January 1967.

System Development Corp., *EOL Display System Evaluation*, Miller, Robert J., 16 August 1967.

System Development Corporation, TRN 176, *An Experimental Study of Two Methods of Indexing Tactical Imagery*, Laymon, Richard S., July 1966.

System Development Corp., SP–2017, *The Idea of a "Look-Out" Institution*, Ozbekhan, Hasan, 26 April 1967.

System Development Corporation, SP–2022, *Toward a Future for Planning,* Adelson, Marvin, June 1966.

System Development Corp., SP–2137, *Multi-Level File Structure As a Frame of Reference for Measuring User Interest,* Anderson, A. A., 12 July 1966.

System Development Corp., SP–2393, *Trends in Computer Hardware,* Fanwick, Charles, 17 March 1966.

System Development Corp., Santa Monica, Calif., SP–2440/000/01, *Security in the Computer Environment,* Dennis, R. L., 18 August 1966.

System Development Corp., SP–2494, *Technology and Man's Future,* Ozkebhan, Hasan, 27 May 1966.

System Development Corp., Santa Monica, Calif., SP–2535, *User Requirements, Personal Indexes, and Computer Support,* Wallace, E. M., 25 July 1966.

System Development Corp., Santa Monica, Calif., SP–3556/000/00, *Guidelines for the Utilization of Statisticians in the Design and Execution of Information Retrieval System Evaluation Studies,* Anderson, A. A., 12 July 1966.

System Development Corp., SP–2557, *Interactive Displays for Document Retrieval,* Borko, H. and Burmaugh, H. P., 4 August 1966.

System Development Corp., SP–2582/000/00, *Computer Software: Developments and Recent Trends in Programming and Operating Systems,* Shaw, Christopher J., 26 August 1966.

System Development Corp., SP–2830, *The Triumph of Technology: "Can" Implies "Ought",* Ozbekhan, Hasan, 6 June 1967.

Tech/Ops CORG, CORG–M–195, *A System for Automated Processing of Tables of Organization and Equipment,* Denet, James, 25 May 1965.

TRW Systems, *A Probe of TRW's Future,* North, H. Q., 5 July 1966.

U. S. Army Electronics Command, Ft. Monmouth, N. J., ECOM 02069–1, *High Density Information Recording and Display Techniques Study, Quarterly Progress Report,* Davis, T. F., August 1966.

U. S. Army Electronics Command, Ft. Monmouth, N. J., ECOM–2760, *Memory-Oriented Processor Study,* Campi, A. V., Cashman, H. J. and Gray, B. R., September 1966.

U. S. Army Materiel Command Technical Forecasting & Objectives Branch, R&D Directorate, *Information Processing Systems for the Field Army,* Darracott, H. T., 29 June 1965.

U. S. Army Missile Command, Redstone Arsenal, Alabama, RG–TR–66–12, *Development of Memory Buffer For Use in A Computer Controlled Memory Exerciser,* Grabney, James R., May 1966.

U. S. Naval Command Systems Support Activity and Planning Research Corp. No. 188, *Analysis and Recommendations Concerning the Reporting Workload in the U.S. Pacific Fleet: Vol. I—Ship Reporting,* 29 November 1965.

U. S. Naval Personnel Research Activity, SRM 67–3, *The Projected Effect of Automation on Future Navy Personnel Requirements: Part I—Specific Implications for the Personnel Structure,* Kaplan, Irving E., August 1966.

U. S. Naval Personnel Research Activity, SRM 67–3, *The Projected Effect of Automation on Future Navy Personnel Requirements: Part 2—Implications for the Navy's Environment, the Nation,* Kaplan, Irving E., August 1966.

U. S. Naval Personnel Research Activity, SRM 67–29, *Personnel Implications of New Technological Developments: Microelectronics and Automation,* Wilson, David A., June 1967.

U. S. Naval Postgraduate School, Monterey, Calif., *Automation and the Navy, Vol. I,* May 1964.

U. S. Naval Postgraduate School, *Thesis: Hybrid Control System Simulation,* Holloway, Lowell J., 1965.

U. S. Naval Postgraduate School, Monterey, Calif., *Management Decision Making and the Computer,* Ruth, Lt. S. R., 1964.

U. S. Naval Postgraduate School, Monterey, Calif., *Automated System Development and Documentation Criteria,* Ziberlein, George V., Jr., 1965.

U. S. Naval Ship Engineering Center, Dept. of the Navy, Washington, D. C., NAVSHIPS 0900–006–5200, *Ship Electronic Equipment Feasibility Study,* August 1966.

U. S. Naval Weapons Laboratory, Dahlgren, Va., NWL MAL–1, *Microfiche Usage in the Technical Library at Naval Weapons Laboratory,* Lyon, C. C., 1 December 1966.

Univac Division of Sperry Rand Corp., *Content-Addressable Memory Techniques: Second Quarterly Engineering Progress Report,* Chow, W F., 31 August 1965.

Univac Division of Sperry Rand Corp., Blue Bell, Pa., *Content-Addressable Memory Techniques: Third Quarterly Engineering Progress Report,* January 1966.

Univac Division of the Sperry Rand Corp., Blue Bell, Pa., *NDRD Memory: Third Interim Technical Report,* Flannery, W. E., March 1966.

Univac Division of Sperry Rand Corp., IR–9–523(1), *Research on the Memory System for Microcircuits: Interim Engineering Progress Report,* 31 July 1966.

Univac Division of Sperry Rand Corp., AFAL–TR–66–306, *30 MHz Low-Power Thin-Film NDRO Memory,* Flannery, W. E., October 1966.

University of California, Berkeley, California, AFOSR 66–0028, *On the Bound to the Memory of a Sequential Machine,* Gill, Arthur, 4 December 1964.

University of Illinois, Urbana, Ill., *Topological Structures of Information Retrieval Systems,* Chien, R. T., *et al.,* October 1966.

University of Pennsylvania, The Moore School of Electrical Engineering, 63–22, *Interim Technical Report: Storage and Retrieval of Technical Information,* Van Dan, Andries, 1 September 1963.

University of Pennsylvania, No. 67–09, *Automatic Introduction of Information into a Remote-Access System: A Physics Library Catalog,* Cabrini, Phillippe J., 1 November 1966.

University of Utah, *Graphical Man/Machine Communications,* Semi-Annual Progress Report for period ending 30 November 1966, Evans, David C., November 1966.

Westinghouse Defense and Space Center, Baltimore, Md., *Survey of Highly Parallel Information Processing Technology and Systems,* Murtha, J. C. and Beadles, R. L., 1 November 1964.

INDICES

AUTHOR INDEX

341

SUBJECT INDEX